HARRIER II
VALIDATING V/STOL

HARRIER II
VALIDATING V/STOL

Lon O. Nordeen

NAVAL INSTITUTE PRESS
Annapolis, Maryland

Naval Institute Press
291 Wood Road
Annapolis, MD 21402

This book was brought to publication with the assistance of the Boeing Company and the Harrier II industry team, including BAe Systems, Rolls-Royce, and Smiths Industries.

Library of Congress Cataloging-in-Publication Data
Nordeen, Lon O., 1953–
Harrier II : validating V/STOL / Lon O. Nordeen.
    p. cm.
Includes bibliographical references and index.
ISBN-13: 978-1-59114-536-3 (alk. paper)
ISBN-10: 1-59114-536-8 (alk. paper)
1. Harrier (Jet fighter plane) 2. United States. Marine Corps—Procurement. 3. Close air support. I. Title.
  UG1242.F5N65 2006
  623.74'63—dc22

                                                                                        2006023870

Printed in the United States of America on acid-free paper ∞

12 11 10 09 08 07 06   8 7 6 5 4 3 2

First printing

Contents

Preface

This book reviews the history of the challenging AV-8B Harrier II program. The goal is to highlight the teamwork, creativity, and innovation that went into the design, development, fielding, and operation of this unique tactical aircraft. Major aircraft programs include many elements. In addition to the technological, military, economic, and political aspects, a key factor is the contributions of the people whose innovative ideas helped the team meet various challenges. This was especially true with the Harrier II program.

The book includes excerpts from interviews and insights from those involved with the program, including former program managers, Harrier II pilots, military commanders, production personnel, and engineers, including those who opposed the program. Major program milestones, technical advancements and challenges, international government/industry collaboration, and Harrier II combat contributions are also highlighted in the book.

Acknowledgments

This book came about due to the desire of a group of program personnel to document the history of the Harrier II as the aircraft reached the end of its production history. Pat Finneran, Dave Bowman, and Robert Feldmann spearheaded the cause, with support from Ted Herman, Jeff Maxwell, Hank Cole III, Jerry Dolvin, and Vince Higbee. Dick Wise led the effort from BAe Systems, with support from John Parker, Ray Searle, and Chris Farara. Mike Gladwin, Russ Hammond, Rick Beckwith, and Michael Ryan from Rolls-Royce and Bob White from Raytheon provided assistance, as did Fred Chana of Smiths Industries.

Dr. Fredrick Allison of the Marine Corps Historical Division and Bert Cooper pointed me in the right direction to find many sources of information. Doug Campbell and David Isby shared their excellent collections of material on military aviation and the development and evolution of close air support. Lt. Col. Lee Schram, Maj. James Coopersmith, and Maj. Robert Sofgee shared their briefings and provided valuable insights. Gary Vangysel and John Valovich set up critical interviews with Marine Corps Harrier II commanding officers and pilots at MCAS Yuma and MCAS Cherry Point and sent me piles of information on Harrier II operations and lessons from past experience.

Lt. Gen. Thomas Miller, USMC (Ret.), gave superb insights about the Marine Corps close air support goals that led to the V/STOL Harrier, and Ed Harper provided behind-the-scenes insights from the Marine Corps, NAVAIR, and industry perspectives.

Lt. Gen. Harold Blot, USMC (Ret.), Maj. Gen. Joe Anderson, USMC (Ret.), Lt. Col. Russ Stromberg, USMC (Ret.), Lt. Col. John Capito, USMC (Ret.), Lt. Col. W. R. Spicer, USMC (Ret.), and Lt. Col. Terry Mattke, USMC (Ret.) all contributed insights concerning the political, economic, developmental, and support aspects of the Harrier and Harrier II. Lt. Col. Mike Hile, USMC (Ret.), Col. Bob Claypool, Col. Mark Savarese, Col. James Dixon, and Col. Lee Buland supplied excellent information and background from recent conflicts.

Ellen LeMond and Kathy Cook provided editorial assistance, and Michael Monahan helped me find photographs and create graphics materials for the book. Finally, thank you to Carol for allowing me to spend the time to complete the task.

The Journey to Capability

This book is a discussion of the development of the Vertical/Short Takeoff and Landing (V/STOL) capability for tactical fixed-wing airplanes, made possible by the technological breakthrough of the Harrier in the late 1960s. It continues to today's situation, where the Harrier II has become the weapon of choice for the ground troops in Iraq. It describes the difficulties in completing this journey that introduced a new capability into a risk-adverse acquisition system; in my opinion, successful only because of the unswerving commitment of the United States Marine Corps. To comprehend this deep-rooted support and the expectations of the end users, one has to understand the problem that required a solution.

In this case we have to go back to 1950, when the United States military was caught unprepared for the Korean conflict. Congress, in order to prevent a reoccurrence of this problem, mandated that the U.S. Marine Corps maintain a state of readiness with three active divisions and wings, all able to deploy on short notice to any clime or place the country may decide. The theory was that the Corps was to give the Army and Air Force the time they needed to deploy their larger forces to the battlefield.

The dilemma that faced the Marine leaders of the time was that two of the highest-priority missions for the military were the protection of NATO and Korea, both armor-rich environments where "heavy" was better; yet rapid deployment favored a light, maneuverable force. The potential solution was to substitute airplanes for artillery, thereby creating a lighter ground element and taking advantage of the self-deployment, high speed, and immense firepower of the aviation units. To be successful, this teaming arrangement made two basic assumptions: (1) that the ground would be able to control the targeting of the assigned air, and (2) that the aviation units would be able to respond in a timely manner and be there when needed.

The air-ground team concept seemed to solve the problem until the Vietnam War, where experience showed that the average time from a call for help to bombs on target was twenty-seven minutes. The aviators were doing their best, but an inefficient command and control system, combined with a shortage of airfields capable of handling the takeoff and landing requirements of the airplanes of the time (the A-4, A-6, F-4, and F-8), prevented the successful completion of the second assumption. Marine air needed to do better, and the goal was to drive the response time down to ten minutes or less.

Not counting the command and control system, the only way to reduce the response time was to: (1) blacken the sky with airplanes, (2) build airports closer to the action, or (3) buy an airplane that could take off and land at forward sites. Number one was considered prohibitively expensive, although that is exactly what was done in the Gulf skirmishes. Number two has been a Marine Corps initiative for more than fifty years, but still creates a significant logistic burden—particularly if the ground forces are on the move. The third method, of having the airplane land at forward sites, required a technology that did not exist in the 1950s, but for the Corps surfaced in the 1960s, with the actual delivery of the first AV-8As in 1971.

The early Harriers proved the concepts that ground-launched response times of seven minutes were achievable and that continuous launch and recovery shipboard operations were well within the capability of the Navy's carriers and LHAs.

The Marines were now convinced that V/STOL tactical airplanes were the only practical solution to avoid response times dictated by airfield locations or launch cycles, and set out to improve the airborne capability of the Harrier.

This is the story of that development, from the program being thirty days from cancellation in 1983 to the present commandant's statement in 2005 that the Harrier II is the airplane of choice for the Marines in Operation Iraqi Freedom.

Enjoy the ride.

Lt. Gen. Harold Blot, USMC (Ret.)

CHAPTER 1

The United States Marine Corps, Close Air Support, and the V/STOL Requirement

With a naval and assault heritage dating back to November 10, 1775, the United States Marine Corps (USMC) is different, a fact reflected in its motto, *Semper Fidelis* ("always faithful"). Marines are proud of being a small, close-knit organization with a reputation for military innovation. The Corps has frequently been "the first to fight," from the American Revolution to the 1847 war with Mexico, World War I, and World War II amphibious assaults against Japanese-held islands across the Pacific.

Marine Corps aviation experience dates back to August 20, 1912, when 1st Lt. Alfred Cunningham flew solo and received his naval aviator wings. Marine aviators contributed to American efforts in World War I. During this conflict aircraft were used for reconnaissance and artillery direction. The French were the first to develop techniques for close coordination between aircraft and infantry. Later the British developed the concept of trench strafing using single-seat fighters such as the Sopwith Camel. Armed with small bombs and machine guns, biplane fighters supported attacks on the western front and were used with great success in Palestine.

Starting in 1917, the Germans deployed specialized two-seat Hannover CL, Halberstadt CL, and Junkers J1 ground attack aircraft in *Schlachstaffel*, or attack squadrons. In the final battles of World War I, from the March 1918 German offensive to the November ceasefire, German and British aircraft flew intensive ground attacks using tactics that would later be known as close air support (CAS) and battlefield air interdiction. Radios were still too large and unreliable for regular use in small combat aircraft. Consequently, most crews were briefed before takeoff to operate against known targets, to support preplanned ground operations, or to respond to very basic visual signals.

The Americans who served with the U.S. Army Air Service were exposed to French, British, and German ground attack concepts. The Marine air-ground team was born during operations in the Dominican Republic, Haiti, and Nicaragua from 1919 to 1933, where pilots and observers flying De Havilland DH-4B, Curtiss SOC-2, and Vought OS2U aircraft provided observation, resupply, dive bombing, and strafing support for Marine ground forces.[1]

The Luftwaffe fielded the Hs-123 and Ju-87 Stuka ground attack aircraft and developed effective interdiction and CAS concepts working with German and allied units during the Spanish Civil War and the early part of World War II. The Luftwaffe CAS played an important role in Germany's successful blitzkrieg offensives against Poland, Norway, Belgium, Holland, France, the Balkans, and Russia. Advancing German units could call to air control centers for CAS from specialized ground support squadrons (*Schlachtgeschwader*, or attack wings, flying the Hs-123 biplane, Ju-87 Stuka, Hs-129, and later FW-190 aircraft) whenever serious opposition was encountered. Air liaison officers in armored cars equipped with radios advanced with the army to guide the aircraft.

The British experimented with air support in the North African campaign after seeing the German success. However, it wasn't until the 1943–44 Sicilian and Italian campaigns that the Allies developed a network of forward air controllers (FACs) fighter-bombers using an airpower planning system to significantly affect the ground battle. (Starting in 1944, FACs were airborne in Piper L-5 spotter aircraft.) This investment was successful in supporting the ground advance in Italy and western Europe. The United Kingdom and United States mostly employed fighters armed with cannon, bombs, and rockets, such as the Hurricane, Typhoon, Tempest, P-47, and A-36/P-51, for CAS; they used light bombers for interdiction.

The debate over the merits of CAS versus interdiction continued throughout the conflict. The U.S. Army Air Corps favored air superiority and interdiction, whereas the Royal Air Force (RAF) increased its emphasis on CAS despite heavy losses. The primary role of the Soviet Air Force in World War II was support for the ground forces. The Soviets used their full spectrum of aircraft—ranging from Yak, Lavochkin, and Lend-Lease P-39 single-seat fighters to specialized attack aircraft such as the well-armored IL-2 Shturmovik and Pe-2 light bomber—in the ground attack and interdiction roles.

In late 1941 and early 1942 the Japanese demonstrated the effectiveness of air power in defeating Allied forces across the Pacific. The American invasion of Guadalcanal, which began on August 7, 1942, was a major lesson for the U.S. Marine Corps. Late on August 8, the U.S. Navy (USN) carriers withdrew in the face of heavy Japanese air attacks. The amphibious ships still unloading pulled anchor and departed and left the Marines ashore without air cover.

The Marine forces suffered under heavy Japanese air, naval, and ground assault and the invasion was in serious danger. On August 20, a squadron of USMC F4F Wildcat fighters and another of SBD Dauntless dive bombers flew into Henderson field on Guadalcanal. Marine air support helped hold back the Japanese. After many months of serious fighting by Army and Marine ground forces and aircraft, along with Navy support, the Americans turned the tide against the Japanese.

Marine commanders vowed never to go into action again without aviation units close at hand to provide air superiority and air support. During the island-hopping campaigns, the Marines slowly refined their CAS doctrine, tactics, and techniques. Forward air controllers with improved radios were assigned directly to infantry battalions to ensure close air-ground cooperation. The FACs and infantry employed smoke and display panels to help pilots identify targets.[2]

New aircraft such as the F4U Corsair fighter-bomber provided air support for ground forces during intense operations against the Japanese. Marine Corps squadrons flew from land bases and aircraft carriers and employed gunfire and bombs, including napalm fire bombs, which proved very effective against caves and hard targets such as fortifications. Pilots and aircrew were trained in pinpoint bombing and employment of weapons when in close proximity to friendly troops.

After World War II, debate on U.S. military force structure in the nuclear age led to the 1947 National Security Act (amended in 1952 by Public Law 416, 82nd Congress), which gave the U.S. Marine Corps the mandate to "include not less than three combat divisions and three airwings, and such other land combat, aviation, and other services as may be organic therein . . . [and] provide fleet marine forces of combined arms, together with supporting air components, for service with the fleet in the seizure and defense of advanced naval bases and for the conduct of such land operations as may be essential to the prosecution of a naval campaign. . . . In addition, the Marine Corps . . . shall perform such other duties as the President may direct."[3]

At the start of the Korean War in the summer of 1950, U.S. Air Force (USAF) aircraft operating from Japan and the few airfields left in Korea provided air support to slow the North Korean invasion. Royal Navy, Royal Australian Navy, and USN and Marine Corps planes flying from aircraft carriers also supported retreating United Nations forces. USMC and U.S. Army units received excellent CAS from Navy and Marine Corsairs and Skyraiders because they possessed established and proven doctrine, communications systems, and tactics.

Once the ground war was stabilized and the September 1950 Inchon invasion turned the tide against the North Korean invaders, Marine aviation units stationed in South Korea came under control of USAF Joint Operations Centers. The USAF, allied air units (South African and Australian forces), USN, and USMC initially did not have a common air doctrine. Marine and Army commanders were often unhappy with the response and coordination following calls for CAS. However, the situation improved as battle commanders, pilots, and ground forces became more experienced.[4]

Korea was also the proving ground for other air innovations. Some Marine fighter squadrons transitioned to Panther jets, which proved effective in ground attacks. The Marine Corps fielded its first helicopters in 1948, and these aircraft played an important role in the Korean War. Initially the focus was on medical evacuation, rescue, and resupply, but later helicopters introduced new air warfare concepts such as vertical assault.

The proven military utility of the helicopter during the early 1950s led Marine commanders to request tactical aircraft that could combine the basing flexibility and responsiveness of the helicopter with the speed, payload, and firepower of a jet-propelled attack aircraft. In 1957 the Marine commandant, Gen. Randolf Pate, sent a letter to the Chief of Naval Operations stating, "All tactical aircraft should possess a short/vertical take off and landing capability as soon as it is technically feasible without sacrificing existing mission capabilities."[5]

Marine Corps helicopter squadrons began support missions for South Vietnamese forces in 1962 in Operation Shufly. USMC ground units deployed to the theater in 1965 and received CAS from fixed-wing aircraft such as the A-4 Skyhawk, A-6A Intruder, F-8E Crusader, and F-4B Phantom, and from UH-1 attack helicopters. The Marines established a forward airbase at Chu Lai, with a short runway to allow A-4s to operate close to the battle zone. Marine operations in Vietnam again demonstrated the benefits of close integration of ground forces with helicopters and fixed-wing strike aircraft providing fire support.

In Vietnam, the Marines were forced to integrate their aviation units into the centralized air control system coordinated by the USAF (directed by the U.S. commander, Gen. William Westmoreland). This change disrupted the Marine air-ground team concept. Many Marine commanders felt this action resulted in air support delays, because they were forced to predict air power requirements, send requests ahead of time, and accept air support from any aircraft available, including USMC, USAF, USN, Australian, and South Vietnamese aircraft.[6]

Results from combat operations in Vietnam underscored the lessons from World War II and Korea; namely, that troops in contact needed bombs on target from fixed-wing air support in less than thirty minutes (ten minutes was the desired goal) for the strike to have any effect on the fighting. The requirement for rapid air support and flexible basing led to the call for a new type of tactical aircraft that could be located close to Marine ground forces, which received most of their support and resupply from vertical-capability helicopters.

As a result, the Marine Corps began looking for a strike aircraft that had V/STOL capability like a helicopter yet had the performance of the much loved A-4 Skyhawk. The A-4 Skyhawk served with twenty active and six reserve VMA (fixed-wing Marine Corps attack) or VMAT (fixed-wing Marine Corps attack training) squadrons from 1957 to 1990, and was the primary Marine CAS aircraft in Vietnam.

The modern Marine Corps is a combined arms force with ground, combat support, and aviation assets that train and fight together to perform primarily amphibious assault missions. The Marine Air-Ground Task Force (MAGTF) commander controls a force ranging in size from the small Marine Expeditionary Unit (Special Operations Capable), or MEU (SOC), composed of a battalion of Marines (1,500 – 2,200) with a composite helicopter squadron and support group of aircraft operating from two to three amphibious ships to a division-size (16,000+) Marine Expeditionary Force (MEF) deployed ashore or on dozens of ships with many assault, support, and tactical aircraft. Aviation combat elements are always part of this team, along with command, ground force, and combat service support elements.

With the goal of increasing mobility, rapid deployment, and efficiency, the Marine Corps streamlined its artillery force in the 1990s and reduced its inventory by more than 50 percent through the retirement of its 8-inch and 155mm self-propelled weapons and the towed 105mm cannon. After this reorganization the Marine Corps fielded only the towed 155mm M198 howitzer.

Because the Marines are a light infantry force with emphasis on assault from the sea, aerial firepower was required to make up for the lack of organic artillery that armies can rely on for fire support. Tactical aircraft have range, firepower, accuracy, and shock action that are far superior to artillery, naval gunfire, and attack helicopters.

There are four major tactical air missions: air superiority, reconnaissance, interdiction, and close air support (CAS). Marine Corps aviation is involved in all of these areas. Interdiction involves the attack of supplies, personnel, and targets from just behind the front line to hundreds of miles behind the battle zone, whereas CAS takes place in close proximity to friendly forces.[7]

CAS is defined as "air action against hostile forces which are in close proximity to friendly forces and which require detailed integration of each mission with fire and movement of those forces."[8]

The Marines are organized in a division–air wing team, in which one aircraft wing is regularly assigned to a division. Marine aircraft wings include fixed-wing fighter-attack aircraft such as the F/A-18A+-D Hornet and V/STOL AV-8B Harrier II; rotary-wing aircraft such as the AH-1W Cobra attack helicopter, CH-46 and CH-53 transport helicopters, V-22 tilt-rotor transports, and UH-1N multimission helicopter; KC-130 C-130 transport and refueling aircraft; unmanned air vehicles; and EA-6B electronic warfare aircraft. The Corps believes both fixed-wing and rotary-wing aircraft have an important role to play in supporting the infantry.

The air and ground force elements of the Marine air-ground team are typically based near each other, regularly coordinate and train together in exercises, and deploy as an air-ground team. The primary roles of Marine Corps attack helicopters are fire suppression, CAS, and escorting transport helicopters. Fixed-wing jet aircraft and attack helicopters often operate together to provide CAS for ground units.

Tactical air control parties operate from battalion to division staff levels and even at the corps level, depending on the situation, to provide ground force commanders with aviation officers to integrate air support. This team includes aviators assigned as forward air controllers, who can be located on the ground with Marine units or in the air (such as in a two-seat F/A-18D). A request for CAS goes up through the air-ground liaison teams at the battalion and regimental fire support coordination centers and air combat element direct air support centers.

The Marine air command and control system integrates all aircraft and missile activity. Preplanned requests are assigned a day or more in advance according to mission assignments. Planned missions assume that target location, target type, strike tactics, timing, and weapons are known in advance.

Preplanned CAS can include either scheduled or on-call missions. Immediate requests for CAS for troops in contact with the enemy comes from the FAC to the direct air support center at the Marine division level, which either diverts aircraft from other missions or calls on other agencies for assistance.

To provide effective CAS, the attacking aircraft needs to operate in an area of local air superiority. Action must be taken by air, artillery, or ground forces to neutralize or suppress enemy air defenses, and the FAC needs to identify the target for the pilot to ensure the safety of nearby friendly forces. The Marines also have air support teams equipped with radars to guide strike aircraft and helicopters for CAS at night and in poor weather conditions.

Modern digital systems in use today allow the FAC to rapidly and securely send the information required for an accurate coordinated attack to pilots of attack aircraft. This information comes in a nine-line brief that includes an initial point (IP) from which to start an attack, the heading to the target, the distance from IP, its elevation, a description, the grid coordinates, the type of systems marking it, the routing for egress from the target, and the location of friendly forces.

Air-ground coordination and responsive CAS have long been goals of the Marine Corps, and it has taken decades to develop these capabilities to the fine art seen in combat in Iraq and Afghanistan.

CHAPTER 2

V/STOL Harrier Heritage

V/STOL tactical aircraft were developed to solve a number of military challenges, including improving runway survivability, reducing tactical nuclear weapons vulnerability, and increasing operational flexibility. There have been a multitude of efforts to design, develop, and field V/STOL aircraft, but only the Harrier family and YAK-36 have made it beyond the concept and prototype stage. The Harrier, the most successful V/STOL jet fighter design, was developed by Hawker Siddeley. This firm had aviation development and production experience dating back to before World War I, including such noted aircraft as the Hawker Hurricane, Typhoon, and Tempest, plus the Sea Hawk and Hunter jet fighters. The Harrier V/STOL jet fighter was designed and developed with company funding.

During the mid-1950s, French engineer Michel Wibault designed a V/STOL jet aircraft called the Gyropter, which could take off and land vertically in a conventional, horizontal attitude. The thrust from the Gyropter's centrally mounted engine was exhausted through four blowers situated around the aircraft's center of gravity. The blowers could be swiveled through 90 degrees to generate lift for takeoff and thrust for conventional flights.

In 1956, Wibault took his concept to Bristol Aero Engines Ltd. Bristol engineers built on his ideas and produced the BE53 V/STOL design, which combined the Orpheus turbojet core, the forward compressor from the Olympus engine, and two rotating exhaust nozzles. After some further design changes, which included the addition of two more rotating nozzles (for a total of four) and counter-rotating engine spools to overcome gyroscopic forces, the basic Pegasus engine design was complete.

In 1957, Hawker Aircraft Ltd. took an interest in the Pegasus and designed around it a V/STOL strike/reconnaissance aircraft. Hawker studied several configurations for a V/STOL fighter known as the P1127. With the help of NASA, Hawker engineers tested a number of design models at the Langley wind tunnel. Design and testing led to the P1127 prototype, and construction began in 1958. The NATO Mutual Weapons Development Program funded engine development.[1]

Ian Milne helped to develop the new Pegasus engine.

> I was the chief performance engineer on the Pegasus in 1959 and part of the Pegasus team headed by John Dale, who was the chief engineer. We not only had the usual constraints of fitting the engine into the aircraft, but also getting the correct aerodynamic cycle so that the ratio to rear thrust matched the aircraft requirements for balance. In the early days the "puffer duct" control system used low-pressure air, but this was heavy and cumbersome and it was soon realized that high-pressure air would have to be used. This of course raised the top temperature and impacted engine life, but this was minimized by using variable bleed and developing a life monitoring system. Many new problems to the V/STOL role emerged during development, and close collaboration with the Hawker team at Kingston was essential. The first engine produced less than 12,000 pounds of thrust. The skills of the team managed to at least double this output within the geometry of the airframe. That was a significant achievement![2]

On October 21, 1960, Hawker test pilot Bill Bedford in the P1127 prototype conducted the first tethered hover at Dunsfold, England. As flight testing continued, the aircraft and engine were modified to increase performance. In December 1961, a P1127 exceeded Mach 1 in a shallow dive.

Development continued, and, in 1962, the UK, U.S. and Federal German Republic governments agreed to fund the development of nine airframes and eighteen engines of an improved P1127 design known as the Hawker Kestrel. In 1964 and 1965 pilots and support personnel formed the Tripartite Squadron and conducted an operational evaluation of the Kestrel aircraft in the United Kingdom. During 1,367 flights the pilots from the three nations, which included German air force, Royal Air Force (RAF), U.S. Air Force (USAF), U.S. Navy, U.S. Army, and NASA pilots (but no U.S. Marine Corps pilots), demonstrated that the V/STOL Kestrel aircraft could effectively perform both the strike and reconnaissance missions. Sorties from remote airfields demonstrated the operational flexibility of the Kestrel V/STOL aircraft and provided an indication of the logistics support necessary to sustain these operations.[3]

During the 1960s, aircraft companies competed in Europe to produce a supersonic V/STOL strike fighter to meet future NATO requirements. The French firm Dassault developed the Mirage III through V, and the United Kingdom pursued the Hawker Siddeley P1154 program. However, in 1965 the joint European requirement collapsed when the French lost to the P1154. The UK government later canceled the supersonic P1154 and supported the purchase of the F-4 Phantom for the Royal Navy and further development of the subsonic

P1127 design for the RAF. The first of sixty production Harrier GR Mk. 1 aircraft flew on December 28, 1967.[4]

Royal Air Force

The RAF purchased more than 150 first-generation Harriers starting in 1965. The Harrier GR Mk. 1 entered squadron service with the RAF in April 1969, and the jet served with No. 1, No. 3, No. 4, and No. 20 squadrons and 233rd Operational Conversion Unit. Initially composed of Harrier GR Mk. 1s powered by 19,000-pound-thrust Pegasus 101 engines, the RAF Harrier force was later upgraded to the GR Mk. 3 configuration. These featured the 21,500-pound-thrust Pegasus 103 engine; a laser ranging and marked target seeker; and improved navigation, attack, and electronic countermeasures (ECM) systems.

RAF pilots amassed more than fifty thousand flight hours and demonstrated the utility of V/STOL operations in their first decade of service. During the 1970s and 1980s the RAF Harrier force provided strike support for NATO from forward bases in Germany, and UK units provided training and prepared for worldwide deployments. German and UK-based Harrier squadrons and the operational training unit regularly deployed to exercises around the world and in support of NATO operations in remote areas such as Norway and Turkey.

A significant part of the RAF Harrier force (two squadrons) was forward deployed to air bases in support of the British Army of the Rhine located near Hanover, West Germany. Harrier GR Mk. 3 aircraft were tasked primarily with offensive air support for NATO forces, which included close air support, battlefield interdiction, and tactical air reconnaissance.

The British, German, and Belgian units that held defensive positions near where the Harrier force was based in northern Germany faced a Soviet/Warsaw Pact air arm with excellent ground attack capability that threatened NATO air bases. Soviet and Warsaw Pact armies also fielded a high level of organic air defense weapons. Thus, UK defense planners had to prepare for repeated attacks against RAF air bases and develop tactics for air support in the face of heavy air defenses.

The Harrier force trained to perform low-level battlefield reconnaissance and interdiction against advancing units behind the battle zone, where air defenses are reduced. A major element of Harrier survivability was the capability to disperse six to eight Harriers away from the main RAF air bases to a multitude of prepared sections of roadways or fields that could be stocked with fuel, ordnance, and support equipment by trucks and helicopters.

Forward-deployed RAF Harrier units have regularly flown more than two hundred strike sorties a day in support of NATO exercises or UK ground forces. RAF support personnel were trained to maintain Harriers and provide remote site self-defense alongside RAF regiments that were assigned both air and ground defense responsibility. Harrier units regularly operated from dispersed forward sites and sustained high sortie rates while improving survivability.[5]

United States Marine Corps

The second customer for the Harrier was the U.S. Marine Corps. The background and history of this program is the focus of Chapter 3.

Royal Navy

UK budget reductions in the 1960s and 1970s led to the retirement of the Royal Navy aircraft carrier HMS *Ark Royal* without a replacement. In 1973, however, the UK ordered the HMS *Invincible,* the first of three through-deck cruisers (V/STOL aircraft carriers by another name for political reasons). The Royal Navy ordered the first of thirty-one FRS.1 Sea Harrier V/STOL fighters in 1975 to arm its new *Invincible*-class aircraft carriers. The Sea Harrier design was based on the GR Mk. 3 Harrier flown by the RAF. The Sea Harrier was slightly longer and heavier than the Harrier and had anticorrosion modifications, a raised cockpit for better pilot visibility, and a revised navigation/attack system that included the Blue Fox radar and the Pegasus 104 engine, which was modified for naval operations. The first Sea Harrier squadron, No. 700A, was formed in 1980 and later became the 899th Squadron. The Royal Navy Fleet Air Arm was later expanded to include squadrons No. 800 and 801. An additional twenty-six Sea Harriers were ordered after the 1982 Falklands War, and deliveries of these aircraft continued until late 1988.

The Royal Navy funded the development of an improved version of the Sea Harrier known as the F/A-2, which included a pulse-Doppler Blue Vixen radar and the capability to fire AIM-120 air-to-air missiles and carry a variety of air-to-ground weapons. Thirty-one FRS.1 Sea Harriers were upgraded, and eighteen new-build F/A-2s were produced.[6]

The Sea Harrier force has been retired and replaced by upgraded versions of the RAF Harrier II in UK service. The plan is to replace the Harrier II with the V/STOL F-35B version of the Joint Strike Fighter.

Sea Harriers and GR Mk. 3 Harriers in the Falkland Island Campaign

The Harrier became famous for its role in the successful British effort to recapture the Falkland Islands from invading Argentine forces in 1982. Between April 2 and June 14, 1982, Argentina and Great Britain fought a short and vicious war to determine who controlled a group of remote islands situated off the coast of Argentina and inhabited by fewer than two thousand British people. The primary goal of Argentina in the conflict was to capture, hold, and control what it called the Malvinas Islands. The British objective was to recapture the Falkland Islands and South Georgia Island and release captured British subjects. The British ground forces ultimately won the terrain, but naval and air forces were required to transport soldiers and equipment to the islands, and air power was essential to support the operation.

The Argentine air force, Fuerza Aerea Argentina (FAA); the Argentine naval air arm, Aviación Naval Argentina (ANA); the Royal Navy; and the Royal Air Force played major roles in the 1982 South Atlantic conflict. Important air warfare aspects included the first combat use of V/STOL tactical aircraft; the first use of air-launched, sea-skimming antiship missiles against warships of a major navy; the first widespread use of sea-based surface-to-air missile (SAM) systems; and the first sustained air attacks against naval forces since World War II.

The British established a multilayered screen of defenses around their task force and ground units following the San Carlos landings. Sea Harriers from the HMS *Hermes* and HMS *Invincible* flew combat air patrol (CAP) along the likely avenues of approach for Argentine attack. Sea Harriers formed the outer perimeter of the Royal Navy air defenses.

Because the small British carriers lacked the capability to carry airborne early warning aircraft, it was necessary to position ships equipped with surveillance radars near the Falklands to give advance warning of strike aircraft and direct Sea Harriers CAP.

In the air intercept role, the Sea Harrier carried two AIM-9L Sidewinder air-to-air missiles and two 30mm Aden cannon. When equipped with two external fuel tanks, the Sea Harrier had a flight time of approximately ninety minutes that allowed thirty to forty-five minutes of CAP time.

Air-to-air combat between British and Argentine aircraft began on May 1, 1982, when two Sea Harriers and two Mirages engaged in a dogfight. The Mirages fired the first missiles at the Sea Harriers (AIM-9B Sidewinders, Matra 550s, or Matra 530s), but a Sea Harrier scored first with an AIM-9L Sidewinder. Most subsequent Sea Harrier air combat victories were against bomb-carrying Mirage/Daggers and A-4 Skyhawks flying at low altitudes and high speeds.

Sea Harriers logged more than 1,100 CAP sorties and were credited with the destruction of twenty Argentine aircraft. No Sea Harriers were lost in air-to-air combat. Confirmed kills included eleven Mirage/Daggers, five A-4 Skyhawks, one Canberra, one C-130, one Pucara, and one helicopter.[7]

The AIM-9L Sidewinder was credited for the destruction of sixteen Argentine aircraft, with another four falling to 30mm cannon. Most Sidewinder shots were from the rear hemisphere. The missile achieved a very respectable success rate of 61 percent (sixteen kills for twenty-six launches).[8]

The Sea Harrier performed excellently despite the fact that it was subsonic, equipped with pulse-only radar incapable of detecting low-flying targets over land, and had relatively limited range and payload performance. Because of the limited number of fighter aircraft available (there were never more than twenty-five Sea Harriers in the South Atlantic at one time) and the lack of airborne early warning platforms, the British were unable to gain air superiority and thus prevent losses. The Sea Harrier performed both air-to-air and air-to-surface missions and achieved a twenty-to-zero air combat record against Argentine air force aircraft during the conflict.[9]

Sea Harriers struck at the Port Stanley and Goose Green airfields with 1,000-pound bombs and BL755 cluster munitions starting on May 1, 1982. Strikes continued, but following the loss of a Sea Harrier and pilot to antiaircraft fire over Goose Green on May 4, tactics were modified.

To reduce vulnerability to the heavy concentration of antiaircraft weapons encountered at Port Stanley and Goose Green, Sea Harriers took to loft bombing. This type of delivery was very inaccurate but was designed to keep pressure on the Argentine troops while limiting losses. Sea Harriers on CAP used their 30mm Aden cannon on May 9 and 16, 1982, to strafe Argentine trawlers and naval patrol craft.

Royal Air Force GR Mk. 3 Harriers arrived in the South Atlantic on May 18 aboard the container ship *Atlantic Conveyor* to augment the force of Sea Harriers. The RAF Harriers operated from the HMS *Hermes* and, later, from a forward operating site near San Carlos.

RAF Harrier pilots took over most of the responsibility for ground-attack operations in support of British ground forces. Harrier pilots flew attacks against airfields at Port Stanley, Goose Green, and Pebble Island, close support strikes, and preplanned strikes against enemy positions. The most common ordnance employed was the 1,000-pound bomb, although BL755 cluster bombs, 2-inch unguided rockets, and laser-guided bombs were also delivered.

The Harriers and Sea Harriers operated routinely against several well-defended targets. Goose Green was defended from air attack by six twin-barrel Rheinmetall 20mm cannon supported by an Israeli-built ELTA radar, two 35mm Oerlikon cannon directed by a Skyguard radar, and SA-7 shoulder-fired missiles. On May 4, 1982, a Sea Harrier striking Goose Green was shot down by 35mm cannon fire. Port Stanley had even heavier defenses, including more than twenty 20mm and 35mm cannon, several fire-control radars, Tiger Cat and Roland antiaircraft missiles batteries, and handheld SA-7 and Blowpipe SAMs.[10]

Three Harrier and two Sea Harrier aircraft were lost to ground defenses during the conflict. One Sea Harrier was lost to antiaircraft fire over Goose Green on May 4, and a second was shot down by a Roland SAM over Port Stanley on June 2. Sea Harriers flew 90 attack sorties during the conflict.[11] Harrier losses included an aircraft destroyed by either an Argentine Blowpipe SAM or cannon fire on May 21, and two downed by antiaircraft fire on May 27 and May 30. The

RAF Harriers flew a total of 126 attack sorties over the Falklands. The aggregate loss rate for Sea Harrier and Harrier strike operations was 2.3 percent (five losses in 216 sorties).[12]

Spanish Navy (Arma Aerea de la Armada)

In 1973 the Spanish navy (Arma Aerea de la Armada) expressed interest in acquiring Harrier aircraft for operations from its aircraft carrier, SNS *Dedalo* (ex–USS *Cabot*). During the late 1970s the Spanish navy procured thirteen Harrier aircraft similar to the U.S. Marine Corps' AV-8A and TAV-8A and designated its aircraft the AV-8S Matador. These aircraft were shipped to McDonnell Douglas in St. Louis, Missouri, for final assembly. The United States provided training for Spanish pilots and support personnel. The 8th Squadron (008 Escuadrilla), based at the Rota naval base, flew the AV-8S and TAV-8S from the SNS *Dedalo* on Atlantic and Mediterranean naval patrols. The Spanish navy replaced the SNS *Dedalo* with the *Principe de Asturias,* a small aircraft carrier based on the U.S. Navy design for a sea control ship.[13]

Indian Navy

The United Kingdom sold twenty-three single-seat FRS.51 Sea Harriers and four Harrier Mk. 60 two-seat aircraft to the Indian navy in the mid-1980s. Two more ex-RAF T. Mk. 4 trainers were delivered in 2003. Two squadrons, No. 300 and No. 551, operate Sea Harriers from their primary base at Goa and the aircraft carrier INS *Vikrant* (ex-HMS *Hercules*) and the INS *Viraat* (ex-HMS *Hermes*).[14]

Unique Advantages of the V/STOL Harrier

Quick Response and High Sortie Rate

Harriers positioned at forward sites near the front lines can respond quickly to calls for strikes against enemy positions. Because they are near the battle area and can be rearmed and refueled quickly, Harriers can fly repeated sorties and deliver far more ordnance than conventional attack aircraft. Forward positioned, the aircraft can "ground loiter" until called upon to strike at the enemy. This adds up to quicker response and significant fuel savings when compared with an attack using conventional fixed-wing aircraft, which in many cases must fly farther and loiter near the target until called in to attack.

Air Combat Capability

The Harrier demonstrated excellent maneuvering agility in air-to-air combat in the Falkland Islands air campaign. This was due to the Sea Harrier's maneuverability, high thrust-to-weight ratio, small size, smokeless engine, cannon, and AIM-9 Sidewinder IR guided air-to-air missile weaponry.

Basing Flexibility and Survivability

The Harrier can operate from a wide variety of sites, including small VTOL pads the size of a tennis court, a short section of road or damaged runway, and conventional runways thousands of feet long. The aircraft can be deployed to small civil airports, road segments, or grass strips near the battle zone in times of tension or conflict. Fuel, ordnance, and maintenance equipment can be airlifted or trucked to these forward sites to allow for continuous operations.

The ability to operate from ship platforms that do not have catapults and arresting gear has also proved to be a significant force multiplier. There are fewer than twenty operational aircraft carriers around the world with catapults and arresting gear that can operate with fixed-wing tactical aircraft. However there are hundreds of ships from which a V/STOL Harrier can operate. The Royal Navy flew Harriers and Sea Harriers from the *Atlantic Conveyor* cargo ship until it was damaged by an Argentine Exocet antiship missile during the 1982 Falkland Islands conflict.

Even if enemy aircraft succeed in damaging runways or air strips, the Harrier's short runway requirement allows it to operate with full weapons loads from airfields or remote sites unusable by conventional attack aircraft. Harrier V/STOL aircraft can be dispersed near an airfield or operate from short strips, which makes enemy targeting extremely difficult. Aircraft can be camouflaged among trees or other suitable terrain to ensure that they are hidden from the prying eyes of enemy reconnaissance aircraft.

Many military planners and political leaders assume that in future military contingencies, host nations near the conflict zone will allow use of air bases and fully support allied air operations, and that these local airfields will be relatively safe from enemy attack. The inaccuracy of this assumption has been demonstrated in dozens of wars, ranging from World War II to conflicts in Afghanistan and Iraq. The highly successful Israeli air attacks using strafing and unguided bombs in the 1967 war destroyed more than 250 Arab aircraft and cratered runways. This conflict is often highlighted as the success story for knocking out an adversary on the ground. However, Anglo-French attacks against Egyptian airbases in 1956, Turkish raids on Cyprus airport in 1974, and a variety of ground attacks on air bases have also met with considerable success.

Most modern tactical aircraft, such as the F-4, Mirage, MiG-21, Tornado, F-15, F-16, F/A-18, Eurofighter, Rafael, and Gripen, require at least 5,000 feet of relatively smooth runway surfaces to take off and land, plus hardened shelters to protect aircraft, support facilities, fuel, and munitions. A typical main operating base has one or two runways (8,000 feet by 150 feet), taxiways capable of supporting flight operations in an emergency, two or three clusters of hardened aircraft shelters to protect aircraft, fuel storage and delivery systems (semihardened tanks with underground pipes or trucks for delivery), a remote and hardened site for munitions, and semihardened support and command and control facilities.

Most NATO bases were developed to operate forty-eight to seventy-two aircraft (two to three squadrons), whereas the Soviets and their allies developed bases to accommodate an air regiment (about thirty-six aircraft). The only tactical aircraft capable of taking off, landing, and maintaining operations with damaged runways are the Harrier, Harrier II, and A-10.

Air Threat

In addition to regular bombs, rockets, and cannon, a number of air forces armed their attack aircraft with specialized antirunway weapons. These weapons included the French Matra Durandal bomb, the Russian BETA B-250 rocket-boosted bomb, and munitions dispensers such as the UK JP-233 or German MW-1, which delivered a mix of cratering weapons and mines to disrupt flight operations. Although Israeli Mirage and Mystere pilots damaged runways with "dibber" bombs and knocked out hundreds of Arab aircraft on the ground with cannon fire during the 1967 war, they never fully shut down Arab air operations.

However, during the 1971 Indo-Pakistan War, continuous Indian Air Force strikes by MiG-21s, Su-7s, and Hunters using Russian-developed anti-runway bombs blasted Tezgaon Air Base in East Pakistan. Even though most of the Pakistan Air Force (PAF) No. 14 Squadron's F-86 Sabres survived the air assault, PAF pilots were unable to contest the damaging Indian air attacks on Pakistani ground forces due to cratered runways.[15]

In June 1982, attacks by British Vulcan bombers and Sea Harriers damaged Stanley airport in the Falkland Islands. During the little-known Operation Empervier in February 1986, French Jaguars closed down Quad Doum airfield in Chad with BAP-100 antirunway bombs.

During the 1991 Gulf War, U.S., UK, and allied strike aircraft conducted a massive counterair campaign against Iraq, which included focused strikes to disrupt fighter operations from many well-defended and hardened air bases. Despite some early losses of A-6Es and Tornados using low altitude strikes, coalition forces persisted, and the Iraqi air force was able to fly only fifty sorties per day on the first few days of the air war.

At the end of the first week of the war, the coalition began a systematic assault against the 600 hardened shelters at Iraqi air bases, using medium altitude attacks with laser-guided bombs. These strikes were devastating. Within two days, Iraqi jets were fleeing to Iran or dispersed to villages in order to survive. By the end of the war, 375 Iraqi hardened aircraft shelters had been destroyed and an estimated 150 aircraft destroyed.[16]

Strike aircraft today in service with U.S. forces and flying with many other nations (such as Su-30s and similar aircraft with advanced guided munitions) have greater accuracy and lethality than the F-111s and Tornados involved in the successful Gulf War strikes. During operations over Kosovo in April 1999, a single USAF B-2 stealth bomber delivered six 2000-pound GPS-guided Joint Direct Attack Munition (JDAM) bombs, which crippled both runways of the Obvra airbase in Serbia. Strikes against seven other air bases in Yugoslavia using a variety of guided weapons ranging from the Tomahawk cruise missile to laser- and TV-guided bombs disrupted operations even if the number of aircraft destroyed was limited. Initial attacks in Afghanistan also targeted airbases and aircraft shelters, and air superiority was rapidly achieved.

Advanced stand-off missiles such as the Tomahawk, JASSM, Apache, and SLAM-ER can destroy any hardened aircraft shelter, command center, or munitions bunker at an air base even in the face of heavy air defenses. Following the initial strikes on fighter bases and suppression of enemy air defense (SEAD) attacks to knock down surface-to-air missiles, strike aircraft can use laser-guided bombs, JDAM, and other weapons to complete the destruction of air bases. Chemical and biological weapons can also be delivered by air to shut down air bases.

Missile Threat

The U.S. Congress in 1999 estimated that 15,450 ballistic missiles were then in service in thirty-four countries and that thirty new types of missiles were in advanced development. An estimated five thousand tactical ballistic missiles have been used in anger during the conflicts of the past fifty years, including the Arab-Israeli conflicts, Gulf War, Iran-Iraq War, Soviet actions in Afghanistan, Yemen civil war, and other conflicts. During the 1973 Arab-Israeli War, several Syrian FROG missiles hit a number of targets, including Ramat David Airbase in northern Israel, causing damage and casualties.

The threat of ballistic missile attack is increasing, more nations are fielding these systems, and they are becoming more accurate due to the availability of GPS and improved inertial guidance systems. Warhead options for ballistic missiles range from nuclear, biological, and chemical to conventional munitions. Even older improved SCUD-class tactical ballistic missiles can be effective against airfields once they are equipped with improved guidance systems and conventional submunition warheads.

As seen in the Gulf War with the SCUD missile strikes, even small numbers of ballistic missile attacks can change the defensive situation. Ballistic missile launchers are mobile and thus hard to detect and knock out. Ballistic missiles have a short time of flight: even the relatively slow SCUD can travel more than two hundred miles in less than five minutes and many newer missiles are much faster. Once detected, incoming ballistic missiles are hard to shoot down. Only a limited number of nations today (the United States, several NATO nations that have bought Patriot batteries, Russia, Israel, and perhaps China) currently field antiballistic missile systems that can shoot down tactical ballistic missiles.

Another widely deployed threat to air bases is cruise missiles, with some 65,000 deployed worldwide in some eighty nations. Although most of the current cruise missiles are antiship weapons, many of these would be very effective in the airfield attack role. According to a 2002 U.S. Congressional study, eighteen nations build cruise missiles today, and twenty-two nations are known to be working on or have the capability to produce cruise missiles that could lead to operational strike systems in the next ten years. Combine a basic airframe with an engine, warhead, and GPS or other commercial guidance technologies, and cruise missiles can be widely deployed for a low unit cost.

The German V-1 missiles were launched in the thousands toward the end of World War II and caused considerable damage despite heavy defenses and their primitive guidance system. The Tomahawk cruise missile has been widely used by U.S. and UK forces since the Gulf War, along with the USAF conventional air-launched cruise missile (CALCM). New systems in advanced development include the Storm Shadow, Taurus, and Joint Air-to-Surface Standoff Missile (JASSM). A basic cruise missile fired in large numbers could prove effective at overwhelming air base defenses. A mass of slow missiles fired at night (seventy-knot unmanned aerial vehicles [UAVs]) would be hard to detect visually or by Doppler radars, and, if armed with chemical, biological, or cluster munitions, could cause significant damage.[17]

Ground Attack

A Rand study identified 645 air base attacks by ground forces during the period from 1940 to 1992; these raids destroyed or damaged two thousand aircraft. Only a quarter of these strikes penetrated the air base, but most used standoff weapons such as rockets, mortars, and artillery. The North Vietnamese and Viet Cong assaulted the ten U.S. air bases in South Vietnam more than five hundred times with rockets, mortars, and commando attacks from 1964 to 1973. These attacks killed hundreds, wounded thousands, and destroyed more than eight hundred aircraft.

Not all anti-airbase attacks go as planned. On the night of September 6, 1965, during the Indo-Pakistan War, 180 Pakistani commandos dropped by parachute from C-130s near the Indian airbases of Halwara, Pathankot, and Adampur. Most of these troops were killed or captured before they could accomplish their mission. However, similar assaults by Afghan forces against Soviet bases, British strikes on Argentine airfields in the Falkland Islands, and other attacks in El Salvador, Grenada, the Philippines, and Africa have met with considerable success.

Air Base Hardening

The Arabs, Israelis, Russians, Americans, and many others reacted to the lessons of the 1967 war and spent billions on improving their air bases to protect against air and ground attacks. Additional sums were also spent on multiple runways, taxiways, and runway repair and air defenses to improve air base survivability. During the 1970s, NATO and the Warsaw Pact made a major investment in this area. NATO funded an upgrade to seventy major operating bases, and alternative airfields were equipped with several types of steel-reinforced, concrete-hardened aircraft shelters (USAF Europe/Korea TAB VEE, and the larger NATO second- and third-generation shelters), which could protect an aircraft from all but a direct hit by a large bomb. Shelters, bunkers, and revetments were built to protect logistics facilities, command and control centers, munitions, storage areas, and airfield support equipment such as fuel trucks and munitions loaders. Alternative airstrips and widened taxiways were constructed at most bases to increase the possibility of operation in the event of attack.

Passive airbase survival efforts included hardening and protective construction, chemical and biological warfare defense capability, camouflage, and concealment and deception programs. NATO air force personnel were also equipped with masks and suits to protect against chemical and biological attacks and collective protection shelters for sustained operations. Investments were also made in detection systems, decontamination equipment, and training. The Soviet Union and Warsaw Pact air arms followed similar airfield upgrades, including the building of concrete, steel- and earth-covered aircraft shelters and hardening. Runways and taxiways were made of concrete slabs so that they were easy to replace if damaged. In addition, tactical aircraft were developed with STOL and rough field operations in mind. The Swedish and Finnish air forces concentrated on the concept of dispersal to prepared strips of highway and alternative civil airfields for wartime operations, whereas the Swiss built aircraft shelters in mountain caves for protection against attack.

Exercises in the United States, United Kingdom, and Europe in the 1970s demonstrated that most NATO forces were not prepared for the task of runway repair. Hardening and aircraft shelters had made it more likely that the runways would be the focus of attacks. Most modern tactical aircraft have small, high-pressure tires, and thus a high wheel loading, which requires multilayered concrete or hardened asphalt runways. Jets can also suck up debris during operations. For successful operations, most tactical aircraft require at least a five-thousand-foot by fifty-foot strip of relatively smooth runway.

Runway repair is a challenging operation: unexploded or delayed-action bombs must be removed or detonated and craters filled and patched with asphalt, concrete, or aluminum matting; runways and taxiways must be cleared of debris. Repair crews must be available with the necessary engineering equipment and supplies at every air base. These crews must be prepared to deal with unexploded bombs and mines and continuing attacks and make difficult repairs while wearing chemical protective gear. NATO and many other air arms expanded their engineering groups and on-base construction materials and fielded additional construction equipment. USAF construction teams fielded armored bulldozers and excavators and remote-control systems to deal with delayed-action bombs and mines.

Active Defenses

Egyptian, Syrian, and Arab forces with experience of the 1967 war not only hardened their airfields with concrete and steel aircraft shelters and multiple runways but also defended them well, using SA-7 SAMs plus 23mm and 57mm antiaircraft batteries on the base and SA-2 and SA-3 missile batteries located in a protective ring around the fields. In addition, large numbers of fighters flew combat air patrols over bases. Egyptian strikes on Israeli airbases in the Sinai during the first few days of the 1973 war shut down several runways and damaged facilities, but the attackers suffered many losses. To reach the air bases, Israeli jets had to penetrate the heavily defended fronts along the Suez Canal and Golan Heights and then get through these terminal defenses.

In 1973 the primary Israeli Air Force airfield attack platform was the F-4E Phantom, which could deliver 12,500-pound free-fall bombs on a long-range strike mission. Although this pre-precision guided munitions load of bombs could damage a runway (which was quickly repaired) and knock out SAM or antiaircraft batteries, unguided bombs had a low probability of kill against a hardened aircraft shelter or ammunition bunker. When the Israelis tried to knock out the Egyptian and Syrian air forces on the ground in the 1973 war, they damaged many runways and slowed Syrian air operations but suffered heavy losses and only knocked out twenty-two aircraft.

NATO, Warsaw Pact, and many other military forces also made sizable investments in air and ground defense to protect air bases from attack. A massive number of fixed and mobile radars were deployed to monitor airspace and detect any potential attack. NATO also fielded its E-3B airborne warning and control system (AWACS) fleet, which could fill gaps and see well into Warsaw Pact airspace. Fighter bombers attempting to penetrate east or west had to face a wall of fighters, surface-to-air missiles, and gunfire, as well as the terminal defenses. NATO forces had large numbers of F-15s, F-16s, Phantoms, and other fighters; parallel lines of HAWK area-defense SAMs along the border backed up by Patriot SAMs plus massive numbers of Rapier, Roland, Chaparral, and Stinger SAMs; and antiaircraft guns around their air bases.

Soviet and Warsaw Pact forces fielded a similar dense air defense. This air defense shield has been reduced in Europe but many other nations still field formidable defenses to protect air bases. In addition, the AWACS in service today with many air arms can vector in F-15s, F-16s, Mirage 2000s, and MiG-29s, all of which have radars capable of detecting low-flying aircraft and firing lethal AIM-120, AA-12, and other advanced air-to-air missiles. Most nations field capable air defenses, and some have advanced Patriot, S300P (SA-10), Antey 2500 (SA-12), or Arrow systems capable of shooting down strike aircraft, cruise missiles, or tactical ballistic missiles.

The USAF, Royal Air Force, and many other air arms have specially trained and well-armed troops stationed at air bases to deal with special operations forces, commandos, and terrorists. In Europe, Korea, and the Middle East, air base defense forces have been on alert for years. Since the September 11, 2001, terrorist attacks in the United States, military forces around the world have increased their defenses against ground and air attacks.

The strikes against Iraq, Yugoslavia, and Afghanistan have demonstrated beyond a doubt that cruise missiles and modern strike aircraft armed with precision-guided munitions have eliminated the defense benefits created by the hardened aircraft shelter and multiple runways. Today a single B-52 or B-2 or a flight of tactical aircraft armed with JDAMs or laser-guided bombs can severely damage an airfield. In a possible conflict between the People's Republic of China and the Republic of China (Taiwan), the threat of attack on air bases is high. Taiwan counts on its large and capable air force (Republic of China Air Force) armed with hundreds of Mirage 2000, F-16A/B, IDF, and F-5E/F interceptors for air and sea defense. However, this air power is concentrated at eight air bases. In addition Taiwan has only about twenty-five (known) military, civil, and highway dispersal runways in the country with a five-thousand-foot operating surface.

The People's Republic of China has more than five hundred tactical ballistic missiles, thousands of strike aircraft, and as many cruise missiles, which can be targeted at these air bases.

This same dangerous situation holds true in a potential surprise conflict between North Korea and South Korea. Although the United States and South Korea hold a major advantage in airpower, the United States has aircraft at only two air bases, and the Republic of Korea (South Korea) has less than a dozen primary airfields. All of these units are located within range of North Korean surface-to-surface missiles, and the threat of attack by North Korean special forces is very real. The risk of air and ground attacks on military air bases or civil airfields around the world is high, especially in light of recent terrorist threats.

Only a few air arms, such as the Swedish air force, Finnish air force, Swiss air force, Royal Air Force, and USMC, have experience with dispersal or remote flight operations. Likewise, only a small number of aircraft, such as the Harrier and Harrier II, have V/STOL capability, but some aircraft, such as the Viggen, Gripen, and F/A-18, have performance that allows STOL operations away from fixed air bases.

CHAPTER 3

The USMC and the Harrier: Overcoming Challenges

Harrier Evaluation

In late 1966, Lt. Gen. Thomas H. Miller, USMC (Ret.), then a colonel, was assigned the Air Weapons Systems Requirements Branch at Marine headquarters. Working under Maj. Gen. K. B. McCutcheon, Deputy Chief of Staff, Aviation, his job was to determine what weapons systems, aircraft, helicopters, bombs, and other equipment the Corps required to do its job.

> In mid-1968 I had a young officer in my office, Lt. Col. John Metzko, who was primarily in charge of the R&D side of my office. Metzko was an unusual guy, he was a great reader and studier. He had his nose in books all the time reviewing R&D, and he was well suited for the job. He came to me one day and said, "I have just seen a film that I have gotten from the British Embassy that describes the latest version of the Kestrel jet also known as the Harrier. I would like to have you come see the film." So we put it on the machine and I watched it and I was flabbergasted! The USMC had followed the P1127 flights, but the USMC didn't get anyone on the Kestrel test team for the flight trials. The main jump was the 15,000-pound-thrust Pegasus engine for the Harrier that made all the difference.[1]

Colonels Miller and Metzko informed Brig. Gen. W. G. Johnson, Assistant Deputy Chief of Staff (Air) HQ USMC, of Harrier capabilities, and contact was made with the UK embassy and the manufacturer, Hawker Siddeley, for additional information. Colonels Miller and Metzko then briefed Maj. Gen. K. B. McCutcheon and showed him the Harrier film. General McCutcheon scheduled a meeting with the commandant of the Marine Corps, General Chapman. After viewing the film the commandant supported finding out more about the Harrier. General Miller noted, "I wanted to take Lieutenant Colonel

Metzko for the evaluation but I could not, as the British were firm on only allowing trained test pilots. So I took Lt. Col. Bud Baker, and we sent our logbooks over to the UK embassy."

General Chapman asked if it would not be smart to send a general officer over on the mission. As Lieutenant General Miller tells the story:

Brigadier General Johnson had fixed-wing flying early in his career, but his primary experience was in helicopters and he was not a test pilot. This forced the fact that Bud Baker and I were the ones that were sent over to do the evaluation. When we left and went over there, we were not cleared at that time to fly. One of the stipulations was we stayed in civilian clothes and no publicity at all about our flights. On the last day of Farnborough one of the UK reps came up and said, "Well I've got some good news and some bad news. You are authorized to fly the plane." I said, "What is the bad news?" "Well, you are limited to no more than ten flights each!" God, I almost laughed in his face as I thought we would be lucky to get two or three flights each! So we made arrangements to go down to [the Hawker Siddeley flight test center at] Dunsfold where the plane was and we stayed in a pub rather than a big hotel.

John Farley was the head pilot for the Harrier at that time, so we sat for two or three days with John, going over the idiosyncrasies of the airplane and everything. Finally John said, instead of going through the routine of flying the airplane conventionally first, we will go ahead and do the "press ups," as they called them. We just have to do them under the overcast. The Harrier was unique in that it had a vertical takeoff, a "suck-down" effect that's caused by the rotation of air through the ducts and then back over the top of the wing. So, the idea was to get out of the ground suck-down effect as quickly as possible. Instead of coming up on the power slowly when you get ready to take off, you went full out and the jet would lift off and then get through the instability. You got about ten feet above the ground and boy, the aircraft shot up just like a cannon.

First we did some runs down the runway to get a feel for the braking stop, which sets the nozzles ahead of the hover position. . . . We'd go up to thirty knots of indicated speed, and then we'd pull the nozzle into the braking stop and come up on the power to slow down. Then, we would go up to sixty knots and try it. We only had a six-thousand-foot runway and we got up to one hundred knots, where you are more than half-way down the runway. Trying to get the jet stopped was a bit touchy. Bud got going through the same process and he gave the jet too much power. He automatically pulled back on the stick and became airborne to about four or five feet off the ground. So Bud was the first American to actually "fly" the Harrier.

We went on and each did four or five hovers in the Harrier. John Farley would say to me, "OK, it's time to come down," since the jet would turn and rotate because I put in rudder and when I went to neutral it would continue until you put in opposite rudder. I had flown helicopters but Bud had not. The Harrier is smooth. You do not have all the vibration of a helicopter, and with the helmet on, it is quiet. We finally were coming to the end of our ten flights so we dropped bombs. I had a lot of experience with dive bombing . . . but I asked how could we use the engine nozzles to help get into proper dive attack position? They called in the engineers and answered our questions about power and speed limitations using nozzle braking in flight.

We each did two hops dropping bombs and using the engine nozzles to slow us down and get into proper angles for an attack. We asked about air-to-air combat and what kind of restrictions did we have? The British engineers finally came back with 92 percent or 93 percent engine rpm at 25,000 feet and no more than 350 knots. So then Bud and I went up the next week. Bud got on my tail and I pulled into a normal hard turn and said, "Bud, are you ready?" When he said, "Yep," I pulled my nozzle into the braking position and heard Bud say, "Oops, where did you go?" I had just disappeared in front of him. This was a very elementary early test, but to me this showed great promise. Certainly there was no modern-day fighter which could have stayed with the Harrier in a close-in air battle.

Colonel Miller and Colonel Baker's flight test report was enthusiastic. They stated in the report that the Harrier could perform the same light attack role as the A-4 Skyhawk was doing in Vietnam and even provide self-defense in air combat. However, the Harrier could fly from a one-thousand-foot strip or amphibious assault ship rather than a six-thousand-foot runway. The Marine Corps saw the promise of a flexible close air support aircraft for protection of its ground forces that could go wherever the Marines went, independent of aircraft carriers or long runways ashore, and would be able to provide responsive air support for the Marine rifleman.

Although the Marine Corps wanted the UK-built Harrier, funds to buy the aircraft had to be identified and support developed. First the Marine Corps had to convince the leaders of the Congress, U.S. Navy, and Naval Air Systems Command (which bought aviation systems for the Marine Corps) that the Harrier was better for the Marine Corps than a U.S. Navy aircraft.

General Miller continues:

After Bud and I got back from the Harrier flight evaluation in the UK, a couple of important things happened. I was the Marine Corps representative to the President's Scientific Advisory Committee on various weapons systems and would attend when they met, which was at least quarterly and sometimes more often. . . . Somehow the word got out that I had flown the Harrier—I think they called looking for me when I was at Farnborough—and the committee wanted to be briefed on it right away.

Dr. Garwin, one of the senior members of the Scientific Advisory Board, called and said they were in session and would like to have you and Lt. Col. Bud Baker brief us on what you found out about the Harrier. I said I can't do that unless the commandant approves it because he has not seen the results yet, so I called General McCutcheon. We got the OK to brief the commandant over lunch, so Bud and I briefed him and he gave us the OK to talk with the Advisory Board. We had not gone to the Navy yet; we had not even told the Navy we had flown the jet. After briefing Commandant General Chapman, [he asked], "Don't you think this is the road we ought to go?"

[I] replied, "General, I would certainly say so because it will do everything the A-4 can do today, only better, so we are not giving up anything going to the Harrier. Now I think we have some obstacles because it is not made here and we have got to deal with the U.S. Navy. I do not know how they are going to respond and I do not know how the civilian industry in this country will respond."

So we started brainstorming and decided we needed to go brief Admiral Connolly and get a team from Patuxent River and make sure one of them was from the Navy and send them over to the UK to get some additional flights in the Harrier. We briefed Admiral Connolly, and he had a guy in his office, Cdr. Bob Thomas, who had commanded an A-4 squadron. Well, Admiral Connolly went for the idea. The team went over and flew the Harrier, and when they came back the strongest supporter was Commander Thomas. He said, "Hell yes, the Harrier will do everything the A-4 will do and a hell of a lot more!"

For two years, Col. Ed Harper, USMC (Ret.), was the program manager for the A-4 Skyhawk for NAVAIR (Naval Air Systems Command). His job was to "keep things going—worry about the financing, managing the contractors—and represent the program in Washington, D.C., with the Navy and Congress. . . . One night I was at a party and a Navy captain from NAVAIR came up and said to me, 'The Marines were over today talking about a new airplane. Would you take on this program as additional duty until we find out what the hell is going to happen to it?' I said, 'Harrier, what is it?' I did not have a clue! That is how it all started."[2]

The Marine Corps had to sell the benefits of the UK-built V/STOL Harrier to the Department of Defense (DoD) and Congress. The U.S. Navy's initial budget request for fiscal year (FY) 1970 did not include a request for Harrier funding. Cols. Tom Miller, Bud Baker, and Edwin Harper were the action officers charged with accompanying General McCutcheon to Congress. Colonel Harper recalls:

He had briefed us. . . . I was to say how we were to buy the airplanes, and Col. Tom Miller could tell how it flew. General McCutcheon was the spokesman. We were told, "Do not volunteer a goddamn thing unless they ask for it and

I tell you to talk." We went over to the Senate office building on a Saturday morning and met with the Senate Armed Services Committee senior members without the staff. They were sitting around. I recall Senator Goldwater was sitting on a table with his feet dangling over the edge. It was very informal. General McCutcheon went through his briefing. We each said our part to describe the program and to buy the aircraft from the British. The general told the Congress that he did not want to buy half a dozen Harriers and have an evaluation because we will never get anywhere. He said, "We want to buy a whole slug of them and get started and have a meaningful program."[3]

Questions asked by the systems analysis branch of the Department of Defense and the U.S. Navy delayed including the Harrier program in the first-draft FY1970 budget. However, support from Congress and the President's Scientific Advisory Group resulted in the addition of funds for the Harrier in a special amendment. General Miller said, "After our brief, the committee [President's Scientific Advisory Committee] was on cloud nine and said, 'Let's go buy these Harriers!' This was great because they provided a lot of push that helped us in the DoD side of the house because we had Russ Murray and others who were not believers in V/STOL."[4]

In 1969, a request for funds for twelve Harriers was added to the 1970 budget request with the support of Congress. The Marines also had to work with U.S. industry to support the purchase of a foreign aircraft or at least prevent any attempts to block the sale. This was especially true because to cover the cost of the Harriers, the Marine Corps planned to cancel seventeen McDonnell Douglas F-4J Phantom II fighters scheduled for purchase in the FY1970 budget.[5]

The U.S. Congress approved $57.6 million for the purchase of twelve Harriers plus support and training expenses in the FY1970 defense budget. This was the initial funding for a planned buy of 114 Harrier V/STOL aircraft for the Marine Corps, which would be delivered over a five-year period. The new aircraft was given the designation AV-8A Harrier for the single-seat aircraft and TAV-8A for the two-seat trainer. However, there was a challenge, as Col. Ed Harper explains:

When the first order [for the Harrier] went through Congress, Representative Mendell Rivers, chairman of the House Armed Services Committee, supported the buy of the first twelve aircraft from the UK but required that later aircraft be produced in the U.S. This got Hawker Siddeley's attention. Executives decided they needed a U.S. company as a licensing partner. A team came to the U.S. and met with NAVAIR and Navy leaders. As the Harrier program leader I followed them around . . . as they made a pitch. The Navy leadership said they do not want to get involved in picking [Hawker Siddelay's] license partner and that [they] should go ahead and do it.

Following these meetings they contacted eight U.S. aviation firms and they boiled it down to three: LTV, Grumman, and McDonnell Douglas. Eventually they settled on McDonnell Douglas Long Beach, which was where the A-4 was made. Hawker Siddeley executives thought it was a good fit since the A-4 was leaving production and the Harrier was the aircraft to replace it. At that time I was going to retire, and I got offers from Grumman, LTV and McDonnell Douglas. I selected McDonnell Douglas, and I had just arrived at Long Beach when Hawker Siddeley arrived to negotiate the license agreement.[6]

Hawker Siddeley and McDonnell Douglas signed a fifteen-year agreement on September 29, 1969, for production and support of the Harrier for the U.S. market. Later the same year, the U.S. and UK governments signed a memorandum of understanding to cooperate on a Harrier improvement program. Rolls-Royce signed an agreement with Pratt & Whitney for the development of the Pegasus engine components in the United States.

Congressman Rivers's changes were taken seriously, says Colonel Harper.

The folks got together, engineers and production people from both companies, and put together a transition plan to bring the program over to the U.S. over a five-year time period. The first year we planned to buy all of the Harriers from the UK. The second year we planned to do final assembly in the U.S. The third year we would build some structure and the fourth even more in the U.S. Finally in the fifth year we would do a lot more work over here.

We had to price all that out and when it came to budget time in the second year, Congressman Rivers became involved. He and his staff said, "We are paying a premium to bring this program to the United States." [The estimate for the plan to buy 114 Harriers with increasing U.S. content was studied in detail and led to a $238.5 million program cost increase.] "We may not buy more than the planned batch so we might as well continue buying them from England. It would be much cheaper." So suddenly there we were without production and the company transferred the program from Long Beach to St. Louis.[7]

During the FY1971 budget debate (which included an order for eighteen AV-8A Harrier aircraft), the House Appropriations Committee stated its concern that the cost of shifting production to the United States was prohibitive and recommended that production remain in the United Kingdom. The other congressional committees supported this plan. In the end all the USMC AV-8A aircraft were purchased from Hawker Siddeley as the prime contractor.

Although this license was never used for USMC AV-8A production, it formed the basis for future cooperative efforts. McDonnell Douglas's initial involvement was basic AV-8A engineering support work with engineering change proposals. By 1972 McDonnell Douglas was designated as the engineering agency and assigned product support responsibility for the USMC's AV-8As.

Close Air Support Debate

While the Marine Corps quietly developed congressional support for the Harrier, roles, mission, and budget debates intensified over the need for multiple aircraft and helicopters to perform close air support. At this time American involvement in the Vietnam War was at its zenith and hundreds of close air support missions were being flown every day by Army and Marine Corps helicopters and U.S. Air Force, Navy, Marine Corps, and South Vietnamese fixed-wing aircraft. The U.S. Army was supporting the development of the advanced Lockheed AH-56A Cheyenne attack helicopter (a program that was later terminated because of development problems), and the U.S. Air Force was pushing the need for the A-X close air support fighter (a competition eventually won by the Fairchild A-10 over the Northrop A-9). The Marine Corps secured funding for the AV-8A Harrier while LTV, with congressional assistance, pushed for additional buys of the A-7D Corsair II fighter bomber for the U.S. Air Force.

In 1970 during debate concerning the FY1971 budget, Rep. George H. Mahon, chairman of the House Appropriations Committee, sent a letter to Secretary of Defense Melvin Laird stating, "There is serious question as to whether or not future Defense budgets can support the development and/or procurement of three separate aircraft weapons systems designed to perform essentially the same mission."[8] Laird responded to Mahon's request with a letter that detailed the tactical requirements of the U.S. Army, U.S. Air Force, and Marine Corps, which led to different aircraft solutions. In effect, the letter argued for the continuation of the Army Cheyenne, Marine Corps Harrier, and U.S. Air Force A-X programs.

Disappointed with the secretary of defense's response, Mahon directed the Office of the Secretary of Defense to "reevaluate the roles and missions and aircraft relative to close air support." Deputy Defense Secretary David Packard took on the task of running a major study on the close air support issue. In addition, the General Accounting Office conducted an independent assessment of the CAS issue and aircraft options.

In March 1971, Senator Howard Cannon, chairman of the Tactical Airpower Subcommittee of the Senate Armed Services Committee, called for a series of hearings to address the CAS issue. The hearings began on October 22, 1971, and continued for seven sessions until November 8, 1971. Deputy Defense Secretary Packard briefed his study concepts and results, which included an overview of CAS and viewpoints from the ground soldiers and airmen, and a review of enemy air defenses and current aircraft and munitions used to perform the mission. The review concluded: "The A-X, Cheyenne, and Harrier offer sufficiently different capabilities for our future forces to justify continuing all three programs at this time."

Interestingly, the Packard study did not significantly examine the roles and mission overlaps or competition in the CAS: "It became apparent quite early in the review that this issue is really secondary." Packard remarked to the Senate at the hearings, "The primary issues are what capabilities are most needed and how to obtain them in the most cost effective manner."[9]

On November 1, 1971, Maj. Gen. H. S. Hill, USMC; and Rear Adm. D. C. Davis, USN, addressed the committee. Major General Hill discussed Marine Corps CAS concepts such as the AV-8A Harrier as compared to the A-4 Skyhawk and other USMC aircraft (for example, attack helicopters). He concluded:

> In the Marine Corps air ground team, we have struck a careful balance in the number and types of various types of supporting arms to enable the Marine ground commander to effectively carry out his mission. . . . Marines have pioneered close air support and devoted primary attention to improvements in development of close air support systems, to include the V/STOL aircraft Harrier . . . development of a responsive command and control system; providing forward air controllers as organic members of the ground force. . . . We are confident that the key factor in the success of our close air support system is the balanced force of air and ground weapons under one Marine Corps operational commander.[10]

Following the hearings, the report from the U.S. Senate's Committee on Armed Services Special Subcommittee on Close Air Support, released April 18, 1972, recommended that the A-X program of prototype development continue, and that procurement of the A-7D continue for the USAF until a fly-off between the A-7D and the A-4M and resolution force structure issues. In addition, the report stated, "There does not appear to the subcommittee to be a valid issue of duplication between the Harrier and the A-X fixed wing aircraft. The Committee sees the Harrier program primarily as an experiment to evaluate the operational utility of V/STOL. . . . The 60 Harrier aircraft ordered through FY1972 will be sufficient for this purpose and [the committee] recommends that no additional Harriers be purchased."[11]

The Marine Corps early on overcame the efforts of the office of Program Analysis and Evaluation (Office of the Secretary of Defense) to stop Harrier procurement. Despite the Senate recommendation to halt procurement at sixty aircraft following the CAS hearings, the Marine Corps was able to secure support for full program funding in 1973 in the Senate and House Armed Services Committee conference meetings. After some negotiations, Congress supported the FY1974 U.S. Navy request for $53.6 million for twelve Harriers, spares, and support, concluding the AV-8A/TAV-8A procurement program.[12]

The U.S. Marine Corps eventually received 102 AV-8As and 8 TAV-8As from 1971 to 1976. All of the AV-8Bs were completed and flight-tested at the Hawker Siddeley plant at Dunsfold, England. Then the new aircraft were taken apart, loaded into U.S. Air Force transports, and flown from the United Kingdom to the United States. After air delivery the AV-8As were reassembled in the United States and delivered to the U.S. Marine Corps.

The AV-8A was similar to the RAF GR Mk. 1 Harrier, except that magnesium components were removed and the Marine Corps aircraft featured U.S. radios and identification, friend or foe (IFF) systems and outer pylons capable of carrying the AIM-9 Sidewinder air-to-air missile for self-defense. The Martin Baker ejection seat was later replaced by the Stencel SIIIS ejection seat.

The first sixty AV-8As were delivered with the Ferranti FE541 inertial navigation/attack suite, but this complex system was later removed and replaced with an attitude heading and reference system and the Smiths Head Up Display (HUD).

The AV-8A was armed with two 30mm Aden cannon mounted in pods below the fuselage and a wide variety of weapons on four under-wing and one under-fuselage pylons. With a vertical takeoff the AV-8A could carry a weapons load of 1,500 pounds and strike a target at a range of 50 miles; with a short takeoff run the Harrier could carry a 3,000-pound payload to more than 200 miles.

All but the first ten AV-8As delivered (which had the Pegasus 10/Mk102-USMC designation F402-RR-400) were powered by the improved Rolls-Royce (Rolls-Royce, or RR, acquired Bristol Siddley Engines in 1966) Pegasus 11/103 F402-RR-401/2 engine, which provided 21,500 pounds of thrust.[13]

Bob Nidiffer has been involved with the Rolls-Royce Pegasus engine for more than thirty years. He started with the AV-8A Harrier program in 1971 at MCAS Beaufort, South Carolina, on August 18, 1971.

> I joined VMA-513 as a young Marine in the engine shop. The squadron had six planes on station. At the time they were the 402 version of the engine, which I think lasted only 300 hours before it needed a major rework. I spent two years with VMA-513 including time overseas in Japan; later I made a Mediterranean cruise to support six Harriers on the USS *Guam*. I joined Rolls-Royce in 1979 and I have worked on the Pegasus ever since. The 402 was pretty basic, and the concept of the engine today has not really changed. What we have done is added new components and features to produce additional thrust and make it more reliable.[14]

The AV-8A Harrier entered service with the U.S. Marine Corps in 1971, and four AV-8As were tested at the U.S. Navy Test Center at Patuxent River, Maryland, as the first USMC squadrons were becoming organized. Unfortunately, on June 18, 1971, one of these aircraft crashed into Chesapeake Bay during a test flight, killing the pilot, Maj. Mike Ripley.

VMA-513, known as the "Flying Nightmares," formerly an F-4 Phantom Squadron, became the first USMC unit to convert to the Harrier. This squadron was declared operational at MCAS Beaufort, South Carolina, in May 1971. This squadron was based at MCAS Beaufort because U.S. Rep. Mendell Rivers (who supported funding for the program) was from South Carolina.

Capt. Bud Orr, USN (Ret.), was in the first Harrier squadron.

Admiral Zumwalt was the CNO, and the word came out he was going to have a Navy pilot in the first Marine Harrier squadron reporting to him about shipboard compatibility. He wanted a landing signal officer, department head and someone who had flown the A-7E because the Harrier had a head-up-display and both aircraft used the HUD as a primary flight instrument. There were five of us who fit the category. After the interviews, I won. VMA-513 has just been recommissioned. It had been decommissioned as an F-4 squadron and recommissioned as the first Harrier squadron. Bud Baker was the Lieutenant Colonel and CO and he had been the right-hand man to Colonel Tom Miller who was the father of the Harrier and a senior officer in the wing at that time. I was the third officer to check into VMA-513 after Lt. Col. Bud Baker and Capt. Toby Griggs. The squadron senior Sergeant Major gave me a lecture about cutting my sideburns and running with the Marines and being one of them; it was the start of three fabulous years for me. . . . Our first planes were delivered in the back of C-141s and the Marines put the wings on and we started flying them. Before that we had all gone through training on CH-46s at MCAS New River to learn about hovering. During my first pressups (hovering) Lt. Gen. [F. George C.] Axtell, commander of the 2nd Marine Air Wing and Col. Tom Miller, his deputy, were sitting on folding chairs on the end of the runway. We checked out night and day.[15]

By the late 1970s, all four Harrier units, three attack squadrons— VMA-513, VMA-542, and VMA-231—and VMAT-203, the training squadron, operated from MCAS Cherry Point, North Carolina. In 1983 VMA-513 moved to Yuma, Arizona.

By the late 1970s, in addition to the V/STOL AV-8A force, the USMC included five squadrons of A-4M Skyhawks (supported by five headquarters and maintenance squadrons and five reserve squadrons with older A-4Fs and two-seat TA-4Fs) for light attack missions. The V/STOL AV-8A light attack aircraft and A-4M Skyhawk squadrons were tasked with providing close support firepower for Marine ground units. Marine A-4M and reserve A-4F Skyhawks had excellent attack capability; however, they needed an 8,000-foot runway for effective operations.

During hundreds of exercises, Harrier pilots and support crews showed that they could take off from roadways, damaged runways, and open ground. Operational exercises in the United States, Europe, and Asia demonstrated that the Harrier could fly more than six sorties a day and deliver weapons in less than twelve minutes from a forward site during simulated battle conditions. Harrier squadrons also shared the task of six-month deployments to Kadena Air Force Base, Okinawa, to provide support for Marines in the Western Pacific.

The Marine Corps bought the Harrier for its basing flexibility and to fulfill CAS needs; others saw the benefits of the aircraft to take on additional missions. In the 1970s the U.S. Navy, Congress, the DoD, and other organizations debated the number of large-deck aircraft carriers and their complement of tactical aircraft that were needed to meet future defense requirements. Adm. Elmo Zumwalt championed the concept of a 15,000-ton Sea Control Ship, similar in concept to the "jeep carrier" from World War II, equipped with Harriers and helicopters, which could perform missions to supplement the larger aircraft carriers.

The AV-8As proved that they could operate from a wide variety of naval vessels, ranging from aircraft carriers to amphibious assault ships. Admiral Zumwalt transformed the Landing Platform, Helicopter (LPH), USS *Guam,* to what was called the interim Sea Control Ship. A detachment from VMA-513 operated from the USS *Guam* in 1972 to demonstrate this concept.

Bud Orr worked with Bud Iles, operations officer of VMA-513 and Sea Control Ship deck manager, to design the landing aids. "We had a single cell from a Fresnel lens that was floating in oil," Orr recalls, "and [it] projected out a three-degree flight path with six degrees of green, a half degree of amber, and four degrees of red. It was pretty antiquated but it worked. I had over 170 landings on the USS *Guam*, 65 of them at night. . . . We had six planes that were attached to the *Guam*. We worked off the coast of South Carolina, and then we deployed to the North Atlantic."[16]

The Harrier pilots flew more than 170 sorties in poor North Atlantic weather. Sorties included the intercept of Soviet Bear and Badger reconnaissance aircraft. This unit deployed again to the same ship on a six-month Mediterranean tour in 1976. VMA-231 sent fourteen aircraft to the aircraft carrier USS *Franklin D. Roosevelt* in 1976 and 1977 for operations alongside two F-4 squadrons, three A-7 squadrons, and an A-6 unit. The Harriers flew independent of the normal carrier launch and recovery cycle and could operate in poor weather that halted conventional aircraft operations.[17]

U.S. Marine pilots were the first to develop the practice of vectoring the AV-8A's nozzles in forward flight—this technique added a new dimension to the aircraft's self-defense capability. During operational readiness training, pilots from VMA-513 and the other squadrons developed air combat techniques flying against F-4J Phantoms and T-38s and F-86 Sabre jets, which simulated potential threats such as the MiG-21 and MiG-17.

Lt. Gen. Harry Blot, USMC (Ret.), recalls:

One of the thoughts we had was that the enemy had developed the capability to knock out runways, and at some point in the battle, the Harrier might be the only aircraft capable of flying. Therefore we wanted to be able to perform the air-to-air mission as well. In fact, I was given the task to see if I could develop the thrust vectoring capability into an air-to-air advantage.... My instructions came from Tom Miller and Bud Baker. The Brits right from the beginning were using thrust vectoring, but they were using it as a last-ditch maneuver. We decided to evaluate this new capability to see if it was valuable in the air-to-air arena. We flew hundreds of sorties against different types of aircraft in conjunction with VX-4, the operational test organization, to determine what the best tactics were and the best way to use thrust vectoring. The tactics we developed are still in use today.[18]

Without aggressive tactics Harrier pilots often lost dogfights to F-4 crews, who could fire radar-guided AIM-7 Sparrows from medium range and also fight well at close range. However, when they started using team tactics and started vectoring the Harrier's engines' nozzles while dog fighting (a technique called VIFF, or vectoring in forward flight) the tables were turned against the Phantoms. VIFF allowed Harrier pilots to decelerate and make eye-watering turns, but this tactic also could leave the user pilot flying slowly and vulnerable to an attack by another fighter.

Safety was an area in which the AV-8A Harrier received a high level of unwelcome attention. Lt. Gen. Harry Blot (Ret.), a test pilot and Harrier commander, first got involved while he was a test pilot at Patuxent River, Maryland. In 1970 he went to England as a part of the evaluation team at RAF Wittering. "We flew five or six flights each," he said, "and then reported the aircraft had the potential to do the Marine Corps mission. The stability and control was fairly lacking in the STOVL regime, but up and away it was a nice honest airplane. So if the Marine Corps wanted to start with this airplane, they needed to hand-pick their pilots."[19] At first the Marines hand-picked pilots for Harrier squadrons. Col. Greg Kuzniewski, USMC (Ret.), started his class to transition to the Harrier in early 1973,

> with people like Mike Ryan and George Goodwin. There were actu-
> ally more astronauts than Harrier pilots. We started off in VMA-513,
> which was the first (and only) USMC Harrier squadron, and then stood up
> VMA-542 and then became the training squadron. Believe it or not, we
> actually were rotating the training responsibility. Since I was a qualified
> Navy LSO, our squadron leadership said, "Why don't you take over train-
> ing and instruct pilots from here on out, since you have over 35 hours in
> the aircraft!" So I collected paperwork and other training material from
> VMA-513 and created a FAM lecture series and flight syllabus. I had
> icons like John Capito and Joe Anderson in my first class. Eventually the
> HQMC moved all Harrier squadrons to MCAS Cherry Point, North

Carolina, to centralize operation after Rep. Mendell Rivers from South Carolina passed away. At Cherry Point, I was transferred to VMAT-203 to help set up the Harrier training squadron again as the pilot training officer under the watchful eye of Major "Nasty" Gibson. As the case with both VMA-513 and VMA-542, we still did not have any two-seat training aircraft; every FAM class was a new and exciting adventure. During this period, VMA-513 was working up for a six-month ship deployment followed by another six months in Iwakuni, Japan. I joined VMA-513 as they arrived in Japan for a year away and then I went on to Naval Postgraduate School in Monterey. So ended my early years in the Harrier program.[20]

Bud Orr says he learned V/STOL aerodynamics from Bud Iles.

I learned why the Harrier did not like to fly in the 30–90 knot range because of its yaw roll coupling and the directionally destabilizing intake momentum drag. Hell, I have a BS in public relations and Master's in counseling, so this was hard learning but I needed it to learn to survive. Iles knew how to fly the Harrier and he kept us in class eight, ten, twelve hours a day teaching us why the plane was negatively stable in the 30–90 knot range and he made us learn to fly it and how to react. He stressed the importance of understanding how the airplane flew and made us think . . . later they brought Bud Iles back to command the Harrier training squadron at Cherry Point.[21]

During the first ten years of operational service (1971–81), the AV-8A Harrier experienced the highest loss rate for a fighter aircraft in naval aviation. This rate was equal to or lower than that experienced by USMC F-4 Phantom and F-8 Crusader communities when those high-performance fighters were first placed into service, and similar to that experienced by the RAF with its Harrier fleet. The AV-8A was challenging to fly in the V/STOL mode, and a Harrier pilot had to follow procedures and maintain his skills and proficiency. The USMC modified its training program for the Harrier, tightening entry requirements and expanding the number of training sorties especially in the two-seat TAV-8A; these changes lowered the Harrier loss rate.[22]

During the 1979–84 period, the USMC worked with McDonnell Douglas to upgrade the sixty surviving AV-8As to the AV-8C configuration to enhance their tactical capability and improve support. The "C" modification added Lift Improvement Devices for increased VTOL performance; life extension modifications; and the fitting of ECM equipment, an inertial navigation system, and ECM equipment.

A major event for the AV-8A proof of concept was an unscheduled deployment aboard the USS *Nassau* in early 1981. Until this deployment the Harrier was perceived in the United States as a Marine Corps–only CAS aircraft. The deployment of the AV-8A on a "Harrier Carrier" to fill a gap in the national defense posture of the United States afforded the V/STOL Harrier a venue to demonstrate its unique flexibility.

Lt. Col. W. R. Spicer, USMC (Ret.), commanding officer of VMA-231 from May 1980 to August 1981, explains the genesis of the Harrier Carrier as an agreement between the United States and its allies requiring the former to keep two carriers (CVA) in the Mediterranean at all times.

> In early 1981 this was not being done; the Navy had one carrier in the Med[iterranean] and one in the Indian Ocean. The Allies had insisted we honor our commitment, and a CVA was not available to fulfill this mission. I cannot verify but only relate this story as told to me by my group commander. At a cocktail party in Washington, D.C., SecNav, CMC [the Commandant of the Marine Corps], and CNO [the Chief of Naval Operations] were discussing this matter, and one of the three said, "What happens if we put a couple of Harrier squadrons on an LHA and send it out there, would that do it?" The question came down the chain of command very quickly, and I received a call from Col. B. J. Palmer, commanding officer of MAG-32. He wanted to know how quickly VMA-231 could get aboard an LHA and head for the Mediterranean. My squadron had only been back from a shipboard deployment to Operation Artic Express a little over 90 days, and I told him 48 hours or as soon as the deck was available. He told me he had recalled VMA-542 from a deployment at 29 Palms and they would be back in 24 hours. Colonel Palmer, Lt. Col. Colonel Drax Williams, and I flew to Norfolk, Virginia, for a meeting with Deputy FMFLant, Maj. Gen. Hal Vincent. He told us we had no restrictions, to use our imagination and to make this work. He told me specifically that since VMA-231 had the most recent ship experience, to take the lead on making the flight deck work like a big deck carrier or better. The USS Nassau was available, and a period of FCLP (field carrier landing practice) and CQ (carrier qualification) was organized very quickly, and we loaded aboard with twenty aircraft. The transit to the Mediterranean was to be our workup, with the expectation to be fully ready for any mission upon entering the Med.
>
> LHA/LPH flight decks are accustomed to operations with aircraft from static positions. Helos operate from spots on the deck, and are towed to and from those positions. The LHA flight deck personnel were not familiar with an aircraft that could maneuver itself on the deck. Since we were to act as a big deck carrier, the Navy had augmented the deck of the USS Nassau with personnel having big deck experience.
>
> When we landed onboard the flight deck, personnel had each aircraft taxi forward and shut down, just like they do on big decks. After the recovery was complete, they "broke the deck" and started dragging each aircraft to the stern of the ship for parking, just like they do on a big deck. We immediately asked to meet with the Air Boss and his officers in flight deck control, so we could use the flight deck model and aircraft models for demonstration purposes. The

lessons we learned on Operation Artic Express had given us a clear picture of what we would need to do with the flight deck organization in order for us to operate in big deck fashion with twenty Harriers.

Maj. Joe Anderson and I told the Air Boss that we would use the inherent mobility of the aircraft to move about the flight deck, and that all launches and recoveries would commence and end from the spot an aircraft was parked. We never wanted to shut down an aircraft on the port side of the foul deck line. We would maintain a clear deck for launch and recovery at all times. By using the aircraft models we demonstrated how we would park six aircraft on the forward starboard side, the forward bone, and the remaining aircraft on the aft starboard side, aft bone, and continue parking aircraft across the stern and up the port side as far as spot eight. This kept spots two through seven clear at all times to launch or recover aircraft. We started all launches at the 300-foot mark, using 50-foot increments thereafter.

We were very fortunate in that Major Anderson, while at Pax River, had done the flying for the development of the Harrier Launch Bulletin for the LHA. Serving as our head LSO, he worked the tower with the Air Boss, and I worked the flight deck teaching the yellow shirts [deck handling crew] and pilots the art of taxiing around the flight deck, to include backing aircraft into parking places when necessary. It was amazing how quickly the flight deck movement came along, and by the time we reached the Med, both pilots and yellow shirts were quite adept at the whole process. The Air Boss was pleased, because our movement greatly reduced the workload for his flight deck personnel. By the time we entered the Med, we could launch eight aircraft in about 100 seconds and recover eight aircraft in a little over two minutes, with near simultaneous landings at spots 2, 4, 6, and 7. As soon as the flight landed, they immediately commenced taxiing to a parking position while the next launch was taxiing into position for takeoff.

In conjunction to our flight deck movement, we were very conscious of the captain's concerns for ship movement and ship maneuvering for flight operations. We met with the captain and the Air Boss, and explained that we understood the problems of maintaining PIM [position of intended movement], SOA [speed of advance], and proposed to him a program for nonstandard recovery. The ship would need to be [facing] into [the] wind for launch because of wind over the deck requirements, but . . . we would recover into the relative wind, allowing him to maintain course and speed so as to maintain PIM and SOA. To accomplish this, we had four recovery patterns—Alpha, Bravo, Charlie, and Delta—all dictated by the relative wind. Alpha was the standard pattern, Bravo for wind from starboard, Charlie for wind from the stern, and Delta for wind from the port. Only the flexibility of the Harrier could allow this, and the captain was very impressed by the flexibility this allowed him in driving the ship. Sixth Fleet came over to see our operation with a group of his staff, and they were most impressed with the flight deck operation, and the speed of launch and recovery.

After their visit, we were put to work screening for the USS *Saratoga*, of Libya. We were tasked to use a bombing range in Bizerte, Tunisia, that had not seen action by American aircraft since WWII, and conducted a surge test during that exercise. From the deck of the USS *Nassau* we flew into the range in Bizerte, approximately 30 miles, dropped ordnance and returned to the ship. We launched three aircraft every 20 minutes, and recovered three every 25 minutes. We surged sixty sorties in eight hours, and took time off for lunch.

The Harrier Carrier proved useful enough that we spent 103 consecutive days at sea operating, but it was worth it because it proved the perfect showcase for the Harrier. It clearly demonstrated the incredible flexibility of the aircraft not only to the Navy, but our allies as well. The Harrier Carrier created real interest in the aircraft from several countries who realized they could have a carrier presence at sea without the requirement for a big deck carrier. I believe this deployment was a major stepping stone for the Marine Corps; the Harrier helped the V/STOL cause, and greatly enhanced investment for advance capability in future Harriers such as the AV-8B.[23]

In fifteen years of operation, the AV-8A proved not only that V/STOL aircraft could meet the CAS requirements of the Marine Corps, but also that the V/STOL concept of operations was practical. As Maj. Gen. Joe Anderson describes it:

In my mind the AV-8A Harrier was like the helicopter in Korea. It could only carry two fully loaded combat Marines, and when you look at that today, you would say that was not significant in terms of combat projection. Well, it was in terms of evolution! The AV-8A was very necessary to take a major power like the United States and a service like the Marine Corps and make it a centerpiece of operations. [The AV-8A] had limited capability, but that's how the first-generation automobile, boat, or other major systems evolved. So the AV-8A was not very forgiving and it was limited in capability, but it brought us into the world of flexible basing and the Marine Corps into the concept of vertical development.[24]

The proof of concept discussed is directly responsible for the development of the AV-8Bs in service with the USMC, the RAF, the Spanish navy, and the Italian navy today. The current eight AV-8B squadrons (seven tactical and one training) are the direct descendants of those first four AV-8A squadrons, are an integral part of the Fleet Marine Force, and have proven their value in several conflicts.

CHAPTER 4

The Challenging Path
to the Harrier II

A lthough convinced by the AV-8A's basing flexibility and rapid response
capabilities, the leaders of the U.S. Marine Corps hoped to improve
the Harrier's performance. In the early 1970s, even as production
deliveries for the GR Mk. 1 continued to the RAF, UK defense staff began
reviewing options to improve the performance of and/or replace the Harrier. In
1973, the U.S. Marine Corps formulated an operational requirement for a new
version of the AV-8A. Development funding was to come from both the U.S. and
British governments, because the Marine Corps and RAF wanted a new version
of the Harrier with improved payload-to-radius ratio and tighter turn rate.

The Marine Corps goal was to replace its light attack force, which
included the V/STOL AV-8A Harrier and conventional A-4M Skyhawk II, with
a force composed entirely of AV-8B Harrier II V/STOLs by the late 1980s. This
led to a bitter fight between the Marine Corps and its congressional and industrial
allies versus the Department of Defense and elements of the Navy and Congress
over whether to buy the AV-8B Harrier II or the F/A-18 Hornet to modernize the
USMC light attack force. The difficult battle continued from 1976 to 1982.

The determination of Marine Corps and industry leaders to achieve the
goal of a more advanced V/STOL CAS aircraft in the form of the Harrier II
to provide air support for the rifleman eventually prevailed, despite economic,
political, technical, and international obstacles. This effort led to a twenty-five-
year development and production program for the Harrier II and an all-V/STOL
Marine Corps light attack force. The similarly challenging debate in the UK over
the best way to replace the Harrier also eventually resulted in the purchase of the
Harrier II.

The U.S. Marine Corps and the U.S. Navy historically have flown
the same aircraft, because the Navy was responsible for developing and

purchasing systems for the two services. However, the Marine Corps has a history of striking out on its own to meet its unique needs, as shown by their use of the F4U Corsair fighter-bomber rather than the F6F Hellcat in World War II, and the debate over the AV-8A Harrier in the 1970s. The Marine Corps even gave up several squadrons of F-4 Phantom fighters to buy V/STOL Harriers to meet its CAS requirements. In the 1970s, the Marine Corps developed and bought an improved version of the Skyhawk—the A-4M—for the light attack role, rather than participate in the more expensive and maintenance-intense carrier-based Navy A-7 program. The Marine Corps also evaded pressure to replace the F-4 with the F-14 (as the Navy was doing) and chose to retain its twelve F-4 squadrons until the lower-cost, multimission F/A-18 Hornet became available in the 1980s.

In May 1973, the U.S. Marine Corps issued a specific operational requirement for a new version of the Harrier. This improved V/STOL aircraft was to have increased payload and mission radius over the AV-8A, accurate first-pass weapons delivery capability, improved vertical takeoff (VTO) and short takeoff (STO) capability, greatly reduced pilot workload, and improved reliability and ease of maintenance.[1]

The industry was awarded a study to develop an advanced Harrier. Unofficially this new aircraft was named the AV-16, to emphasize the goal of achieving twice the AV-8A's range and payload. Ed Harper, the McDonnell Douglas Harrier II program manager and former USMC Harrier program manager, recalls that "Dick Marsh, the program manager at NAVAIR, called us up one day and said to get the four companies together (Hawker Siddeley, McDonnell Douglas, Rolls-Royce, and Pratt & Whitney) and we will design an improved version of the Harrier. He gave us a contract for $1 million. So we gave the British some of the money too. We started a year-long study and a wind tunnel model."[2] This program eventually became known as the AV-8B Harrier II. Considerable experience was gained with the AV-16 study. The new aircraft was to be powered by a Pegasus 15 turbofan engine with increased thrust (24,000 pounds) and to have a larger wing and avionics improvements.

Ray Searle was the first British Aerospace Harrier II program manager.

The AV-16A was supposed to be an improved performance AV-8A. . . . In order to do that and get the extra performance, the idea was that Pratt & Whitney would put a bigger fan on the engine under a license agreement with Rolls-Royce. British Aerospace and McDonnell Douglas would put together an airframe configuration that would help make [up] the extra performance. That included a bigger wing and a raised cockpit. This program took off in early 1973. Larry Smith from MacAir (McDonnell Douglas) came over to the UK with a few guys and met with John Fozard and we all wrote out a program of work to secure a proposal from the two governments. I was surprised to find

[out] in the meeting that we would swap some engineers on a more perma-
nent basis, and John Fozard said, "I volunteer Ray Searle." So in June 1973 I
found myself in St. Louis. I knew as much as anyone except for John Fozard
about the Harrier because I had worked so long in his office and I knew all the
players in the UK . . . we put together a proposal in six months; it was a very
rapid program. We came up with four configurations of the aircraft. But the
program died a natural death. It turned out the MOD [Ministry of Defence]
future systems was using a slush fund but it had not secured any more money
and the U.S. also ran through its funds.[3]

The total development cost of the new aircraft and engine was estimated
to be more than $650 million, and funding was not available. In June 1974 UK
funding for the engine was eliminated, and the 1975 UK Defense White Paper
did not include this cooperative program.

Starting in 1974, separate programs to enhance the Harrier's performance
began in the United Kingdom and the United States. In the United Kingdom,
Hawker Siddeley (later known as British Aerospace and eventually BAe Systems)
focused on the development of the Sea Harrier. This new design incorporated a
radar and other advancements to the basic Harrier for the Royal Navy, intended
to operate from the three Invincible Class V/STOL aircraft carriers (which were
similar in concept to the U.S. Navy Sea Control Ship, but larger and armed with
the Sea Dart self-defense SAM system). The United Kingdom also funded
an upgrade of the RAF Harrier to the GR Mk. 3 configuration, including an
improved avionics suite.[4]

A joint U.S. Navy–Marine Corps Chief of Naval Operations Executive
Board met in late 1974 and terminated the AV-16A project, because the
United Kingdom had eliminated funding and the estimated costs for the
upgraded engine and total system had grown to more than $700 million.[5]
McDonnell Douglas then had to invest in the technology and carry the program
along until the Marine Corps could convince the Department of Defense, the
U.S. Navy, and Congress of the benefits of funding a lower-cost advanced Harrier
development program.

The U.S. Navy at this time was seriously considering the Sea Control Ship
concept as a force multiplier to support its large-deck aircraft carrier force. It estimated a need for fifty-seven V/STOL aircraft to equip these new small aircraft
carriers. In addition, U.S. Navy planners projected a requirement for 336 new
V/STOL aircraft to modernize the AV-8A and A-4 light attack aircraft in the
Marine Corps fleet.

Congress was asked to fund research to develop V/STOL fighter
attack and multimission aircraft. Development studies for engines and several
airframe designs were awarded on a competitive basis. Ed Harper recalls the first

big exercise, when the Navy came out with a fresh proposal for a new V/STOL aircraft.

> We quickly put together a proposal for a warmed-over Harrier North American won that competition with the thrust-augmented wing concept (XFV-12A prototype, which was funded 1972–77 but never flew successfully). That is when McDonnell Douglas management—George Graff, Bob Little, and others—nearly wrote the Harrier off. They said, "You made a good effort, we got the license, we tried to get into full production, we tried to win an R&D competition but we lost—so no more new business development funding for you guys." I was told [that] we have a little budget left and we were down to a team of only ten guys. If you can bring in some money, you can stay alive, otherwise you are going out of business. . . . We ran around and convinced NAVAIR that the British Harrier maintenance publications would not be useful in the United States and they had to be rewritten. We got a few small ECPs [engineering change proposal contracts] to rewrite Harrier publications. It kept us alive. We were able to keep the 10 guys together and added a few . . . we were able to rework a 15 percent wind tunnel model. Larry Smith and Tom Lacy and others put it into the low-speed tunnel at MacAir and tested new ideas. . . . From then on we never looked back.[6]

The U.S. Navy favored the Rockwell XVF-12A thrust-augmented wing design for its future V/STOL jet fighter. NASA also awarded contracts to study lift plus lift/cruise multi-engine V/STOL designs; this was the VTOL configuration employed by the Soviet Union in the YAK-36 Forger. The Marine Corps focused on the advanced Harrier, which they considered to be a relatively low-risk and low-cost V/STOL option.

Budgetary realities forced McDonnell Douglas to follow the "minimum change" approach for the advanced Harrier design. In early 1975, McDonnell Douglas announced that it was committed to developing an improved V/STOL aircraft called the AV-8+. A series of wind tunnel tests using a model from the AV-16 program proved that improved performance could be obtained through weight reduction, new wing designs, and airframe upgrades.

YAV-8B, Demonstration of the Harrier II Design

Despite successful wind tunnel testing, the U.S. Navy decision makers wanted confirmation with flight hardware before committing to an enhanced Harrier development program. The Navy agreed to provide McDonnell Douglas with two AV-8A aircraft to create YAV-8B prototypes. The initial studies for the YAV-8B program were initiated in May 1975 under guidelines from NAVAIR Harrier Program Management Organization (PMA-257) with the full support of the Marine Corps.[7]

This development and testing program was intended primarily to advance V/STOL technology and verify AV-8+ design enhancements. McDonnell Douglas and Hawker Siddeley engineers researched a number of concepts for improving Harrier performance without the benefit of the higher-thrust Pegasus 15 engine. Composites were used to eliminate weight in the wing and fuselage of the design, and new aerodynamic concepts were tested. Design concepts were verified through more than 4,000 hours of wind tunnel testing of models and use of a modified full-scale AV-8A with a new wing and other features, which "flew" in the low-speed NASA wind tunnel at the Ames Research Center in California. Two AV-8As were fitted with composite wings with a supercritical airfoil, modified air inlets, lift improvement strakes, and new exhaust nozzles for a full flight-test program to confirm wind tunnel and engineering analysis.

"Larry Smith wasn't a guy to give up easily," says Ray Searle,

> and with a little bit of IRAD [internal research and development] money from McDonnell Douglas and a lot of searching around, the team managed to put together enough funds to start on development of what became the AV-8B. They got money from NASA to develop and test a carbon fiber wing. And NASA funding paid to test wing configurations in the NASA Ames Wind Tunnel. To be fair, most of the configuration was developed in St. Louis. . . . To bring the risk down, NAVAIR wanted to have Hawker Siddeley [British Aerospace] as a participating partner in some way or another. As the program went ahead two configurations of wing were tested. One was the supercritical wing and the other the sonic rooftop wing. The sonic rooftop wing was a British design. Small-scale designs of both wings were tested at the NASA Ames wind tunnel. We (Hawker Siddeley) actually built the wind tunnel model wing that went on the McDonnell Douglas wind tunnel fuselage model. Both wings were tested. Information coming out of the testing was mixed. The McDonnell Douglas wing was quite good; in fact it was very good until it started to hit the Mach number drag rise. The sonic rooftop wing went deeper into Mach and therefore would give you a higher maximum speed, but it did not carry as much fuel. The sonic rooftop wing was more maneuverable, but we did not have the money to fully develop the sonic rooftop wing so we had to go with the more tested supercritical wing.[8]

The YAV-8B development program included two phases. Phase I (April 1, 1976, through October 31, 1976) assessed advanced technology previously developed in V/STOL studies and developed a program plan for transition into Phase II. The AV-8B Full-Scale Wind Tunnel Program was completed on September 18, 1976; over the course of this program, the AV-8B VTO and STO performance capabilities were demonstrated, inlet characteristics were documented, the high lift configuration was optimized, and the stability and control characteristics were shown to equal or exceed those of the AV-8A. Phase II involved wind tunnel and flight testing of the YAV-8B prototypes to verify results.

The Controversial Harrier II

The Defense Systems Acquisition Review Council (DSARC) reviewed the advanced Harrier development program in a meeting held on March 26, 1976. In this review, the DSARC approved the program, but also suggested changes that extended the development period and added $122 million, including adding two R&D aircraft, restructuring the production schedule, increasing reliability and maintainability activity, and enacting design changes to improve capability and add new weapons. On July 27, 1976, Deputy Secretary of Defense William P. Clements approved the Harrier II development plan.[9]

In the late 1960s and early 1970s, the Marine Corps successfully worked with the U.S. Navy, Congress, and industry to procure the AV-8A Harrier in order to meet its CAS goals. The procurement of the UK-built AV-8A Harrier was controversial, and the Program Analysis & Evaluation branch of the Office of the Secretary of Defense (PA&E) opposed this procurement (as did some members of Congress and their staff), but they were overruled. Harrier opponents were determined to make their case more aggressively this time.

While the U.S. Marine Corps and the Navy requested funding for Harrier II development, the Department of Defense reviewed and approved the program; congressional support was strong. In 1976 PA&E opposed the program and recommended that it be cancelled. The opposition to the development of an advanced Harrier was led by Russell Murray II, assistant secretary of defense for PA&E.[10]

Every year the U.S. government goes through a long and complex process to develop, review, and approve its annual budget. For the defense budget this process starts with the planning, programming, and budgeting cycle, which involves the Department of Defense, the Joint Chiefs of Staff, and military branches (USAF, Army, and Navy, which includes USMC systems). After significant review by the services, the Office of the Secretary of Defense, and the Office of Management and Budget, the defense budget is submitted to the president for review by his staff. The budget is then integrated into the annual federal budget, which must be submitted to Congress on or before the fifteenth day on which Congress meets in each year (this usually occurs in February). Congress then holds hearings and reviews the budget submitted by the president. Programs must go through both the House of Representatives and the Senate authorization and appropriations committees for approval and enactment. This complex process includes many reviews and approvals, any of which could disrupt or halt development or procurement programs.

By the mid-1970s the Harrier was in service and proving the utility of V/STOL from land bases and ships. Congress continued to favor the Harrier and added funds to meet Marine Corps desires for an advanced Harrier, even though the U.S. Navy offered only lukewarm support. Marine Corps coordination with the U.S. Navy and Congress, along with industry lobbying, ensured continued development funding for the Harrier II program, including $60.3 million in the draft FY1978 budget plan.

The election of Jimmy Carter as U.S. president in 1976 brought a new team to Washington. In early 1977 the new staff brought in by President Carter reviewed the defense budget plans established by the Ford administration and the military services. The Harrier's accident rate provided ammunition for program critics who sought funds for competing programs or who had an axe to grind with the Marine Corps and/or the industry team. Following program reviews, Dr. Harold Brown, then secretary of defense, elected to curtail the U.S. Navy V/STOL development program and instead focus on conventional fixed-wing aircraft (especially the problem-plagued F-14 fighter program) and additional nuclear-powered aircraft carriers.

The secretary of defense recommended delaying the AV-8B Harrier II development program and cutting Harrier II development funding from the draft FY1979 defense budget. An analysis paper by Russell Murray stated, "The AV-8B is a small, single-engine, subsonic aircraft of British lineage, developed as an improvement over the Marines' current AV-8A. The Harrier is a relatively undistinguished aircraft in all aspects save one—its unique ability to use very short runways, at some sacrifice in range and payload."[11]

The Carter defense plan called for the purchase of an additional twenty-four A-4M Skyhawk II aircraft to sustain the Marine Corps light attack force, and acceleration of the development of the F/A-18 Hornet strike fighter for the Navy and the Marine Corps in the FY1979 budget. Some officials within the DoD, the Carter administration, and the U.S. Navy sought to end the AV-8B development program and to fill the Marine Corps light strike/CAS requirement with Hornets in order to reduce the number of aircraft in service and to save money.

The Hornet was in advanced development at the time as the replacement for the U.S. Navy A-7 light attack aircraft and for U.S. Navy and Marine Corps F-4 fighters. Although the new F/A-18 could perform both fighter and attack missions, it was in competition with the F-14 for the air defense role and could not fulfill the critical Marine Corps V/STOL mission requirements. This situation initiated an ongoing battle between DoD, the Office of Management and Budget, and elements of the U.S. Navy versus the Marine Corps, Congress, and aerospace industry representatives.[12]

Lt. Gen. Tom Miller, the first U.S. pilot to fly the Harrier, was now the DCS/Aviation (Deputy Chief of Staff, Aviation) for the U.S. Marine Corps. He spearheaded the campaign to save the AV-8B program.

> We were constantly being hit again on specifications by Russ Murray that we were giving up too much in order to have V/STOL. We, for some reason, could not impress upon anybody but the Congress the importance of this 30 minute rule [air support needs to arrive within 30 minutes of the call or it will not impact the course of battle]. . . . Really this was the path General McCutcheon and Commandant General Chapman set in motion when they signed off on the Quantico studies [in 1963], which called for a long-range plan for an all–Marine Corps tactical V/STOL force as soon as technology would permit it. Unfortunately, there was still an ongoing battle over roles and missions.[13]

The AV-8B development program was the Marine Corps number-one aviation program in the late 1970s. Many senior Marines felt that the Corps was not receiving its fair share of aviation development and procurement funding from the U.S. Navy. There has often been friction between the U.S. Navy and Marine Corps over budget issues since the Navy is responsible for funding Marine programs. In the 1970s, the Navy's aviation budget funded production of the F-14; development of the F/A-18 Hornet, which included funding for the U.S. Marine Corps; development of the Harrier II; and procurement of large numbers of CH-53, UH-1H, and AH-1J Cobra helicopters. The Navy was primarily concerned about maintaining aviation force levels and desired an all-F-14 fighter force, for the A-18 to replace the A-7 in the attack force, and for the Marine Corps to receive the F-18 fighters and either the A-18 or AV-8B for its light attack force. (Initially there were to be two versions of the Hornet, the F-18 for the fighter mission and the A-18 for the attack mission, but eventually the advanced crew station and systems allowed for a single version to perform both missions—thus the F/A-18 designation.)

In 1977, Secretary of Defense Harold Brown directed that a study be conducted to compare the costs and benefits of the AV-8B for the Marine Corps CAS mission versus the A-18 proposed by the DoD. Entitled "An Evaluation of the Comparative Cost Effectiveness of the AV-8B and A-18 Aircraft in Support of Marine Corps Light Attack Requirements Including Amphibious Operations," the evaluation (known as the 8-18 study) was conducted by the Office of the Secretary of the Navy for Program and Analysis, along with representatives of both the U.S. Navy and the Marine Corps. A detailed analysis of several potential conflict scenarios in the Middle East, Korea, the Persian Gulf, and Europe reviewed the tactical and cost aspects of the two aircraft.

The study found that the ten- and fifteen-year costs of the two aircraft were roughly equal, and that relative effectiveness of these aircraft depended upon scenarios and employment assumptions. For CAS scenarios, the AV-8B had substantial advantages over the A-18, because of its flexible basing, responsiveness, and operational survivability. The commandant, Gen. Louis H. Wilson, and other senior Marine Corps officers briefed Congress on the results of the 8-18 study and successful YAV-8B test program to Congress. In response to a question from Sen. Gary Hart (D-CO) concerning which aircraft he would prefer, General Wilson said, "Of course we obviously need the F-18 as much as we need the AV-8B for our attack aircraft. But I testified last year, and I believe this still holds, if I am pushed to the point toward which I am now being pushed, we could hold off modernizing our fighters. Therefore I would take the AV-8B."[14]

The Carter administration continued to oppose the Harrier II. Unhappy with the results of the 8-18 study conducted by the Navy and the Marine Corps, Brown instructed his staff to conduct another evaluation. Russ Murray and the PA&E staff contested nearly every element of the 8-18 study and concluded that the F/A-18 Hornet was the more effective aircraft. Funding for the Harrier II program was restored in the FY1979 budget by Congress, which appropriated $123 million for AV-8B development. The Department of Defense, however, impounded $108 million of this funding and delayed the program until congressional pressure released the funds.[15]

During discussions on the FY1980 budget in early 1979, Secretary of Defense Harold Brown told Rep. Jack Edwards (R-AL), a Harrier II supporter, "My cancellation of this program shows how I feel about this program. The AV-8B is basically an updated AV-8A designed to correct many of the deficiencies seen in the earlier aircraft. The AV-8B does not represent an advance in the state-of-the-art V/STOL technology, nor does it provide the capability the Navy desires for sea-based operations. We feel that these aircraft (two YAV-8B prototypes and the Marines' AV-8As) will be sufficient to explore V/STOL operations to the extent possible with either AV-8A or AV-8B aircraft."[16]

CHAPTER 5

Harrier II Development and Demonstration

YAV-8B Prototype—Flight Demonstration

The flight demonstration phase of the YAV-8B program was a thirty-two-month effort from November 1, 1976, through June 1979. Test program objectives achieved in the flight demonstration program included demonstration of improved payload radius and takeoff performance, improved reliability and maintainability, increased external load capability (more store stations), increased propulsion system efficiency through inlet and nozzle improvements, satisfactory handling throughout the operational flight envelope, and flight experience with production-relevant components and systems.

Major program stages included designing, manufacturing, and flight-testing two YAV-8B aircraft. Two prototype aircraft were produced by significantly modifying AV-8As into the YAV-8B configuration. The first of these was delivered in November 1978, fifty-three days ahead of schedule. The YAV-8B prototypes incorporated AV-8B aerodynamic advancements, including an improved inlet with a larger auxiliary inlet system for increased jet lift; lift improvement devices for additional vertical lift; and a new, larger, higher-aspect ratio wing. The supercritical airfoil wing incorporated a positive circulation flap to achieve high lift when performing takeoffs and landings. The wing structural elements were mostly composite materials.

The aircraft retained the F402 Pegasus 11 series engine, but incorporated a new gearbox and zero-scarf forward nozzles. These changes resulted in mission performance about twice that of the AV-8A, based on range and payload. The YAV-8B also incorporated selective system modifications, which improved reliability and maintainability, permitting a brief flight demonstration program to validate the improved mission availability of the AV-8B.

The first YAV-8B took off for the first time with McDonnell Douglas test pilot Charlie Plummer at the controls on November 9, 1978, and the second YAV-8B flew on February 17, 1979. Flight tests of the two prototypes demonstrated that the modifications did substantially improve range and payload capability and flying quality over the AV-8A. The aircraft was more stable, in ground effect and during vertical takeoff and landing, than the AV-8A and also reduced pilot workload. Vertical landings in 25-knot winds, gusting to 35 knots, were found to be easy and comfortable. Maneuvering in a hover was smooth, positive, and precise; height capture was easy and precise; and the aircraft was very stable in roll. Slow approaches and slow landings were comfortable with low workload, hardly noticeable ground effect on longitudinal trim, and good control on runway after touchdown. YAV-8B flight testing was flown by McDonnell Douglas test pilots Charlie Plummer and Jackie Jackson, as well as British Aerospace test pilot John Farley, with oversight from U.S. Navy and USMC personnel.[1]

The two YAV-8B prototypes demonstrated their improved performance during 451 flights over two and a half years. Jackie Jackson flew as a test pilot with McDonnell Douglas (Boeing) from 1982 to 2004 and is the high-time Harrier II pilot, with more than five thousand flight hours. "The Harrier II built on the positive benefits of the Harrier," he says, "and added improved flight characteristics. For example, as compared to the wing on the AV-8A or Sea Harrier, which quit generating lift at approximately 96 knots, the wing on the YAV-8B and Harrier IIs generated lift down to 42 knots. This increased stability and allowed the aircraft to be easier to fly and left more conventional flight characteristics from flight to hover. Demonstrating this was a big step in heading down the road toward production as we know it."[2]

The success of the YAV-8B prototype flight and wind tunnel test program led to a Defense Systems Acquisition Council Review (DSARC II) and approval of the full-scale development contract that was awarded in April 1979. This decision supported development of the AV-8B Harrier II and production of four development aircraft.[3]

Col. Richard H. Priest flew the YAV-8B test aircraft. "The YAV-8B provided a valuable test bed for the weapons separation work during full-scale development," he says. "It was, however, challenging to attain the end points at high dive angles and airspeeds, because while the YAV-8B had a composite with a supercritical airfoil, it was missing the AV-8B Harrier II cockpit and the full stability augmentation of that aircraft."[4]

Despite the "minimum change" philosophy behind its development, the AV-8B pushed the edge of the technology envelope. Major Harrier II improvements over the AV-8A include a larger wing with a supercritical airfoil, which reduced transonic drag; improved maneuvering performance; and greater volume for fuel. The Harrier II carries 7,759 pounds of internal fuel, 50 percent more than the AV-8A. The AV-8B also includes larger flaps and ailerons, which improve short takeoff, landing, and turn performance, as well as leading-edge root extensions ahead of the wing to enhance maneuverability. The aircraft features new air intakes to improve vertical takeoff and landing and cruise performance, lift improvement devices under the fuselage to enhance vertical lift, and a lengthened rear fuselage to allow for additional equipment. The wing, forward fuselage, horizontal stabilizer, rudder, flaps, ailerons, and most access doors are now composed of composite materials. A more powerful reaction control system and stability augmentation and attitude hold systems have improved hover and slow-speed flight characteristics and pilot workload. The AV-8B has been fitted with a much-improved cockpit and upgraded avionics suite, including the angle-rate bombing system.[5]

Harrier II Composite Success Achieved

The AV-8B includes an all-carbon/epoxy composite wing with metal used only for the leading edge, wing tip, and fasteners. Its upper and lower Harrier II wing skins are 28 feet long and composed of a one-piece composite structure. Spars and other structural members, which constitute the wing torque box, ailerons, and flap substructures, are made of woven carbon epoxy cloth. Most of the wing torque box serves as an integral fuel tank. Control surfaces have carbon/epoxy skins, which are bolted to the composite substructure. The wing weighs 330 pounds less than a comparable wing produced with conventional materials. This wing has proved to be so strong that it has been reused in the remanufacture program, which converted day-attack Harrier IIs into the Harrier II Plus with APG-65 radar.[6]

The AV-8B Harrier II is one of the best demonstrations of the potential benefits of composites in tactical aircraft. The Harrier redesign program goal called for the development of an aircraft with significantly greater range, payload, and weapons delivery effectiveness than its predecessor, the first-generation AV-8A Harrier V/STOL tactical aircraft. The Harrier II, however, is powered by essentially the same power plant (that is, the Rolls-Royce Pegasus II vectored thrust turbofan) as the earlier aircraft. In the AV-8B, composites were used extensively to reduce weight and eliminate metal fatigue characteristics.

The AV-8B's forward fuselage also extensively utilizes carbon/epoxy material. The left and right shells, floor, pressure bulkheads, skin panels, and stiffener frames are fabricated of carbon/epoxy cloth and tape. The fuselage is composed of only 88 parts held together by 2,450 fasteners, versus the 237 parts and 6,440 fasteners of the AV-8A forward fuselage. The composite structure weighs 56 pounds less than a similar metallic counterpart.[7]

In addition to the wing and forward fuselage, the AV-8B's horizontal stabilizer (tailplane) is constructed of carbon/epoxy material. Like the wing, the stabilizer is made of a combination of aluminum, titanium, and composite materials. However, unlike the wing, the lower stabilizer skin is cocured with integral spars, saving 46 pounds compared to metal. Other AV-8B carbon/epoxy applications include the rudder and lift improvement device strakes and fence.

The AV-8B also uses a high-temperature-resistant composite resin material in places where the operating temperature exceeds that suitable for epoxy materials. Both carbon and glass bismalemide composite applications are found in areas where hot engine exhaust impinges on the aircraft structure. More than 26 percent of the Harrier II's structural weight is composite material. The application of composites has reduced the aircraft's weight by about 500 pounds. Benefits from the new wing, redesigned air intakes, lift improvement devices, and weight-saving efforts have effectively doubled the Harrier II's range and payload performance over its predecessor.

Development of the composite manufacturing techniques employed in the manufacture of the Harrier II was a challenge. Jerry Kauffman supervised the development of the AV-8B composite facilities and managed the production of these parts.

> It took quite a while to develop the correct manufacturing techniques to achieve success. We had to work hard with close coordination between design, tooling, test, and production teams to create the complex parts for the Harrier II and ensure quality control. Some of the early Harrier II wings suffered delaminations due to incorrect manufacture. X-ray and nondestructive testing showed that some of the wings on early production lot Harrier IIs delivered to the U.S. Marine Corps and RAF Harrier IIs were in need of repair. To correct the problem, we sent teams to the field, and these wings were injected with resin and fitted with additional fasteners and repair plates. We keep learning and eventually we refined our techniques, but it was an art more than a science.[8]

Harrier II Program

Congressional actions continued program funding even in the face of FY 1979–81 DoD and Carter administration cuts and delay tactics. Spearheaded by supporters, including Sen. John Stennis (D-MS), who was the chairman of the Senate Armed Services Committee, Sen. Gary Hart, (D-CO), Sen. Barry Goldwater (R-AZ), Rep. Bruce Vento (D-MN), and many other elected representatives who supported the Marine Corps, Harrier II funding continued. The road to success on the Harrier II for the Marine Corps was not an easy one, as Ed

Harper explains: "The Marine Corps supported us all the time. They wanted to keep the program going, and without Marine support we would have been dead a half dozen times. The Navy was dragging its feet. They did not want to spend budget on an airplane that they felt they did not need and didn't like. The Marines did a lot of backdoor work and Congress saved the program several times."[9]

By late 1980, the DoD and Navy ended their three-year effort to halt the Harrier II program. Funding for the development and production program was included in the Pentagon's 1981 budget and the five-year defense plan. The Marine Corps set its requirement for the Harrier II at 336 production aircraft to replace eight squadrons of AV-8A Harriers and A-4M Skyhawk IIs in the light strike role, plus training, attrition, and pipeline aircraft for maintenance and modifications.

Four full-scale AV-8B aircraft and eight pilot production aircraft were ordered in FY1982. Compared to the YAV-8B prototypes that were used for the initial flight test development efforts, the four full-scale development aircraft had a similar composite wing, new composite forward fuselage, an 18-inch extension of the aft fuselage, a 5-inch taller vertical tail, and a totally new avionics suite. The production rate ramped up quickly, with twenty-one Harrier IIs ordered in FY1983, twenty-seven in FY1984, thirty-two in FY1985, forty-six in FY1986, forty-two in FY1987, and twenty-four for FY1988–91.[10]

The Harrier II test program began on November 5, 1981, at St. Louis with the first flight of the first full-scale development. This aircraft, FDS-1, was the primary performance and handling qualities test aircraft; FDS-2 was used to test the propulsion systems and structural capabilities. A third aircraft was used for avionics and spin testing, and the fourth aircraft was used for maintenance testing and the trial for the 25mm GAU-12/U gun system.

In mid-1982, flight testing of the AV-8B began at the U.S. Navy Air Test Center at Patuxent River, Maryland. Fred Chana worked on the Harrier II as a flight test engineer and later in senior positions for both Boeing and Smiths.

> I came to the Harrier II program as a lead engineer in the flight test division at the very beginning of the Full-Scale Development Program. I am proud to have been part of a team that completed a technically challenging flight test program safely, on schedule and within budget. The "high angle of attack" portion conducted at Edwards Air Force Base was particularly challenging. We ran a simulation of most of the test points in the St. Louis AV-8B simulator before starting the actual flight tests. We recorded data on various types of flight control departures and spins and recovery techniques. This data was then used during the flight test program for pilot briefings and post-flight comparisons. The flight data matched almost perfectly, which was a tribute to the fidelity of the simulation modeling. With this confidence in the simulation, we were able to minimize the actual number of flight test points. We sure put

Bill Lowe—the test pilot for this portion of testing—through some wild rides during the program, and the plane and pilot performed like champs.[11]

The Initial Operational Test and Evaluation (IOT&E) by VX-5 pilots started later in the same year. Early testing revealed the need for dozens of structural and systems changes for the AV-8B to meet its performance requirements. Enhancements were made, but the aircraft still did not pass the second set test and evaluation flights, which were flown by a mix of U.S. Navy, USMC, and contractor test pilots in late 1982 and early 1983. Lt. Col. Russ Stromberg, USMC (Ret.), flew Harrier II test flights as a major assigned to the U.S. Naval Air Test Center.

> If you want to get into how MacAir screwed up on the AV-8B and how they salvaged it, I can tell you my view. The initial AV-8B design was based, in part, on AV-8A drag data received from Hawker Siddeley who designed the Harrier. The MacAir engineers misinterpreted this data, in part because of bookkeeping differences between the United States and the United Kingdom. They had built the F-101 and 5,000 F-4s and most of the engineers were focused on high-performance century-series fighters with supersonic performance. Thus they did not ask the right questions. So the drag estimates they were making for the AV-8B were made off the wrong baseline. In addition, they promised great performance from the new supercritical wing. Actual performance fell short of promised. You took a bunch of guys from the century-series fighter mentality and they had to adjust to a generational shift. Look at the performance of the F-16 and the F/A-18 compared to the fighters that came before them. It was a new concept. . . . Frankly, the team did a great adjustment. People build airplanes, companies don't. To make it work, we had to adjust the performance model, which we did. And McDonnell Douglas fixed the inlets and did other things to reduce drag and achieve greater performance. And we formed a team, measured the AV-8B weapons delivery performance, and made adjustments to the weapons delivery system OFPs [operational flight programs]. The weapons delivery accuracy of the AV-8B was orders of magnitude better than the AV-8A and equal to the F/A-18. . . . We had this phenomenal team! Superb people like Ed Harper (McDonnell Douglas Harrier II program manager), Hank Wall (McDonnell Douglas Harrier II chief of avionics), USMC officers Lt. Col. Joe Anderson (Class Desk), Col. Harry Blot (AV-8B program manager), Lt. Col. Pat Finneran (APP) [Aviation Plans and Programs], Lt. Col. Terry Mattke (APW) [Aviation Weapons Requirements Branch] and many others all working together. . . . Another guy who is an unsung hero is Bill Frailey (McDonnell Douglas avionics engineer). He took a bunch of young pilots (like myself) who initially tried to pound the AV-8B design back into the Stone Age with steam gauge instruments (as in the cockpit of the AV-8A and A-4) and forced us into the new world of sophisticated modern weapons systems that offered combat capabilities we had no idea existed—he never gave up. The AV-8B, in my opinion, demonstrated what you can do if you have the

right people with the right commitment in the right place at the right time. That is the real story of the AV-8B.[12]

Jackie Jackson, one of the McDonnell Douglas Harrier II test pilots, adds:

We had to do a full-load flight test program on aircraft B2 to confirm what the AV-8B could do. Since the AV-8B had a composite wing, tail, and some of the fuselage, we had to perform a 100 percent loads survey, which was generally not done on an aircraft, to confirm that the composite elements were sound enough to be on a combat aircraft. In testing we found we needed to make changes to the aircraft, and thus weight and drag went up compared to our predictions. To get Ps back up we worked a lengthy test effort. We flew a lot of tufted flights to look at improvements. We changed things on the wing, such as the placement of the vortex generators and placement of the antennas for the RWR [radar warning receiver], and we filled in some hollow points to get the drag down. The inlet was very big and we took too much airflow from the 404/406 engine to supply other things (cooling, generators, and so on) and it was difficult for the engine to produce the thrust we needed. On the inlet, the second row of blow in doors did not prove necessary. In fact they were a detriment because [they] cut back on the surge margin for the engine. It cost us almost a year, as we had to come back and eliminate the second row of doors, change the inlet shape, and make other changes. Compared to the first two Harrier IIs, the production AV-8B day-attack aircraft had a longer fuselage and many other changes.[13]

In the late 1970s, the UK government evaluated options for an improved Harrier. Ray Searle elaborates:

The RAF realized that their Harriers were starting to wear out and they needed to fund a new airplane. Now we got into the dilemma, which any government has to ask to make a quotation for a new airplane, particularly if it is seen to be a foreign airplane. So BAe [British Aerospace] was asked for a GR Mk. 5 based on the AV-8B and a GR Mk. 5 based on the GR. Mk. 3 Harrier with a "big wing," as it was called; the metal wing—we called it the "sonic rooftop wing." The differences in the two airplanes were that the overall performance of the AV-8B was slightly superior in most aspects except for speed. The AV-8B is slower than the AV-8A, due to the supercritical wing. The rooftop wing would give us a higher speed and it would give us similar handling. It was a little heavier and would not carry as much fuel. So overall the performance from the AV-8B was likely to be better, except for speed. Because there was no development program, the cost of the AV-8B was cheaper, even though the per-aircraft cost was a little higher. By this time I was project manager for the Harrier at BAe and we went with the proposal for the GR Mk. 5 based on the AV-8B.[14]

In August 1981 the United Kingdom announced its intent to order sixty GR Mk. 5 Harrier IIs to replace the RAF's GR Mk. 3 first-generation Harrier. Design of the airframe and weapons system was managed by McDonnell Douglas, which also acted as the prime contractor for the AV-8Bs delivered to the U.S. Marine Corps with British Aerospace as principal subcontractor responsible for the aft center, aft fuselage, and reaction control system. For the RAF's GR Mk. 5, the roles of the two companies were reversed, with British Aerospace as prime contractor and producer of the center aft and aft fuselage, stabilators, and final assembly (test). Rolls-Royce was responsible for the production of all Pegasus engines for AV-8Bs and GR Mk. 5s. The Harrier II production-sharing agreement had McDonnell Douglas responsible for building the forward and forward center section of the fuselage and the wings for all Harrier II aircraft, and the stabilators for U.S. Marines Corps aircraft. More than one hundred U.S. and British firms participated in the Harrier II program.[15]

The AV-8B was an international program, with U.S., British, and industrial firms from many other nations participating in development, production, and support. The team was headed by the McDonnell Douglas corporation (now Boeing) as prime contractor. British Aerospace (Kingston-Brough Division) was the principal subcontractor. As developer of the Harrier and Sea Harrier, British Aerospace (BAe) brought extensive experience to the program. Rolls-Royce (Bristol) provided the proven Pegasus engine. In July 1981 MacAir and BAe signed a teaming and license agreement that covered the Harrier II and its derivatives.

Darryl Carpenter, a McDonnell Douglas engineer, worked on the Harrier for twenty-five years—the AV-8A, AV-8C, YAV-8B, Harrier II, and then the Harrier II Plus.

> I was involved with the YAV-8B right after it was flying and the Harrier II with a lot of fatigue testing, element testing, component testing, and full-scale testing, and I did a lot of work when we had problems with the wing. One thing that stands out in my memory about the Harrier II program: it was always very challenging. I enjoyed that very much. We always had a short schedule to get things built and do the testing. It was always a tight budget with the Harrier II. There was never enough money, but we always found ways to get it done. The other thing I think that stands out about the Harrier program [is that]we had risk takers—calculated risk takers—especially in the development area. When the Harrier II was developed, it was on the leading edge. The leading edge of first composites that were going to be used in critical components like the wing, stabilator, rudder, forward fuselage, and other pieces were like never before. With budgets as they were, there were guys who took risks, but they worked out and I think it was because they had the foresight. It was a risk but we would get it to work and we did. . . . We had a lot of collaboration with BAe at the engineering level, and things at that level went very well. I can't say how things worked at the upper levels of management, but the program worked well, so I have to assume they were good. With engineers you will get differences, and we worked through them. We came up with what we felt

were the best technical answers, and what was right for the airplane. We saw a lot of the British Aerospace engineers and made a lot of friendships and some I still keep in contact with. I think it was good to see how another company did things.[16]

CHAPTER 6

Into Service

The first major milestone for the Harrier II was a demanding operational evaluation (OPEVAL), which all U.S. Navy aircraft must successfully complete before entering service. During OPEVAL a team of four pilots, each of whom had more than a thousand hours of fleet experience flying the Harrier, and a team of support personnel fly and maintain the aircraft in a variety of conditions to simulate combat.

The AV-8B Harrier II OPEVAL ran from August 31, 1984, to March 30, 1985. The testing was divided into two phases. Graded aspects during OPEVAL included pilot and AV-8B aircraft capability to navigate, acquire targets, deliver a variety of weapons, evade and survive defenses, and fly to projected range and payload performance. Reliability, maintainability, supportability, safety, and other factors were also evaluated.

In the first phase (August, 31, 1984, to February 1, 1985), operational test and evaluation pilots flew CAS, deep air support (DAS), battlefield interdiction, and armed reconnaissance missions. These missions were flown at the Naval Air Test Center of China Lake, California; Canadian Forces Base (CFB) Cold Lake, Canada; Marine Corps Base Camp Pendleton, California; Marine Corps Air Station (MCAS) Yuma, Arizona; and off the coast of California flying from the USS *Belleau Wood*. During the first phase of OPEVAL, 318 sorties and 315 flight hours were flown. Test results showed that the AV-8B could effectively perform its missions from austere bases and ships and sustain a sortie rate of six to eight per aircraft per day. On one day, two aircraft flew ten sorties in a six-hour period.

The first portion of the OPEVAL was tightly structured to test the accuracy and flexibility of the weapons system. This included flights to evaluate the electro-optical Angle-Rate Bombing System (ARBS) and inertial platform, which projected weapons delivery solutions on an HUD. OPEVAL pilots demonstrated the excellent navigation capability and bombing accuracy of the AV-8B. The Harrier II's 25mm cannon proved to be very accurate.

During the operations from MCAS Yuma the AV-8Bs flew CAS missions with A-4Ms, A-6Es, F-4Js, and AV-8Cs against a variety of ground and air threats. The AV-8B demonstrated very good weapons delivery accuracy— better than requirements. The aircraft also proved to have a high level of survivability against Stinger teams and Improved HAWK missile batteries, which represented potential Russian surface-to-air threats, and F-4 fighters as air-to-air adversaries.

The second phase of OPEVAL testing included AV-8B pilots flying fighter escort, combat air patrol, and deck-launched intercept missions in simulated combat flying from MCAS Yuma. Harrier II pilots flew 210 sorties and 231 flight hours during Phase II of the OPEVAL (February 25 to March 8, 1985). AV-8B OPEVAL pilots fought against other pilots flying F-4s, F-14s, F/A-18s, A-4s, and AV-8Cs simulating a variety of potential airborne adversaries.

The AV-8B Harrier II OPEVAL pilots armed with the 25mm cannon and AIM-9L/M Sidewinder IR guided air-to-air missiles achieved more than twice as many simulated victories as losses during simulated close in-air combat. When AV-8B OPEVAL pilots fought against adversary aircraft that were firing beyond visual range missiles (F-4Js, F/A-18s, and F-14s) the results were not as good. Yet the AV-8B OPEVAL pilots showed that they could fight and survive against all threats and still perform their primary strike mission.

The OPEVAL test team evaluated shortfalls identified earlier in the 1982 IOT&E, Phase I, and confirmed that all of the critical deficiencies, ten of twelve major deficiencies, and fifty of fifty-seven minor deficiencies had been corrected and/or had solutions implemented. Although the team identified a number of deficiencies that still needed to be addressed by the contractor team and the Marine Corps, the overall evaluation was deemed a major success. As Rear Adm. E. W. Carter III concludes, "I have not changed my standards. OPEVAL of the AV-8B was tough and demanding. The results speak for themselves. They also bespeak the professionalism of the AV-8B project management. I still feel admiration and appreciation . . . for [those who made] this the best OPEVAL in my almost three years as COMOPTEVFOR [Commander, Operational Test and Evaluation Force]."[1]

McDonnell test pilot Jackie Jackson offers specifics:

The airplane on up and away did pretty well. It was the only aircraft that went into production with a supercritical wing made out of composites. The improvements in the Harrier II aircraft added weight and the [Pegasus]-406 engine (the same engine that powered the AV-8A Harrier) had reached its growth potential. The Rolls-Royce engine was a real thoroughbred, and it produces a lot of thrust. But you have to fly the aircraft on its engine when you are in hover. One of the downsides of the -406 engine was the large number of inspections it required. Also thrust deteriorated as it increased its time in service. The -406 engine was underpowered for the day attack airframe. . . . flying a day-attack aircraft with a typical weapons load and an average -406 engine on a hot day, you would struggle to achieve 480 knots. For a while we suggested that pilots start their run at 320 knots and accelerate to 450 plus. One benefit with the supercritical wing and the -406 engine: we lowered the corner speed to 360 knots, which was a big step better than the AV-8A Harrier.[2]

VMAT-203 Hawks: Training Harrier II Pilots

The first unit to receive the AV-8B Harrier II outside of the test community was VMAT-203, the Hawks. Located at MCAS Cherry Point, North Carolina, the training squadron for the Harrier and Harrier II received its first AV-8B on December 12, 1983. VMAT-203 had flown the AV-8A/TAV-8A since 1975 and had graduated nearly three hundred Harrier pilots by the early 1980s. During 1980–82 the Harrier training squadron graduated between fifteen and twenty pilots per year to staff the three Marine Corps AV-8A Harrier squadrons.

A massive expansion of training operations was still required to achieve the goal of the rapid transition of the Marine Corps V/STOL force from the three V/STOL AV-8A Harrier squadrons (and the conversion of six A-4M units) to eight fielded Harrier II fleet squadrons. Each of the eight fleet squadrons was to be equipped with twenty AV-8Bs and thirty pilots. VMAT-203 was expanded to forty-five instructors and thirty aircraft in order to graduate and/or retrain more than seventy-five pilots per year in the mid-1980s. The squadron received the first twelve pilot production Harrier IIs and a large number of initial production aircraft, for a total of more than two dozen Harrier IIs, while the six remaining TAV-8A trainers were worked hard.

Harrier II pilots came from AV-8A Harrier, A-4 Skyhawk, and F-4 Phantom squadrons, as well as from staff assignments or new Marine Corps pilots who graduated from the naval aviation pilot training program. Training for the AV-8B Harrier II was significantly different than training pilots for transition to the AV-8A Harrier. AV-8A Harrier pilot training for the Marine Corps took twenty-eight weeks and included four weeks of ground school and instruction, a week of helicopter training, and then twenty-three weeks of flight training, which included seventy Harrier sorties. The syllabus for the Harrier II was completely redesigned to reflect the improved handling qualities and advanced avionics suite of the AV-8B.[3]

Maj. Gen. Mike Ryan (Ret.), then a lieutenant colonel, served first as the VMAT-203 executive officer and later as the commanding officer (1982–85).

I loved flying the plane. I thought it was a lot of fun! The AV-8A was more fun than flying the AV-8B; much less capable, but a lot more fun. The AV-8A was not a hard plane to fly; it was not an unsafe airplane or anything like that. But it wasn't a very forgiving airplane. The AV-8B would forgive you. And almost all pilots would say [that because of] the good work McDonnell Douglas and British Aerospace did on it, the airplane would help you. You needed less skill to fly the AV-8B than the AV-8A. But when you have a lot of systems on an airplane, you have to have a plane that's pilot-friendly if it is a single-place airplane. The pilot has to operate all the weapons systems and fly.[4]

The Harrier II training program was thirty weeks long: two weeks in the classroom reviewing systems and two weeks of squadron procedures, followed by eighty hours in the simulator and twelve sorties in the TAV-8A/B. Student pilots were able to build experience by flying a realistic Evans & Sutherland CT5A Visual Reference simulator system designed to replicate the Harrier II flying characteristics. Then the student pilots flew approximately eighty sorties in the AV-8B before they were ready for the transition to an operational Harrier II squadron for additional tactical training.

The new AV-8B syllabus eliminated the helicopter training phase previously used to instruct Harrier pilots and incorporated a larger number of training sorties on both two-seat and single-seat aircraft to better prepare new pilots for the demanding V/STOL flight environment and operational missions. Pilots converting to the Harrier II from A-4 or F-4 squadrons went through a twelve-week course that included five TAV-8A flights and fourteen AV-8B sorties before moving to an operational unit.

Pilot conversion was improved considerably when VMAT-203 was able to replace the aging TAV-8A two-seat trainers with the more capable TAV-8Bs. The first TAV-8B Harrier II jet trainer (the sixty-fourth Harrier II airframe built) flew on November 21, 1986. Following the flight test program, in July 1987 TAV-8Bs finally began arriving at VMAT-203 to support the training program. The TAV-8B has the same controls, displays, and improved handling qualities as the AV-8B.[5]

Lt. Col. John Capito (Ret.) served as executive officer (XO) under Lieutenant Colonel Ryan and then assumed command of the Hawks (1983–87). VMAT-203 was tasked with planning for the arrival of and transition to the AV-8B Harrier II, he explains, in addition to training AV-8A pilots.

This task was made difficult for many reasons. The AV-8A aircraft, especially the two-seater, was experiencing a very difficult maintenance cycle during 1983 to 1985. The squadron was preparing to relocate from a small hangar to a large, new facility and with that move also pick up all the maintenance training for the AV-8B program. This was a first for the Harrier community, and was a concept only just recently perfected by the

F/A-18 training squadron at NAS [Naval Air Station] Lemoore. AV-8B maintenance training brought with it new challenges such as curriculum development, instructor training and a large number of students into the administrative section of VMAT-203. This "FRAMP" (Fleet Replacement Aviation Maintenance Program) effort also required a dedicated aircraft from the operational side to be utilized daily for "hands-on" maintenance training. . . .

Each of these obstacles was met head on, and for the most part overcome through the hard work, teamplay, and dedication of people in every organization. VMAT-203 worked directly with NAVAIR (specifically Jo Ann Puglisi), McDonnell Douglas (Hank Wall and many others), Headquarters Marine Corps (Kathryn . . . and others) to plan for the build-up and receipt of aircraft and people. There was a definite lack of animosity and bureaucracy and an abundance of "Let's make this program successful" and can-do attitude evident at all levels. As the XO/CO from 1983/87 it was a real pleasure to come to work every day. It was finally time for the Harrier community to put its best foot forward and I believe that it did so at every level. It always seemed to me that VMAT-203 acted like a hopper. Others poured in a certain amount of people, aircraft, parts, equipment, money, hardware, and support, and our job was to turn out the final product—either a fleet pilot or maintainer. It was truly a heady time to be in the squadron.[6]

From 1985 to 1987, VMAT-203 flew more than twelve thousand flight hours, trained approximately 147 pilots (including three general officers and a future assistant commandant of the Marine Corps), and provided the maintenance personnel for the AV-8B Harrier II squadrons.

USMC Harrier II Service Introduction

Marine Air Group 32 (part of the Second Marine Aircraft Wing), located at MCAS Cherry Point, North Carolina, included the training unit VMAT-203, the first operational AV-8B Harrier II squadron VMA-331, and (by 1987) three other fleet AV-8B squadrons. Lt. Col. James R. Cranford was the commander of VMA-331 (the Bumblebees), the first Harrier II unit. This Marine squadron dates to 1940 and fought in the Pacific during World War II and during the Korean War. The unit flew the A-4 Skyhawk for more than two decades, and VMA-331 received the last production A-4M Skyhawk II in 1979. In 1983 the squadron was decommissioned as an A-4 unit and initiated training for the Harrier II.

The squadron was recommissioned with the Harrier II on January 30, 1985, at MCAS Cherry Point. VMA-331 was certified as having reached its initial operating capability in August 1985, with an initial complement of fifteen AV-8B aircraft, twenty-one pilots, and more than two hundred maintenance personnel.

VMA-331 pilots and support crews honed their skills at home and on deployments. In March 1986 a group of eight VMA-331 crews made the first nonstop transatlantic flight of 3,500 miles from MCAS Cherry Point to NAS Rota, Spain, for an exercise. On October 23, 1986, six VMA-331 AV-8B pilots completed day-carrier and (for the first time) night-carrier qualifications from the amphibious assault ship USS *Belleau Wood*. On June 10, 1989, VMA-331 became the first Harrier II squadron to deploy as a full unit to Japan for an extended assignment.

Lieutenant Colonel Cranford says of the AV-8B's performance: "With 1,200 feet of runway, even on a hot day, a Harrier II can take off at 31,000 pounds and take with it 9,200 pounds of weapons on seven hard points."

> I am very impressed. In many ways, it is like buying a new car: you occasionally have to resolve minor maintenance problems . . . but I think we have a fantastic airplane in the AV-8B. Because it is such a stable airplane, the workload in taking off and landing is greatly reduced. The airplane's weapons delivery system is fantastic—especially in the air-to-ground role, which is what being a Marine attack pilot is all about. It is really accurate. Even in the hottest situation, when you are extremely busy with ground fire and SAMs and even enemy fighters, you can roll in, acquire the target with the Angle Rate Bombing System and knock it out. You can have a wing down, you can be sliding and slewing, you can be fast or slow, but the bombs will go where you want to out them. You do not have to worry about accuracy; they will be on target.[7]

Reviewing VMA-331's initial experience with the new Harrier II, Lieutenant Colonel Cranford adds, "Perhaps two things have helped us the most. First, the behavior of the aircraft in the air has been outstanding. Second, we have had our own new simulators. Together these two factors have made the whole training task a lot easier."[8]

The second squadron to convert to the Harrier II was VMA-231, which previously flew the AV-8A. This squadron was also part of MAG-32 (Second Marine Aircraft Wing) located at MCAS Cherry Point. The "Ace of Spades" squadron traces its history back to 1919. In August 1985 VMA-231 pilots flew their last AV-8A sortie, and on September 19, 1985, the squadron transitioned to the Harrier II. A year later VMA-231 sent a twelve-aircraft deployment to Europe to participate in NATO operations, and in November 1986, six AV-8Bs operated from the USS *Saipan* in the Mediterranean Sea. During 1987 and 1988, pilots and support crews from VMA-231 deployed detachments to the USS *Saipan* and the USS *Nassau*, and in June 1990, the entire squadron flew to Japan for a western Pacific (WESTPAC) deployment.[9]

VMA-542—the "Flying Tigers"—were established as a night-fighter squadron back in 1944 and fought in the Pacific during World War II. Later the squadron was equipped with the F-4 Phantom IIs, and the unit flew thousands of sorties in Vietnam. In 1972 VMA-542 became the second USMC squadron to fly the AV-8A Harrier. VMA-542 transitioned as the third Harrier II squadron in May 1986 under the command of Lt. Col. John W. Cox. Following a period of transition and training, VMA-542 deployed in 1988 on the USS *Guam* for operations in the Mediterranean. The squadron moved to Iwakuni, Japan, for WESTPAC operations from December 1989 to May 1990.[10]

VMA-223—"the Bulldogs"—was established in 1942 and became famous for WWII operations over Guadalcanal and the Philippines flying the F4F Wildcat and F4U Corsair fighters. Equipped with the A-4 Skyhawk, the unit spent more than four years in Vietnam providing CAS for U.S., South Vietnamese, and allied forces. In 1975 VMA-223 reequipped with the A-4M Skyhawk, and in 1977 the squadron moved from forward deployment in Japan to MCAS Cherry Point.

The Bulldogs transitioned from the Skyhawk in October 1987 and became MAG-32's (Marine Air Group-32) fourth Harrier II squadron. "It was extremely rewarding to be the commanding officer of VMA-223 during the squadron's transition to the AV-8B, says Lt. Col. Richard H. Priest "I was anxious to see how the 'A-4 Forever' fraternity would take to the new aircraft. It was great to be in the ready room and hear the enthusiasm of the new Harrier II pilots discussing the combat capabilities of the AV-8B and the basing flexibility that V/STOL provides."[11] In May 1989, the squadron deployed on the USS *Nassau* to the Mediterranean, and in September 1998 the squadron went to CFB Cold Lake, Alberta, for training with the Canadians. An early 1990 deployment on the USS *Saipan* included armed air support for the evacuation of personnel from Liberia during Operation Sharp Edge.

VMA-513 was based at Yuma and was the first Marine Corps squadron of Marine Aircraft Group 13 (MAG-13), Third Marine Aircraft Wing, to reequip with the AV-8B Harrier II. VMA-513, created in 1944, was equipped with the Corsair during World War II. The unit also saw action over Korea as a night-fighter squadron flying the F3D Skynight. The squadron, later equipped with the F-4B Phantom, saw extensive combat in Vietnam. In 1971 VMA-513 transitioned from the F-4B to become the first AV-8A squadron, operating from MCAS Beaufort.[12] In early 1987 pilots and support personnel from VMA-513 ("the Nightmares," part of MAG-13 located at MCAS Yuma) started their training at VMAT-203 for the transition from the AV-8A to the AV-8B Harrier II. In August 1987 the squadron was declared operational with the AV-8B.

In March 1989, VMA-311 ("the Tomcats," part of MAG-13 located at MCAS Yuma) transitioned from the A-4M to the AV-8B Harrier II. The Tomcat squadron was established in 1942, and its pilots flew Corsairs in the Pacific in World War II, Panther jets in the Korean War, and A-4 Skyhawks over Vietnam from 1965 to 1973. In the 1980s the squadron transitioned to the A-4M and was deployed for several overseas exercises, including an assignment in Japan. The Tomcats received the Marine Corps Aviation Association's Lawson Sanderson Award in 1988 as the best attack squadron in the Marine Corps. VMA-311 was the last USMC attack squadron to be equipped with the AV-8B day-attack Harrier II.[13]

The VMA-214's long and proud history dates to its establishment in 1942 as Marine Fighter Squadron 214. The "Black Sheep" squadron is famous for flying the F4U Corsair in World War II under the command of Maj. Gregory Boyington. The squadron flew Corsairs in the CAS role during the Korean War; later the unit was equipped with the F9F Panther, F2H Banshee, and FJ-4B Fury jet fighters. In 1962 the unit converted to an attack squadron and began its tenure of nearly three decades flying the A-4 Skyhawk, including two years of combat in the Vietnam War. VMA-214 was the first USMC squadron to transition to the AV-8B Harrier II night-attack aircraft from the A-4M. This transition began in late 1989.[14]

VMA-211 was established in 1937 flying Grumman F3F biplanes. The unit is famous for its 1941 defense of Wake Island flying the F4F Wildcat. Renamed the Wake Island Avengers, the squadron was reconstituted flying F4U Corsairs in 1943. The unit saw extensive service during the Vietnam War flying the A-4 Skyhawk. In September 1987 VMA-211 reached the milestone of flying the Skyhawk for three decades. The squadron made the last overseas deployment of the A-4M in 1989. In late 1989 the VMA-211 squadron began phasing out the Skyhawk, and in June 1990 it received its first AV-8B night-attack aircraft.[15]

Spanish Navy Air Arm Harrier Experience

The Spanish Navy became a Harrier operator in 1976, when the service received a dozen AV-8A and TAV-8A Matador aircraft via the U.S. government as a by-product of continuing political friction between Spain and the United Kingdom. A following order for five Harriers was placed in 1977, and these came directly from the UK production line. Spanish AV-8S and TAV-8S aircraft served with the 8th Squadron based at Rota.[16]

Between 1970 and 1988 the Spanish Navy operated the aircraft carrier *Dedalo* (formerly the USS *Cabot*). The AV-8S version of the first-generation Harrier provided air defense and strike support for the Spanish fleet. In 1988 the *Dedalo* was retired and Harriers started flying from a new aircraft carrier, the *Principe de Asturias*, built by the Bazan shipyard in Spain. This fourteen-thousand-ton ship was built using plans first developed by the United States for a Sea Control Ship designed to support operations of six to ten V/STOL Harrier aircraft and six to ten helicopters.

In 1983 the Spanish Navy ordered twelve Harrier IIs from the United States to form a second V/STOL squadron. The 9th (Cobra) Squadron was commissioned when the first EAV-8B day-attack aircraft was delivered on October 6, 1987. Spanish Navy pilots receive their training from the U.S. Navy; the two services and the U.S. Marine Corps have maintained a close working relationship.[17]

United Kingdom Harrier–Harrier II Evolution

The United Kingdom started out with a mixed attitude toward the AV-8B. Proud as they were of the revolutionary V/STOL Harrier, it was a bit of a challenge for the RAF, the MOD, and British industry to acknowledge that American funding and support were needed in order to move forward with the development and production of the more advanced AV-8B Harrier II for the RAF.

After the Spitfire, the UK-developed Harrier was the most famous evidence of British aviation creativity. The RAF Harrier was famous for aggressive ground attack operations in support of NATO and air shows worldwide. All of the U.S. Marine Corps AV-8As and TAV-8As were produced by British Aerospace, and British industry developed the Sea Harrier for fleet air defense. British designed V/STOL aircraft carriers equipped with Sea Harrier fighters had emerged victorious against Argentine Dagger and Skyhawk fighters in 1982 combat over the South Atlantic. RAF Harriers provided support for the successful amphibious assault that recaptured the Falkland Islands in 1982.

By the late 1970s the first-generation Harrier had reached the end of its growth capability, and the necessary funding for a replacement was unavailable. The British MOD was already committed to a multitude of other programs in addition to maintaining naval, army, and air structures to meet their NATO commitments.

The UK Air Staff Requirement (ASR) 409 set standards for an aircraft to replace the Harrier GR Mk. 3. Initially the RAF voiced concerns about the turn-rate performance and top speed of the AV-8B. It was compared to the "big-wing Harrier" (a paper design).

U.K. industry defense company executives worried that they would lose out by joining a cooperative program with the Americans.[18]

John Parker was the BAe Systems Harrier II program manager.

When the UK wanted to replace their [GR Mk. 3] aircraft with a more advanced Harrier, they had two options. One was the indigenous "big wing Harrier," which was a totally British product based on the GR Mk. 3 with a bigger wing. The other was to take the AV-8B and make some changes and modifications to make it suitable to the European operating environment. I think the issue at the working level was [whether] we were giving our heritage to the Americans. That was the debate. My view was that if we did not join with the Americans, the Harrier line would finish in 1979 or so with the delivery of the last GR Mk. 3 or Sea Harrier. But the Marine Corps production of the AV-8B was just starting. Wasn't it better to get a good percentage of a program than a hundred percent of nothing? I think the emotions were reduced when they realized that we would be assembling one hundred advanced Harriers in the UK between Kingston and Dunsfold. . . .

An RAF exchange officer had flown the AV-8B. He was delighted with the bubble canopy and improved performance. In the early days here, the Harrier was perceived by cynics as a very good circus act, but it could not carry a cigarette across a football field. When the advanced Harrier came along we could double the payload or the range and so it became a significant platform. . . . I do not think the RAF pilot cared [whether] he flew our engineer's "big-wing Harrier" or an AV-8B modified for the European scenario. But when the MOD made the political decision to go with the AV-8B, the thing was that the aircraft was proven; it had completed a significant amount of fatigue testing and systems testing. A lot of this work had been done in the UK—particularly the Pegasus engine work. So why would you want to go down a different route and have to start over and pay for all the development and testing again?[19]

The RAF determined that—with modifications—the AV-8B could meet the ASR409 requirements. Hawker Siddeley (BAe Systems) and McDonnell Douglas (Boeing) set forth a partnership agreement in the initial Harrier teaming. Despite nearly all of the business on the initial buy of 110 Harriers going to British industry, this agreement served as the basis for the Harrier II plan.

The U.S. Marine Corps planned to buy 336 AV-8Bs with final assembly in St. Louis, Missouri, and the RAF planned to purchase sixty Harrier IIs from the Kingston and Dunsfold (Surrey) factories. This work-share agreement brought substantial industrial benefits to the United Kingdom, British Aerospace, and other European aerospace companies. Rolls-Royce maintained its sole position as the designer and builder of the vectored-thrust Pegasus turbofan engine common to all variants of the Harrier and Harrier II.

British Aerospace became the prime contractor for all RAF GR Mk. 5/5A Harrier II aircraft, with McDonnell Douglas as the principal subcontractor. The UK version of the Harrier II aircraft featured a significant number of changes from the Marine Corps AV-8B design, including thicker wing and air intake leading edges to improve resistance to damage from bird strikes, which are common in the low-level European operating environment.

The RAF aircraft also used a Rolls-Royce Pegasus 11-21E or Mk. 105 engine, which incorporated a digital engine control system, UK-developed Zeus internally mounted electronic countermeasures (ECM) systems, BOL chaff dispensers, a Plessey missile approach warning system, a Martin Baker Type 12 ejection seat, a Ferranti moving-map cockpit display, FIN1075 inertial navigation system (INS), two additional stores stations on the wing for AIM-9 Sidewinder air-to-air missiles, and many other changes for RAF tactical requirements. In addition, the RAF funded the development of a new 25mm version of the ADEN revolver cannon rather than buy the General Electric (GE) gun of the AV-8B. Concerns about turn rate of the AV-8B led to the testing of various configurations of leading-edge root extensions (LERX) to enhance turn rate and high angle of attack performance. These were then also fitted to USMC, Spanish, and RAF Harrier IIs.[20]

The first of two development GR Mk. 5 aircraft ZD318 first took to the air on April 30, 1985, flown by BAe chief test pilot Mike Snelling. An initial batch of forty-one GR Mk. 5 aircraft were built and delivered to the RAF. In June 1989 the first of the GR Mk. 5A aircraft, with provisions for later retrofit of night-attack systems, was delivered into storage until the retrofit could be undertaken.

RAF Harrier IIs weighed more than U.S. Marine Corps AV-8Bs, due to the modified systems and structure, and the changes resulted in a number of challenges. The Ferranti INS suffered initial reliability problems and was replaced for a time by the Litton AN/AS-130 INS used by the U.S. Marine Corps. The ECM suite and the ADEN 25mm cannon ran into problems. The ADEN cannon never successfully passed its development testing.

Lt. Cdr. Taylor Scott, a BAe test pilot, took off on a sortie in the afternoon of October 22, 1987, and a malfunction of his ejection seat pulled him out of the cockpit with fatal results. The aircraft continued, with a USAF C-5A flying in formation, until the Harrier II crashed in the Atlantic after running out of fuel. As a result of this accident, the RAF Harrier II fleet was grounded for four months until the cause was determined and modifications to the ejection seat incorporated. In 1988 a government review found that the changes required by the RAF to make the Harrier II meet its requirements had delayed introduction of the GR Mk. 5 by two years and added more than $70 million to the program costs.[21]

The first operational GR Mk. 5, ZD233, was delivered to No. 233 Operational Conversion Unit Squadron at RAF Wittering in July 1987, under the command of Wing Cdr. Peter Day. Most of the initial order of forty-three GR Mk. 5s were delivered from May 1988 to February 1989. In mid-1988 operational conversion of crews and support personnel from the GR Mk. 3 to the GR Mk. 5 started. Nineteen GR Mk. 5A aircraft were built in 1989 and were de-livered with an empty forward-looking infrared (FLIR) housing in the nose and updated night-attack systems and cockpit displays. These aircraft were stored at RAF Shawbury until systems were available for them to be fully converted into the full GR Mk. 7 night-attack configuration.

Pilots converting to the Harrier II in the late 1980s and early 1990s started with ground classroom training, followed by a week flying Gazelle helicopters to gain perspective on vertical and hovering flight characteristics. After several flights in the T Mk. 4/4A two-seat trainer, student pilots flew about fifteen hours on the GR Mk. 3. Pilots then spent more time in the classroom learning Harrier II aspects and also "flying" the Harrier Avionics Systems Trainers and more sophisticated simulators. Pilots then flew thirty-six training sorties in the

GR Mk. 5 to become familiar with the aircraft and its systems and learn combat techniques. This was followed by about ten weapons delivery sorties to perfect techniques using the ARBS and Continuously Computed Impact Pointing delivery modes and simulated combat profiles.[22]

Initially the RAF planned to modernize its fleet of T Mk. 4/4A two-seat trainers. However, as pilot training continued, the limited benefit of flying the aging Harrier trainer was noted. Experiences from RAF exchange pilots who had flown with the U.S. Marine Corps pilot training program pointed to the benefits of flying the TAV-8B, in that its cockpit layout and handling characteristics more closely replicated the single-seat Harrier II. In February 1990 the MOD, with full RAF support, decided to procure fourteen T Mk. 10 Harrier II aircraft that could be used for training and—if necessary—operational missions, as they were to be fitted with night-attack systems and a full weapons suite.

The motto of the RAF No. 1 Squadron, "First in all things," seems appropriate, as this unit was the first to put the Harrier into service in 1969. No. 1 Squadron, located at RAF Wittering, flew the GR Mk. 1 and Mk. 3 Harrier and its crews provided support for the 1982 invasion of the Falkland Islands. In late 1988 No.1 Squadron was the first to receive the GR Mk. 5. The conversion continued into December 1989 when the unit was declared operational under the leadership of Wing Cdr. Ian Harvey. During the first year of operations, Harrier II crews of No. 1 Squadron supported flight testing, were the first to fire the AIM-9 Sidewinder, and made several operational training deployments in support of NATO training to Denmark, Sicily, Norway, and Greece.[23]

The RAF's No. 3 Squadron became the second RAF Harrier II unit. In 1972 this squadron converted to the GR Mk. 1 and later the GR Mk. 3 Harrier and served as a front-line unit with RAF Germany. The squadron began its conversion to the GR Mk. 5 in 1989 and reached full conversion in April 1990 under the command of Wing Cdr. Peter Moules, when based at RAF Gutersloh, Germany.[24]

The RAF's No. IV Squadron became the first to put into service the GR Mk. 7 night-attack Harrier II. This conversion began in mid-1990 under the command of Wing Cdr. Malcolm White. This squadron, another RAF Germany unit located at Gutersloh, had flown the GR Mk. 1 and Mk. 3 Harrier since 1970.[25]

The GR Mk. 5s enhanced the capability of the V/STOL force assigned to RAF Germany, due to added range, payload, greater weapons capability, enhanced survivability, and improved flying characteristics. Squadrons continued to utilize the remote site operational concept developed and perfected with the Harriers. However, the mission emphasis moved from CAS to battlefield interdiction, as the Harrier II had greater range and survivability against both ground and air threats.

Since the Harrier II was delivered to the Marine Corps in November 1983, the Spanish Navy in 1987, and the RAF in 1989, pilots and support crews have operated worldwide, exploring every facet of the missions that it is required to perform, whether patrolling with a Marine Expeditionary Unit, supporting NATO exercises in Norway, or taking off from a ship in the Mediterranean. Harrier IIs have successfully operated in every basing mode and every climate envisioned for Marine Corps V/STOL attack in wartime. Operations have been conducted from major airbases and grass fields, from country roads and ships' decks, and from deserted airfields under actual combat conditions.

The AV-8B has set new standards of interoperability with its operation from carriers of the Spanish Navy. During 1986, Marines of VMA-331 participated in joint operations with the Spanish Navy, operating from the Spanish Navy carrier *Principe de Asturias*. Since then the Marine Harriers have demonstrated operations aboard the Italian Navy carrier *Giuseppe Garibaldi* and participated in joint exercises in the Mediterranean with both navies.

By 1990 the USMC had retired its AV-8As, transitioned most of the A-4Ms to reserve squadrons, and fielded an AV-8B Harrier II V/STOL strike force that included MAG-32 with four squadrons plus the large operational training unit (VMA-331, VMA-231, VMA-542, VMA-223, and VMAT-203) at MCAS Cherry Point, and MAG-13 with four squadrons (VMA-311 and VMA-513 operational; VMA-214 and VMA-211 still in training taking delivery of the AV-8B night-attack variant of the Harrier II) at MCAS Yuma. These squadrons regularly deployed to Iwakuni and Okinawa, Japan, on U.S. Navy amphibious assault ships in support of Marine Expeditionary Unit operations and in support of training operations and exercises around the world.

The Spanish Naval Air Arm's 9th Squadron was operational with twelve EAV-8B Harrier II aircraft operating from Rota. Harrier IIs and older AV-8S Harriers of the Spanish Naval Air Arm regularly operate from their new aircraft carrier the *Principe de Asturias*.

The RAF had Harrier IIs flying with three squadrons by the end of 1990. No. 233 Operational Conversion Unit (OCU) was operating at a high level in order to speed the transition of personnel from the GR Mk. 3 to the GR Mk. 5. No. 1 Squadron was fully operational with its force of GR Mk. 5s in the United Kingdom, while the No. 3 and IV squadrons were building up to operational capability in RAF Germany.[26]

CHAPTER 7

V/STOL Flexibility Demonstrated: Operation Desert Shield/ Desert Storm

Iraqi forces invaded Kuwait in a surprise assault on August 2, 1990. The Iraqi invasion of Kuwait and the subsequent coalition effort to drive out Iraqi forces (1990–91) has become known as the Gulf War. During this conflict coalition aircraft flew more than a hundred thousand sorties, swept the skies of Iraqi aircraft, and delivered eighty-eight thousand tons of weapons, which disrupted the defenses and paved the way for the highly successful ground offensive. In the Gulf War air power—including the first combat use of the U.S. Marine Corps AV-8B Harrier II—had a positive impact on the outcome of the conflict and made a significant contribution to low U.S. and allied casualties.

Iraq may have emerged victorious from the Iran-Iraq War (1980–88) but the country and its armed forces were war weary, having sustained one hundred and fifty thousand fatalities, four hundred thousand wounded, and fifty thousand troops captured during the conflict. Basra, the nation's second largest city, was in ruins, and Baghdad and many other cities had suffered due to Iranian SCUD missile attacks and air strikes. In addition Iraq owed an enormous debt of more than $70 billion to Saudi Arabia, Kuwait, the Gulf states, the Soviet Union, France, and other nations.

Rather than standing down and rebuilding after this costly conflict, Saddam Hussein sustained mobilization of the Iraqi army, which at the time was the fifth largest in the world. Iraqi oil revenues were reduced after the war, due to a world-wide oversupply of oil. As a result, Saddam Hussein made little effort to pay off his war debts. By early 1990 Iraq was on the verge of bankruptcy, as creditors were calling in their loans. At a February 1990 meeting of the Gulf Cooperation Council in Amman, Jordan, Saddam Hussein made it known that he did not intend to repay the $37 billion owed to the Gulf states for defending the Arabs against the Persians.

In May 1990, during an Arab League meeting in Baghdad, Hussein again pressed for an immediate loan from neighboring Kuwait. On July 17, Saddam Hussein publicly threatened to attack Kuwait unless his demands were met. In this televised speech he listed several disputes with Kuwait: demands for more loans, a long-standing border issue, and a demand for a decrease in Kuwaiti oil production. On July 30, Iraqi, Kuwaiti, and Saudi representatives met in Jeddah, Saudi Arabia, to discuss the issues and seek a resolution to the escalating Iraqi threats. Kuwait agreed to reduce its oil production and refrain from placing its armed forces on full alert, but the talks failed to reach an agreement.

At this time Iraq fielded the largest army in the Middle East, with more than eight hundred thousand troops, forty-seven hundred tanks, and thirty-seven hundred artillery pieces. Many of these troops had seen combat during the Iran-Iraq War. Saddam Hussein assigned three of his top Republican Guard divisions (Al Medina, Hammurabi, and Tawakalna) for the invasion of Kuwait. The Republican Guard invasion force was supported by Army Air Corps Mi-24s and Gazelle attack helicopters, which flew escort for Iraqi convoys, and Mi-8 transport helicopters carrying commandos. Iraqi air force fighter-bombers flying from bases around Basra and An Nasiriyah struck Kuwait air force and army bases and other Kuwaiti targets.

The invasion caught most of the Kuwaiti military by surprise. The Emir of Kuwait had lowered the military alert status in an attempt to give Saddam Hussein no cause to attack. Saudi and Egyptian leaders were caught equally by surprise, as they felt Iraq was bluffing to secure addition loans and oil production concessions. Many Kuwaiti military officers and civilians were on their summer holiday when the invasion started. The first warning of attack came early on August 2, 1990, when the approach of many vehicles from the north was detected by Kuwaiti balloon-borne early warning radars.

At around 1:00 A.M. on August 2, Iraqi Republican Guard divisions, with more than one hundred and twenty thousand troops and three hundred tanks, drove into Kuwait. Their goal was to seize the Kuwaiti oil fields; knock out the small twenty-thousand-man military—army, air force (which only fielded forty jet fighters), and navy; garrison Kuwait City; and take up positions along the Saudi border to stop Saudi or coalition actions. Kuwaiti forces fought back and inflicted casualties, but they were soon overrun. A raid by armor and helicopters against the palace nearly resulted in the capture of the Emir of Kuwait, but an aggressive defense by the guards allowed him and his family to escape.

By late in the day on August 3, Iraqi forces had taken up positions in much of Kuwait, and they next began consolidating their control, preparing defensive fortifications, and looting. Iraqi forces had seized Kuwait and a quarter of the world's oil supply, and there was no reason to believe that these forces would not continue their drive into Saudi Arabia. Saddam Hussein announced that Kuwait had become Iraq's nineteenth province. In late August and early September Republican Guard forces in Kuwait had pulled back to positions in southern Iraq and were replaced by ten divisions (about a hundred and fifty thousand troops) of the regular Iraqi army that fortified the Kuwait-Saudi border and the coastal area.

In addition, Saddam Hussein ordered that foreign nationals in Kuwait be rounded up and placed at potential targets as "human shields" to deter attacks, using international television coverage to make his threats known. Clearly Hussein intended to retain its control of Kuwait. Iraqi army units in Kuwait and southern Iraq dug in and prepared for attack by the aircraft and ground forces of the coalition. To defeat Iraqi forces, the coalition would have to tackle not only units in Kuwait, but also take on Iraqi home defenses to isolate the battle zone and disrupt Iraqi resupply and command and control capability.

Operation Desert Shield

On August 2, 1990, the United Nations Security Council passed Resolution 660, which condemned the invasion and called for an immediate Iraqi withdrawal. U.S. President George H. W. Bush signed an executive order declaring a national emergency and ordered the U.S. Central Command to prepare for the defense of Saudi Arabia and to initiate planning to drive Iraqi units out of Kuwait. He also ordered the U.S. Navy carrier battle groups *Independence* and *Eisenhower* to head toward the Persian Gulf. Saudi Arabia and the Gulf Cooperative Council rushed military units to positions along the Saudi-Kuwaiti border to defend against a possible Iraqi thrust, but these small forces would constitute merely a speed bump in the face of a determined Iraqi attack.

On August 6, Saudi King Fahad met with U.S. Secretary of Defense Richard Chaney and Gen. Norman Schwartzkopf and invited the United States and other nations to send military forces to Saudi Arabia. Traditionally Saudi Arabia has been a closed kingdom, harboring two of the most sacred Muslim shrines. In the past the kingdom did not allow foreign troops on its soil unless there was an emergency. A day later American fighters began arriving at airfields in Saudi Arabia, along with transport aircraft carrying elements of the U.S. Army 82nd airborne division and the USMC.

U.S. and allied ground forces were in defensive positions in Saudi Arabia within a week of the invasion. Aircraft and ground forces from the United Kingdom, France, and many other nations were also on the way. The deployment of airpower into the region to deter any further attacks by Iraq was rapid; within a week there were more than three hundred allied aircraft available, and within a month more than twelve hundred had arrived.

Within days of the Iraqi invasion of Kuwait, U.S. Marine Corps air and ground units were on their way to the region to forestall any attempt by Iraq to move into Saudi Arabia. By August 15, maritime prepositioning ships, which carry U.S. Marine Corps equipment, had sailed to the region and met up with Marine units that had been airlifted from the United States. The first U.S. Marine Corps tactical aviation to arrive were the AV-8B Harrier IIs, which had the task of providing CAS.

During the 1980s and early 1990s, the four squadrons of AV-8A Harrier aircraft and five A-4M Skyhawk units transitioned to the AV-8B Harrier II. This gave the Marine Corps an all-V/STOL light-attack force consisting of eight squadrons of sixteen to twenty aircraft each, plus a large training squadron. All of these squadrons could operate from amphibious assault ships and/or short strips near the front lines to support Marine riflemen and coalition ground forces.

When the invasion of Kuwait occurred, the last two Harrier II squadrons were still in the process of converting to the then-new night-attack version of the aircraft. Six other USMC VMA squadrons flew the day-attack version of the AV-8B, while VMAT-203, the Harrier II training unit, operated a mix of AV-8Bs and TAV-8B two-seat trainer aircraft.

The primary attack sensor of the AV-8B day-attack aircraft was the Angle Rate Bombing System (ARBS), an electro-optical contrast tracker that the pilot operated using his integrated controls and displays. Once the pilot had locked the sensor onto a potential target, the ARBS system sends angle-rate data to the central computer, which provided weapons solution and weapons delivery symbology to the pilot via the Head Up Display (HUD). Pilots could also employ continuously computed impact point delivery for bomb delivery via the HUD. USMC AV-8Bs were equipped with six wing weapons stations, a centerline pylon, and attachment points for a 25mm cannon and ammunition. The aircraft can carry up to 9,200 pounds of external payload.[1]

After the Iraqi invasion, once the alert for potential deployment came, USMC squadron personnel worked around the clock to prepare for the call to action. Support equipment was packed, aircraft serviced, and personal preparations made. Harrier IIs scheduled to deploy to the Gulf were painted with a new two-tone gray camouflage paint scheme to better match the desert sky background. On August 18 and 19, the MCAS Yuma–based VMA-311 (led by Lt. Col. Dick White), and VMA-542 from MCAS Cherry Point (led by Lt. Col. T. N. Herman) flew across the Atlantic on the first leg of their journey to the Gulf.

"Our night crossing was very tough," says Lieutenant Colonel White. "Few of my pilots had ever refueled at night, and none had ever operated with

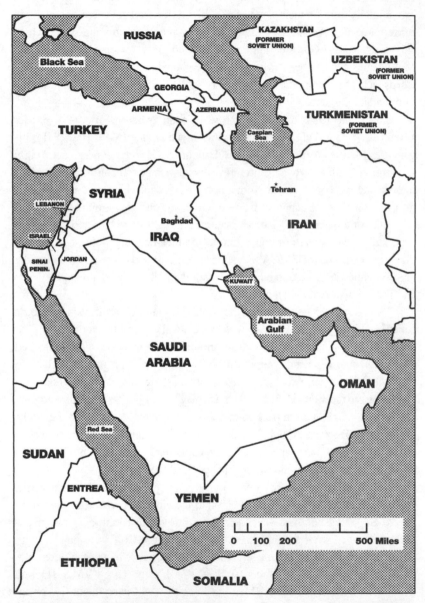

Map showing the Kuwait and Arabian Gulf region. During the Gulf War of 1990–91, U.S. Marine Corps AV-8Bs flew from bases in northern Saudi Arabia and from U.S. Navy amphibious assault ships operating in the Arabian Gulf. *M. Monahan*

a KC-10 tanker. It was dark, stormy, and you could see St. Elmo's Fire all round the aircraft. We did eleven refuelings to stay topped off, most at night, and arrived in Rota after eight and a half grueling hours."[2]

The aircraft each carried two external fuel tanks and were armed with the 25mm cannon and two AIM-9M Sidewinder air-to-air missiles. After a night of rest, the pilots of the two squadrons then flew on to Bahrain. U.S. Air Force C-5s and C-141s and civilian transports brought in the two squadrons' support personnel and equipment. Within twenty-four hours the AV-8B pilots were sitting alert and flying training missions.

After three days, VMA-311 moved from Bahrain to King Abdul Aziz airfield, an austere facility located about one hundred miles from the Kuwaiti border, near the Saudi Arabian coast. A soccer stadium located nearby was used to support the Marines, and tents were set up in the parking lot for living quarters, storage, and maintenance. Fuel was stored in rubber bladders and ammunition was stacked in the shipping containers nearby.

As Lieutenant Colonel White describes it:

> We arrived right after the 82nd Airborne, and there was still a fear that Saddam was not stopping at Kuwait, but would move on to the economic center of Saudi Arabia. The Marine Commandant was concerned about his troop—the Harrier is the grunts' aircraft—and we got the word to be the first in. . . . General Walter Boomer [commander of all Marine forces in theater] visited us within twenty-four hours of when we arrived. I remember he walked down the row of jets and patted their noses like they were race horses. He asked if we were ready, and I said, "We can be over your heads in five minutes."

White's unit received many visits from the media and Marine ground commanders: "The media would ask what we were doing up here," he recalls. "We were the closest jets to the action because that's what we're designed to do—not sit 300 miles to the rear."[3]

After facilities were established and expanded, Lt. Col. Ted Herman and the VMA-542 "Tigers" also deployed from Bahrain to the King Abdul Aziz facility. The forty AV-8Bs flew training flights over the desert; at all times there were four Harrier IIs armed and ready to launch to support U.S. allied forces. In late August VMA-331 from MCAS Cherry Point under the command of Lt. Col. Gerry Fitzgerald, deployed on the amphibious assault ship USS *Nassau*. Twenty more of VMA-331's aircraft arrived, aboard the USS *Nassau*, at the Persian Gulf during the first week of September.

The USS *Nassau* arrived in the Persian Gulf with the many other vessels of the U.S. Marine Corps' 4th Expeditionary Brigade. The pilots of VMA-331 flew training sorties off the USS *Nassau* and participated in several amphibious exercises, which helped convince Saddam Hussein and his generals that the Marines would assault Kuwait from the sea.

A series of United Nations resolutions, in combination with invitations of support from the leaders of the government of Kuwait in exile, Saudi Arabia, and the Gulf Cooperation Council (GCC) as well as massive negative publicity, created a significant worldwide condemnation of the Iraqi invasion and commitments to support the liberation of Kuwait. The leaders of the United States, Kuwait, Saudi Arabia, and GCC countries worked in concert to develop a coalition that would eventually include more than fifty nations. UN Resolution 665 enacted an embargo against Iraq, which was enforced by naval, air, and land forces. Military forces intended to halt Iraqi aggression and retake Kuwait (including land, air, sea, support) came from the United States, Saudi Arabia, the United Kingdom, France, Egypt, Syria, Kuwait, Bahrain, Qatar, the United Arab Emirates, Canada, Italy, Bangladesh, Morocco, Senegal, Nigeria, Pakistan, South Korea, the Netherlands, New Zealand, Spain, Portugal, Australia, Greece, Poland, and the Czech Republic. Saudi Arabia, the GCC, and other nations of the region such as Egypt provided basing, port facilities, and logistical assistance.

During an August 29, 1990, interview in Baghdad with CBS anchor Dan Rather, Saddam Hussein remarked, "The U.S. depends on its Air Force" and "The Air Force has never decided a war." The Iraqi leader underestimated the strong international reaction to his invasion of Kuwait and the rapid development of a coalition under U.S. leadership. He also did not understand the dramatic reform and technology upgrade that American forces had undergone since the Vietnam War. From available evidence it seems that Saddam Hussein perceived U.S. and allied military capabilities as being only moderately stronger than those of Iraq.

In the 1980s the United States developed new operational concepts, such as the air-land battle and deep strike doctrines, which called for a war of rapid maneuver, simultaneous strikes against air defenses, and command and control to overwhelm the ability of an adversary to react. This doctrine was designed to defeat numerically superior Soviet and Warsaw Pact forces in Europe.

The U.S. Air Force, Navy, Marine Corps, and Army fielded a host of new weapons and support systems to support fast-moving offensive operations. These systems and the new operational doctrines gave the coalition superior intelligence, command control, communications, and systems to disrupt Iraqi air defenses and accurately destroy point targets. As important as these systems were, U.S. and their allied forces had also the advantage of previous training in realistic simulated combat in a desert operating environment like that of Kuwait and Iraq. Many U.S. and allied air crew and mission planners had flown in the Nevada desert during a set of realistic training exercises known as Operation Red Flag. Ground forces had fought at the Army National Training Center and USMC training facility at Twenty Nine Palms in the California desert.[4]

Another factor contributing to the superiority of the coalition over Iraq was the availability of air bases and fueling and support facilities in Saudi Arabia and the GCC countries. Saddam Hussein did not interfere with the nearly six-month-long massive buildup of coalition ground, air, and naval forces except for unsuccessful political and propaganda efforts to break up the Arabian component of the coalition and threats to launch missile attacks on Israel, Saudi Arabia, and the GCC countries in the event of war.

By mid-September the coalition had, on the ground or in transport, sufficient land, air, and sea forces to delay or deter any Iraqi thrust into Saudi Arabia. Leaders thus began to focus on the plans to build up the larger assault forces needed to tackle the Iraqi forces and retake Kuwait. U.S.-allied ground forces in position included combat forces from the Royal Saudi Land Forces, Royal Saudi National Guard, Bahrain, Oman, Qatar, the United Arab Emirates, Egypt, Syria, Great Britain, and France, plus U.S. Army and USMC units. Most of these forces were located along the border between Saudi Arabia and Kuwait running from King Khalid City in the west to Dhahran in the southeast.

More than fifty U.S.-allied naval vessels and three carrier battle groups were patrolling in the Arabian Gulf, Red Sea, and surrounding ocean areas. As a result of the size of coalition forces and for political reasons, Saudi Lt. Gen. Khaled bin Sultan became the commander of theater operations and joint forces, and General Schwarzkopf headed U.S. forces. USAF Lt. Gen. Charles A. Horner was appointed commander of air defenses and joint force air component commander in charge of planning and exercising the air operations. More than fifteen hundred combat and support aircraft and helicopters from Argentina, Belgium, Canada, France, the GCC countries, Italy, Kuwait, Saudi Arabia, the United States, and Great Britain were in the region.

Because political efforts had failed to achieve results and combat seemed inevitable, on November 6 U.S. President George H. W. Bush called for a substantial increase in American forces in the region. Soon about one hundred ships carrying additional ground and air units, suppliers, and support systems were en route to the region or returning for additional supplies. This stage included the deployment of several heavy armored divisions from Europe and the boosting of air and naval forces. Arab and European contingents also deployed more ground and air units. Eventually the coalition fielded six hundred thousand troops, twenty-three hundred tanks, fifteen hundred helicopters, and a hundred and fifty naval vessels to the region.[5]

A second wave of AV-8Bs was sent to support U.S. Marine Corps and allied ground forces late in 1990. VMA-231, under the command of Lt. Col. W. R. Jones, had been deployed to Iwakuni, Japan, since June. In December 1990, this squadron flew from Japan to MCAS Cherry Point and then on to King Abdul Aziz airfield, a total distance of eighteen thousand miles (28,967 km).

Lieutenant Colonel Jones says:

KC-10s were a lifesaver. That is the first time I have really done long-range tanking with the KC-10. It takes all the worry out of getting where you are going. They both guide you and give you gas all the way. . . . When we left Japan we had a different paint job. We took the ghost grey from the Hornet squadrons that were right there and then we took another can of that ghost grey and a Styrofoam coffee cup full of black, dumped it in, and made another shade of grey. We used basically the same camouflage pattern. We also painted the intakes gloss white. What that does is kill the shadow. The huge intake of the Harrier, head on, looks like a dot, a very clear black dot head on from three to five miles. The bright white in there kills the shadow. This makes the airplane harder to see.[6]

A detachment of six AV-8Bs from MCAS Yuma–based VMA-513 deployed to the Arabian Gulf on the USS *Tarawa*. This ship arrived in theater as part of the 5th Marine Expeditionary Brigade. The remaining fourteen Harrier IIs of VMA-513, under the command of Maj. C. S. Patton, moved to Japan to take the place of VMA-231. By January 1991 the King Abdul Aziz airfield was a crowded and busy place. More than thirty-five hundred Marines, sixty AV-8Bs, and twenty OV-10 Bronco forward air control aircraft were located at the site. The Marines built a parallel taxiway with AM-2 metal matting to allow for better dispersal and thus ease runway congestion.

Of the Harrier II's V/STOL performance, Lieutenant Colonel Jones notes:

Even though it was a seven-thousand-foot runway, we didn't use much of it. Most ground rolls, even with maximum fuel and weapons, were maybe one thousand feet and that is because the pilot just kept it on the ground. . . . We had three eight-plane strikes, one from each squadron; all arrived back at the base almost simultaneously one day. On the single seven-thousand-foot runway all twenty-four aircraft landed within three and a half minutes. This demonstrated the flexibility of the airplane, and as the original British designer said, It is better to stop, and then land, than to land and then stop.[7]

Farther north, at the ARAMCO facility near Tanajib, the Marines prepared a forward operating site from which AV-8Bs could fly, rearm, and refuel. The concrete parking area at this location could hold up to a dozen Harrier IIs at one time. Because this base was only five minutes by air from the Kuwait border, AV-8Bs located here could respond to a call for assistance in a matter of minutes.

Planning for the air campaign against Iraqi forces was initiated on August 3, 1990, by the U.S. Air Force component of U.S. Central Command (CENTAF). By late August a detailed air attack plan (which included involvement by all U.S. services) entitled Operation Instant Thunder was being briefed to the U.S. Joint Chiefs of Staff. In September UK RAF staff was asked to participate and later representatives from the Royal Saudi Air Force (RSAF) and other air forces joined the team.

The plan called for a four-phase offensive air campaign. Phase I was a strategic campaign against Iraq, Phase II focused on destroying Iraqi air defenses in the Kuwait theater of operations (KTO), Phase III's goal was the neutralization of the Republican Guard and isolation of the KTO, and Phase IV was to provide support for the ground offensive to force Iraqi units out of Kuwait.

Once the overall plan was approved, a daily air tasking order (ATO) for every allied unit was created. An ATO is a two-hundred page, two-section document covering daily sortie assignments and providing communications frequencies and the assignment of all support missions such as tankers, suppression of enemy air defenses (SEAD), and so on. The Joint Forces Air Attack Campaign (JFAAC) objectives included:

1. Isolate and incapacitate Iraqi leadership through attacks on command and control facilities, telecommunications and electrical power systems

2. Seize and maintain air superiority through assault of Iraqi air defense radars and command and control centers, air defense sites and airbases

3. Destroy Iraq's nuclear, biological and chemical capabilities and offensive systems such as SCUD launchers, bombers and fighter-bombers

4. Render Iraqi military forces ineffective in the KTO and southern Iraq through destruction of transportation systems and combat systems.[8]

By January 1991 time had run out for Iraq. On January 12 the U.S. Congress authorized the use of force against Iraq, and three days later the UN deadline for Iraqi withdrawal from Kuwait passed. The coalition fielded the greatest force of ground, naval, and air units seen in action since the Korean War. Approximately twenty-four hundred fixed-wing aircraft from nine nations plus fourteen hundred helicopters were ready for action. This force included naval aircraft from three aircraft carriers (USS *Saratoga,* USS *America,* USS *John F. Kennedy*) in the Red Sea, three aircraft carriers and two amphibious assault ships in the Arabian Gulf (USS *Ranger,* USS *Midway,* USS *Theodore Roosevelt,* USS *Nassau,* and USS *Tarawa*), plus aircraft based in Saudi Arabia, Bahrain, Qatar, UAE, Oman, and Turkey. Aircrews and support personnel had practiced the types of missions they would fly in war. Although this resulted in a number of accidents, coalition air power was ready for action.

In January the weather in the region was cooler, and the coalition had by then secured an accurate assessment of Iraqi dispositions. The air assault into Iraq would be led by F-117s, F-15Es, F-111s, A-6Es, A-7s, F/A-18s, and Tornados, all of which had nighttime precision-strike capability. These strike aircraft were assisted by an armada of support systems, including air superiority fighters in the form of USAF and Royal Saudi Air Force (RSAF) F-15s, USN F-14s, RAF and RSAF Tornado F3s, French Mirage 2000s, and EA-6B, EF-111, and F-4G electronic attack and defense suppression aircraft, USAF KC-10 and KC-135, RAF VC-10s, and USMC KC-130s tankers, plus surveillance and reconnaissance aircraft like the E-3A AWACS, RF-4Cs, and EC-130s. Unmanned BQM-74 drones and Tactical Air-Launched Decoys (TALD) were used to stimulate Baghdad's air defenses so that antiradiation High Speed Anti-Radiation Missiles (HARMs) and similar British Air Launched Anti-Radiation Missiles (ALARMs) could knock out radar. Other aircraft, such as USAF B-52s, F-16s, A-10s, USN/ USMC F/A-18s, A-7s, AV-8Bs, and allied Jaguars, concentrated on Phases II and III of the air campaign, attacking Iraqi forces in Kuwait and southern Iraq to pave the way for the ground offensive. A massive fleet of transports and helicopters was busy moving forward supplies, while attack helicopters patrolled along the border, ready to attack Iraqi positions.

As the January 15, 1991, UN deadline approached, U.S. Marine maintenance crews worked feverishly to prepare their AV-8Bs for action. The weather during this period was cool, and it even rained several times in December and January. The rain turned the sand into mud that stuck to everything. When it was dry and windy, the air was filled with swirling sand, which got into everything.

Vacuum cleaners were used to suck the fine sand out of cockpits, access panels, and air intakes. Support crews worked twelve hours on and twelve hours off, six days a week. With no place to go and no beer to drink, there was little else to concentrate on but the job, writing home, and watching CNN.

During Operation Desert Shield, USMC AV-8Bs located on the USS *Nassau* and USS *Tarawa* flew training and support sorties and participated in several exercises. Land- and sea-based AV-8Bs working with Marine Forward Air Controllers practiced day and night CAS in conjunction with U.S. Marine and Army, British, and Arab contingent forces. In addition AV-8B pilots flew armed reconnaissance, air-to-air, and air-to-ground training sorties.

Lieutenant General Boomer counted on Marine aircraft, especially the AV-8Bs, to suppress and destroy Iraqi artillery, rocket launchers, and Frog missiles, which were viewed as the primary threat to U.S.-allied ground forces. Iraqi artillery and rockets outnumbered and outranged those in service with allied forces, and allied commanders suspected that these indirect fire weapons were capable of delivering chemical munitions.

Initially the AV-8Bs were scheduled to be held in reserve during the first phases of the air war. This decision was made in order to reserve the jump jets for the battlefield preparation phase and ground assault. The AV-8Bs on the USS *Nassau* and USS *Tarawa* operating in the Arabian Gulf likewise were held back to provide CAS for any Marine ground raids or amphibious assaults. Alert aircraft at King Abdul Aziz airfield and on the two amphibious ships were nevertheless armed and standing by, in case they were called into action.

However, just after dawn on January 17, 1991, a Marine OV-10 aircraft spotted an Iraqi 122mm artillery battery shelling the town of Khafji and the nearby oil refinery. A prompt call for air support by AV-8Bs from VMA-311 led to the launch of its alert aircraft at 0830 that morning. "The call was made to the guys right up there next to the border, who do this for a living," said Lieutenant Colonel White. "Four VMA-311 aircraft on alert responded to the call and attacked the Iraqi artillery battery with thousand-pound bombs and cannon fire. . . . The grunts, who were about seven miles away, and the OV-10 flying out over the water watched the attack through binoculars and telescopes. They saw the thousand-pounders being dropped inside the revetments and watched the artillery pieces going end over end. The strikes completely destroyed all six artillery pieces and silenced the shelling of Khafji."[9]

Harrier IIs from VMA-542 and VMA-231 followed suit with their alert aircraft and all three divisions engaged and destroyed Iraqi artillery positions. AV-8B strikes against Iraqi artillery and other targets in Kuwait continued until the ceasefire on February 28.

Starting the next day, Marine Harrier IIs flew regular strikes against Iraqi positions in southern Kuwait to prepare the battlefield. AV-8B pilots flew three basic mission types: preplanned strikes, CAS with direction from a FAC, and armed reconnaissance. Daily ATOs directed the Harrier IIs against known targets in Kuwait, such as artillery batteries, command posts, armor concentrations, and defensive fortifications.

Frequently AV-8B pilots would work in conjunction with a ground-based or airborne FAC flying in a two-seat F/A-18D. The FAC would pinpoint priority targets with smoke rockets and direct strikes by radio. Sometimes flights of AV-8Bs were assigned to fly armed reconnaissance over a fifteen-mile-square section of terrain in southern Kuwait with clearance to bomb any target that presented itself. Most AV-8B sorties lasted a little more than an hour. Sections of two aircraft would take off, climb to twenty thousand feet, and reach the target area in about twenty minutes. Then they would orbit and talk with the FAC for directions or seek out their targets visually. The pilots would make one or more bomb runs and then return to their base.

Most attacks were made from medium altitude using 30 degrees or greater dive delivery tactics with the pilots pulling out above the effective altitude of smaller antiaircraft guns and shoulder-fired SAMs, which were the primary threat in the southern Kuwait area, where most Harrier II attack missions were flown. Chaff and flares were released during the dive and pull-out to decoy Iraqi missiles. Because the AV-8B was an accurate bomber, most of the weapons delivered were unguided "dumb" bombs.

"After the first days we dropped our Sidewinders so we normally went out with six Rockeye, six Mk-82s (five-hundred-pound bombs) or sometimes four Mk-83s (thousand-pound bombs)," says Lieutenant Colonel Jones. "Occasionally we would carry an ALQ-164 defensive electronic countermeasures pod on the centerline. By the way, the gun also worked extremely well. We fired in excess of twenty thousand rounds in our squadron alone. The charts don't give accurate numbers for 30- degree deliveries, with the pilot squeezing the trigger at ten thousand feet. We found it works just fine. It tends to keep the antiaircraft gunners' heads down too!"[10]

The Harrier IIs also employed napalm bombs, which were dropped just before the ground war to set Iraqi fire trench defenses aflame. Fuel air explosive weapons were also used, as were a number of AGM-65 Laser Maverick air-to-ground missiles.

At the peak of Operation Desert Storm, which took place between January 16 and February 27, 1991, a section of Harriers took off or recovered every fifteen minutes, and at least one or two more sections operated from Tanajib. Tanajib operations provided continuous cover for the battle, interspersing ground-loitering assets with airborne assets and providing response times of as little as ten minutes. Sorties flown included deep air strikes in the north of Kuwait, with the aircraft flying up to 210 miles one way without need of tankers. Other sorties were helicopter-escort, CAS, and armed reconnaissance. Normal ordnance loads consisted of fully loaded guns, four to six MK 20 Rockeyes or MK 82 HE, two to four MK 83 HE, or two laser-guided Maverick missiles with guns and two bombs. MK 77 fire bombs were employed during the later stages of the war, before the ground war began.

Aircraft were "pit turned" (the pilot remaining with the aircraft for two or three sorties) to reduce turnaround time and work for the maintenance crews. Missions were regularly cycled through the forward site at Tanajib to increase response time and the capability to generate sorties. Pilots were routinely scheduled for two or three flights per day, but the vagaries of weather and needs of the supported forces occasionally necessitated changing the ATO schedules. Overall a pilot averaged one day off the flight schedule approximately every fourth or fifth day.

Tactics included high angle dive attacks at 45 to 60 degrees and ordnance-dropping at eight thousand to thirteen thousand feet to defeat antiaircraft defenses. Constraints in the weapons delivery software precluded dropping MK 20 Rockeyes above approximately twelve thousand feet using the automatic weapons release (AUTO) or continuously computed impact point (CCIP) modes—this restriction was common to all "systems" aircraft, as MK 20 logic was not designed to drop from such altitudes. Workaround methods were developed and ordnance was delivered from virtually all altitudes and in all modes, including classic "lay downs" with napalm. The angle rate bombing set—TV computer system (ARBS) six-power TV—proved to be valuable in debriefing and bomb damage assessment. The GAU-12 25mm gun was reliable, highly accurate, and lethal.[11]

Lieutenant Colonel White called southern Kuwait a "Harrier hunting ground." He said that after January 18, 1991, "There was not a five-minute time block that Harriers weren't expending ordnance on target. I tell you there was no rest for those (Iraqi) gents . . . I think that had a lot to do with the incredibly low casualty figures sustained by our troops. When you looked down on Kuwait, the entire country was an armed camp. . . . There was no problem finding targets—the problem was, [whether] this target [had] really been destroyed, and which tank is it that you want me to hit."[12]

As the date for the ground offensive approached, the six AV-8Bs of VMA-513 Detachment B moved ashore to the King Abdul Aziz airfield from the USS *Tarawa*. The Harriers of VMA-331 on the USS *Nassau* went into action on February 20 against Iraqi targets on Faylaka Island. With the start of the ground offensive on February 24, land- and sea-based AV-8Bs flew hundreds of missions a day in direct support of advancing Marine and U.S.-allied units. As Lieutenant Colonel Jones tells it:

> They didn't fly a lot of missions, mostly because they were used as a threat from an amphibious raid, or an amphibious landing north of Kuwait City. They got some pretty impressive numbers though; once they got into the war, they got in in a big way. Starting about February 25 that twenty-plane squadron was flying at a rate of 72 sorties per day. And you can only get some fourteen Harrier IIs on the deck of an LHA [amphibious assault ship]. They got only fifty-six of the scheduled seventy-two sorties out because they were cut back by the weather. The weather got awful when the ground war kicked off. Every one of the missions they did fly carried ordnance and they were really flying those jets hard. They did very, very well.[13]

Availability of the Harrier force was extremely high. Aircraft were consistently available to surge to as high as one hundred sixty sorties a day among the sixty-six land-based AV-8s. Sortie rates of 3.6 per aircraft were anticipated, but the aircraft usually averaged less than two per day, due to the large numbers of other aircraft in the extremely small theater of operations. On one occasion, with merely an hour's notice, thirty additional AV-8 sorties were launched from the King Abdul Aziz airfield in a surge effort to counter Iraqi forces. No conventional aircraft were available to react that quickly; the basing concept of the V/STOL aircraft—which puts living and maintenance spaces in close proximity to the aircraft as well as to the battle area—allowed for such a surge. Readiness rates throughout the war averaged 90 percent mission-capable and 84.1 percent full mission-capable; given trained personnel and proper funding/logistics, the Harrier proved to be as reliable as any aircraft in the inventory.

The exemplary readiness of the airplanes was punctuated by the feats of VMA-231, which arrived from its eighteen-thousand-mile transit with only two aircraft in need of unscheduled maintenance. VMA-231 flew highs of 904 hours during December and 966 hours in February. Overall, maintenance crews were able to hold five to ten aircraft per squadron in maintenance reserve and meet or exceed the demands of the schedule; airplanes actually got better during the war! Foreign object damage (FOD) rates were low to nonexistent; the rate of 0.359 was considerably lower than during peacetime, in garrison. At King Abdul Aziz airfield, two engines received FOD by maintenance error and three more received minor, blendable damage; anticipated accelerated wear and damage from sand ingestion never occurred, nor did sand and dust adversely affect avionics equipment.

The AV-8Bs averaged about two sorties a day, but the Marine squadrons could have sustained a rate of 3.5 sorties. "The Harriers were supplying more airpower than they could possibly use," said Capt. John Downey, a pilot who flew with VMA-311. "We didn't even break a sweat. On one internal surge exercise early on, we completed fifty-four sorties in four hours."[14]

Threats ranged from MANPAD (man portable air defenses) SA-7/14 IR (infrared) missiles and radar/optical-guided SA-2/3/6/8/9s. Antiaircraft artillery (AAA) ranging from small arms to 100mm antiaircraft cannon completed the gamut of enemy air defenses. The SA-7/14 proved to be the Iraqis' most effective weapon, accounting for numerous hits on U.S.-allied aircraft.

Lt. Russ Sanborn was assigned in January 1990 to his first operational squadron tour with VMA-231.

We flew two missions a day and dropped incredible amounts of ordnance from January 16 to March 6. We were nervous yet excited at the same time. Our focus was on being professional and doing a good job. As you come down the chute (for a bombing run), you have fifteen seconds where you are not avoiding missiles or anything else. . . . There were handheld (SAM-7 missiles) all over the place. A bad thing is you can't see them, but on the same note, they have a hard time seeing you as you come down the chute (because of the small size and the fast rate of speed of the Harrier's approach). In order to get a lock on a plane they have to spot it first. I came down the chute, rolled in, hit my target dead on, was spotted and tracked by an Iraqi handheld, and was hit in my hot left nozzle as I was just about into the safe zone. . . . I froze for a split second in disbelief. Firelights and warning lights were going off and smoke filled the cockpit and the plane started spinning upside down, which was a big clue that something went really wrong. It all happened instantly—from the time I heard the initial hit to when I ejected from the cockpit. I remember seeing fire from the rockets shooting my seat out of the cockpit and the plane getting farther away.

I blacked out for about five seconds because of the g-forces, and woke up startled, when my parachute snapped open. I immediately went into action, all the training flooded into my mind. As I floated down I chambered a round and got the radio to contact my wingman. For some reason my radio didn't work. It was not my day . . . I wasn't making conscious decisions any more; it was all my training that took over. I spun myself around and saw that I was going to land about ten miles behind enemy lines. I was a little scared, but more than anything, pumped and ready to hit the ground. . . . After the Iraqis blew my aircraft out of the sky, everyone was able to see my parachute and tracked me down to the desert floor . . . I had my 9mm (pistol) with me. . . . John Wayne might have stood there and shot it out with them but I'm not that good.

After Lieutenant Sanborn was captured he was beaten and eventually taken to Baghdad, where he suffered from brutal interrogations including regular beating. He was put into a cell next to British commandos and suffered from food poisoning. After twenty-six days, he was turned over to the Red Cross and flown out of Baghdad.[15]

Iraqi shoulder-fired SAMs were responsible for the downing of four AV-8Bs, leading to the capture of three Marine pilots and the death of another pilot. A fifth AV-8B and pilot were lost due to unknown causes during a night attack. The rotating nozzles that allowed for V/STOL flight were a vulnerability, because IR missiles homed in on these heat sources and impacted or detonated close to the engine and fuselage of the AV-8B. Tactics employed to reduce the AV-8B's vulnerability to IR-homing SAM included flying at night and higher altitudes, releasing more expendables (chaff and flares). A missile-approach warning device was planned for future installation into the AV-8B. These measures to improve Harrier II survivability had been previously identified and were already in development when the conflict broke out.[16]

Kuwait was overrun in several days by vastly more powerful Iraqi forces, but Kuwaiti air force fighters and air defense units downed more than twenty Iraqi aircraft and helicopters. The United States and more than thirty other nations responded to the Kuwaiti, Saudi Arabian, and United Nations requests for support and assistance. Critical aspects to the success of the coalition were its political resolve and the availability of airfields, port facilities, housing, and assistance provided by Saudi Arabia, Bahrain, the United Arab Emirates, Qatar, Oman, Egypt, and other nations. After six months of preparation, the coalition began a massive air campaign, which ran for forty-three days. This air assault was the biggest coalition effort since World War II, and made a major contribution to smashing Iraq's air, ground, and naval defenses and paved the way for a hundred-hour invasion of Kuwait. Air attacks crippled Iraq's economy through the selective destruction of strategic targets such as electrical power systems, oil refining and storage facilities, and transportation networks.

By the end of the conflict coalition aircraft had flown nearly 109,876 sorties, delivered 88,500 tons of ordnance, and shot down some thirty-eight Iraqi aircraft. The USAF flew 63 percent of these missions, U.S. Navy 24 percent, coalition forces 16 percent (RSAF 6.5 percent, RAF 5.1 percent, Armée de l'Air 2.1 percent), and the USMC 14 percent. Coalition losses included thirty-eight aircraft and helicopters lost, forty-eight damaged, and thirty destroyed due to accidents or operational problems. Coalition air and ground forces lost fewer than 250 people killed during combat and a similar number killed through accidents. Iraqi loss figures ran from ten thousand to one hundred thousand killed and sixty-five thousand captured, giving the Gulf War one of the most lopsided loss rates in history.[17]

Air-to-Ground Operations

In forty-three days approximately twenty-five hundred aircraft from sixteen nations flew a total of 126,645 (support and combat) sorties. The air element of the United Nations forces providing combat aircraft for action against Iraq included Saudi Arabia, Kuwait, Qatar, the United Arab Emirates, Great Britain, France, Canada, Italy, and the United States. These air arms flew about sixty-five thousand combat sorties, of which forty-five thousand were attack missions. Coalition aircraft delivered ninety-six thousand tons of munitions (162,000 unguided bombs), but only seventy-four hundred tons (ninety-five hundred) of these were precision-guided weapons. Due to the effective defense suppression effort, medium altitude tactics, and other factors, coalition forces lost only thirty-eight aircraft in combat during these attacks (an additional forty-eight suffered damage and twenty-eight aircraft were lost in operational accidents). The combat loss ratio of about one aircraft for every two thousand sorties was far better than that experienced over North Vietnam and in the Arab-Israeli conflicts.[18]

The bulk of coalition aircraft—USN/USMC AV-8Bs, F/A-18s, A-7Es; USAF F-16s, RAF/Italian/RSAF Tornados; British/French Jaguars; Kuwaiti; UAE, and French Mirage fighters; Saudi F-5Es; and Kuwati A-4s—delivered unguided bombs. USAF B-52s dropped about 29 percent of the 82,000 tons of unguided weapons dropped during the conflict. The bulk of the munitions delivered against Iraqi targets were conventional general purpose and cluster bombs ranging from the 500-pound Mk-82 to the 2,000-pound Mk-84 and various types of cluster munitions (Mk-20 Rockeye, CBU-58/78, BL-755, and so on). These weapons were effective when they hit their targets, but delivery of these munitions from medium altitude reduced their effectiveness, due to the effects of wind and targeting—some estimates placed the hit total of unguided munitions at around 25 percent.

By February 27, 1991, when Harrier II attack missions ended due to the ceasefire, the eighty-six Marine AV-8Bs deployed to the Gulf had flown 9,353 sorties for 11,120 hours during Operations Desert Shield and Desert Storm. The U.S. Marine Corps AV-8Bs flew 3,380 combat sorties for a total of 4,038 hours and 5.95 million pounds of ordnance delivered.

The summaries of each squadron's combat sorties follow:

- VMA-231—987 sorties
- VMA-311—975 sorties
- VMA-331—242 sorties
- VMA-513—103 sorties
- VMA-542—1,037 sorties[19]

At the end of the hostilities, AV-8B aircraft were redeployed to the United States by a combination of sealift and strategic tanker. With only one field carrier landing practice period (FCLP) per pilot, VMA-231 and two-thirds of VMA-542 flew to Rota, Spain, and embarked on the USS *Saratoga* and the USS *Kennedy* for the ten-day nonflying Atlantic transit to the continental United States. Two hundred miles from the U.S. coast, the shipboard AV-8s flew off the carriers, once again illustrating the extreme versatility of the airplane and confirming the viability of V/STOL operations.

CHAPTER 8

Night Attack:
Improving the Harrier II

Even before the 1990–91 Gulf War, the U.S. and British governments had funded McDonnell Douglas and British Aerospace to develop improvements for the Harrier II. With its electro-optical ARBS, the AV-8B was essentially a daylight, visual light-attack aircraft optimized for CAS and strike missions. The team was examining many options to upgrade the Harrier II, including systems to enable the pilot to fly and fight at night, additional self-defense systems to improve the aircraft's survivability, and the addition of a new engine with higher thrust and enhanced reliability.

During the late 1970s and early 1980s, a number of U.S. and European firms developed new technologies that enhanced the capabilities of tactical aircraft to effectively fly and perform their missions at night and in conditions of suboptimal visibility. The FLIR systems, such as the Electro-optical Viewing System (EVS) on the B-52G/H and the TRAM on the A-6E, gave these aircraft more accurate navigation and bombing capability than with radar.

On the A-6E two-seat attack aircraft, the FLIR was mounted under the nose of the aircraft in a rotating turret and was used for both navigation and target designation for the delivery of conventional and laser-guided bombs. A FLIR system looks at the temperature of objects, a method especially effective after dark when objects cool at different rates. The FLIR consists of a lens and an array of IR detectors over which an image is passed via a lens. The results of the scan are projected on a TV-like screen in the cockpit or on the HUD for improved pilot visibility. Most first-generation FLIRs (as employed on the A-6E, the F-111, and the B-52) were complex, expensive, heavy, and reliant on a weapons systems operator or dedicated naval flight officer for effective operation.

In the 1980s the U.S. government focused on the development of the common module FLIR to meet its future night-vision needs. The USAF funded Lockheed to develop the pod-mounted Low Altitude Navigation and Targeting Infrared for Night (LANTIRN) system for night attack using laser-guided munitions. This extensive suite included a FLIR, navigation radar, and laser designator in two pods for the F-15E and eventually F-14B/D fighters. Many single-seat F-16Cs and two-seat F-16Ds were fitted with the single-pod version of LANTIRN, which included the FLIR and laser designator but no navigation radar.

The space- and weight-sensitive tactical aircraft like the V/STOL Harrier II required innovative solutions for installing a night-attack system. Electronics technology had advanced to the point where a FLIR could be mounted in the nose of the Harrier II, with the processed imagery projected into the HUD and/or color cockpit displays so that the pilot could detect potential targets and navigate effectively. The fixed FLIR on the AV-8B Night Attack variant was employed mostly for navigation, but it could also be used for target detection.

In addition, companies in the United States and Europe had developed night-vision goggles (NVGs), which are mounted on a pilot's helmet to provide effective intensification of ambient light for operations in the dark. NVGs have an image intensifier tube for each eye, which produces a bright monochromatic green image under conditions where the unaided eye could not detect anything. With NVGs, a pilot can "see" in the dark, increase the element of surprise, and reduce vulnerability to threat systems.[1]

Although the performance of NVGs has improved and weight has decreased over time (including the recent fourth-generation systems), limitations include the need for some ambient light, a limited field of view (which can lead to pilot disorientation), and a loss of situational awareness. Training is required to ensure effective employment of NVGs by pilots.

Initially NVGs were tested and perfected on slower helicopters. In the United Kingdom, RAF pilots also conducted the "Nightbird" test program, flying two-seat Hunters and Harriers with NVGs and test versions of a GEC-Marconi FLIR. The USMC secured funding for research projects to test these new systems on fighter aircraft under operational conditions at the Naval Air Test Center at China Lake, California.

Lt. Col. Terry Mattke, USMC (Ret.), was an exchange officer flying Harriers with the RAF.

> As a result of the contacts I developed then, in mid-1982 I was invited to the United Kingdom to fly a two-seat Hawker Hunter fitted with NVGs. In addition, I saw test versions of the Marconi FLIR. This was a tremendous new capability. After returning to the United States, I briefed Maj. Gen. William Fitch, DCS Aviation for the USMC, on the system and how it could be added to the Harrier II. General Fitch had flown more than one hundred missions over North Vietnam at night and was very aware of our limited night strike

capability. After the briefing, the general said, "Make it happen" . . . so I went around in the fall of 1982 and swept up $750,000 from the USMC, Coast Guard, and USAF Reserve for a program to demonstrate this capability on a tactical aircraft.[2]

. . . Russ Stromberg was stationed at NAS China Lake at this time, and he identified a YA-7F two-seat jet which was about to go into overhaul. Through personal contact, he secured this aircraft. I brought a team composed of engineers, marketing and program personnel from McDonnell Douglas, Vought, and GEC-Marconi quietly to China Lake on a need-to-know basis. We put the marketing and business people in one room to work out arrangements while Russ stayed with the engineers in another room. At the end of three hours or so, we had an agreement and the engineers had created cockpit drawings for the changes needed to work with NVGs and hang a FLIR in a pod under the wing and wire it up. Through hard work, nine months later we had a two-seat jet ready to fly with NVGs and the FLIR. General Fitch told us to find a naval officer test pilot to fly the aircraft since it was a Navy jet that we had quietly taken control of. He flew the systems and it worked very well.[3]

. . . A few weeks later we organized a briefing in Washington, D.C., led by General Fitch, which included a two-star admiral in charge of USN funding, the captain-level program manager for the A-7, and several other senior officers. The Navy was amazed and not real happy that we had pulled off this secret and successful development program using one of their aircraft. General Fitch briefed SECNAV [Secretary of the Navy] John Lehman (who had served as an A-6 bombardier navigator) and got him to fly in the aircraft. After the flight the SECNAV secured full funding for the program to integrate night attack into the Harrier and later the Hornet, and made it number two on the U.S. Navy research and development list of critical programs. That is how we got night attack into the AV-8B![4]

In mid-1984, McDonnell Douglas engineers started looking into how to integrate night attack systems into the AV-8B. Clint Moore, a senior engineer on the program, visited China Lake in the early 1980s, to see a technology demonstration of the future night attack systems.

Hank Wall and I were aware that several of these first-generation technologies were beginning to mature into usable products. Most were targeted for larger attack aircraft having weapons systems operators as well as pilots, due to their complexity and the immaturity of the systems integration. After our meetings with the program sponsors and test pilots, we began to realize that not only were several parallel new technology developments going to be required, but the USMC pilots intended to fly this aircraft at night in the same manner that they were flying in daytime. This meant that all functions of flying, navigating, and prosecuting the ground attack had to be accomplished by a single pilot flying "heads up," looking out of the cockpit. This single-operator system was a new approach that required precise systems integration to ensure first pilot safety, and then adequate capability to perform accurate weapons delivery to achieve a kill against a target on the first pass. This was a big task for the Harrier II engineering team to pull off. It required a lot more from the Marine Corps pilots also, since they had to be pilots, weapons systems operators, and navigators at night.[5]

McDonnell Douglas engineers, with support from British Aerospace and GEC-Marconi, started a program to integrate a FLIR in the nose of the AV-8B and project the imagery onto a new HUD. In addition the AV-8B Night Attack cockpit featured a digital moving map and new cockpit lighting, which allowed for use of NVGs. Ben Park served as the AV-8B Night Attack program manager.

> We had an interesting challenge in figuring out where to put the navigation FLIR. Previous planes had put it on the bottom, but we found that would not work on the Harrier II because of the hot air coming out of the nose puffer duct—basically it obliterated the FLIR picture, so the pilot would not be able to use the FLIR on takeoff and landing. So we found a spot on top of the nose barrel that did not restrict the pilot's over the nose vision and also did not add much drag to the aircraft. As with any decision on the design of an aircraft, it turned out to be a compromise. The night-attack system worked because of the integration of the FLIR imagery and night-vision goggles with the moving map. The FLIR had a narrow field of view; the NVGs provided a wide field of view and allowed the pilot to move his head around. One system by itself did not work. Also, the fact that the FLIR relied upon IR energy and the NVGs upon light energy seemed to give the pilot the best of both worlds. The moving map was also crucial to the formula, because it was easy to get disoriented without having a God's-eye view of where the airplane was. In a single-seat airplane like the Harrier II, this was very important. It was definitely an exciting time in my life to be involved in this program.[6]

The concept was approved by the Harrier II program office in late 1984. Col. Lewis C. Watt, USMC (Ret.), NAVAIR Harrier II program manager, says of development challenges:

> One of the finer management efforts I have ever witnessed occurred during the AV-8B Night Attack development. Sperry, as the subcontractor to McDonnell Douglas, was developing the moving map, critical to the overall system, and always on the critical path. With a few months to go before integration of the moving map, the merger which became UNISYS occurred. The new UNISYS team, however, did not want the division that included the Albuquerque shop of Sperry where the map work was being done. So this leading-edge work was accomplished by folks who literally had no company sign on their building, and no clue about their future. The result? Sperry was on time, on cost, and technically excellent. That's the kind of dedication and the quality of management we had working in those days. Honeywell subsequently acquired the division.[7]

Following engineering and testing, a prototype was built. In June 1987 the first Harrier II Night Attack prototype (the 87th AV-8B produced, modified to include night-attack capability) rolled off the assembly line in St. Louis, Missouri. Testing confirmed that these improvements allowed pilots to effectively fly and fight at night. In addition, the USMC Night Attack Harrier II incorporated a larger Leading-Edge Root Extension (LERX) for improved turn rate and agility, and four more chaff/flare dispensers in the upper aft fuselage.[8]

The USMC received its first of sixty-six production AV-8B Night Attack aircraft in September 1989 with initial deliveries going to USMC squadrons located at MCAS Yuma. The RAF also bought the Night Attack aircraft, which they designated the GR Mk. 7 Harrier II. Earlier production GR Mk. 5 aircraft were upgraded to include night-attack systems and features.

A key element of further growth for the Harrier II was development of a new higher-thrust version of the Pegasus turbofan engine. David J. Martin was a lead engineer at Rolls-Royce. "Since entry into service in 1969 (the F402-RR-402)," he says, "the Pegasus engine thrust has been enhanced by about 15 percent and the thrust-to-weight ratio by about 7 percent. In that time a major increase in overhaul life has been achieved, from two hundred hours for the initial engine to five hundred hours on the -406A engine. . . . The main technologies available to improve Pegasus were improved fan aerodynamics and single-crystal cast materials for turbine blading. These two technologies were doubly important because it was agreed not to change the engine envelope."[9]

Col. Lewis C. Watt (Ret.) adds:

> Gene Newbold [from Rolls-Royce] had done a superb job of selling the engine upgrade in Washington, D.C. The final signature, however, had to come from the SECNAV, John Lehman, who had a plateful of other ways to spend the U.S. Navy's money. In the final briefing to Mr. Lehman, he challenged every reason I offered for funding the -408. I finally offered the explanation that the upgrade would support the additional weight of the radar, radar would cement sales to the Italians and additional sales to Spain, and those sales would keep the production line open. Mr. Lehman said something like, "Why didn't you say so!" And he signed the approval. In the room were several U.S. Navy flag officers, a well-known Assistant SECNAV, and Maj. Gen. Keith Smith, Deputy Chief of Staff, Aviation programs (DCS AIR) for the Marine Corps. The intake of breath around the room was audible as the document was signed. I realized later that Major General Smith and I were the only ones in the room who wanted that paper signed. The AV-8B does not, after all, have a tail hook![10]

In 1986, Rolls-Royce received funding for a new F402-RR-408 engine that provided additional thrust and reliability enhancements. Mike Gladwin was then director of Pegasus programs at Rolls-Royce.

The introduction of the -408 (improved thrust Pegasus engine) totally changed the way in which the aircraft was operated. I don't think people recognize that this was a very structured program. The concept of growing the aircraft after introduction to service was totally dependent upon the ability to be able to carry more sensors, weapons, and payload. We were looking to do this and there were two people who really pushed this. The first was Ed Harper, the McDonnell Douglas program manager. And the other was Gene Newbold of Rolls-Royce. Gene was selling the airplane and not just the engine. We managed to secure funding due to these two men,. along with help from many others. . . . [A] program like the Harrier II is essentially an aircraft built around an engine. So you are bound to have lots of complex interactions between the two, especially with a very short intake, because of the fundamental design of the engine and aircraft. We did some interesting work in the 1970s that showed if we could add a longer intake, adding a foot or so, we could generate two to three thousand pounds of additional thrust. But we were stuck with the aircraft as it was because of the critical element of balance during takeoff, landing, and hover. So we had an interesting challenge, and with the -408 we added a revised fan and better combustor and we moved to an electronic control system. Nobody thinks about it now, but the so-called DEC [Digital Engine Control] systems were the first fully digital control system to fly in a combat aircraft.[11]

In June 1989, British Aerospace test pilot Heinz Frick flew the first -408 prototype engine in an RAF GR Mk. 5 with a special blue, black, and white paint job from the company airfield at Dunsfold. More than sixty flights by Rolls-Royce, British Aerospace, RAF, and Marine Corps test pilots confirmed the new engine's improved performance. In the summer and fall of 1989, the test aircraft achieved four new V/STOL time-to-height records.[12]

By early 1990, the first AV-8B Night Attack aircraft fitted with the Rolls-Royce F402-RR-408 version of the Pegasus turbofan engine started flight-testing. This new version of the vectored-thrust Pegasus passed an abbreviated flight-test program with excellent results.

Soon after the AV-8B Night Attack aircraft with the -408 engine entered service with Marine Corps fleet squadrons VMA-211 and VMA 214, based at Yuma, problems began to appear. On a bombing sortie an engine surged but the pilot was able to make it back to base. Subsequent disassembly and inspection of the engine showed that the High Pressure Compressor (HPC) Vanes had rubbed the HPC Rotor Spacers, causing holes to be burned in the titanium spacers when the engine was hot and under high "g" loading. Soon the same thing happened on a second new AV-8B Night Attack Harrier II. However, in this case the engine caught fire and the pilot had to eject. In early 1991 all -408 Harrier II aircraft were grounded.[13]

The engine problem halted deliveries of Harrier II Night Attack aircraft to the U.S. Marine Corps. Operational training at the night-attack squadrons

VMA-211 and VMA-214 was delayed until the earlier -406A Pegasus engines could be installed.

Rolls-Royce quickly identified the problems that caused contact between the HPC Vanes and the HPC Rotor Spacers. A modification program was instituted, which included changing the HPC Stator Vanes from titanium to high-temperature resistant steel, increasing the HPC blade tip-to-case clearance, and other changes. All of the -408 engines had to be returned to the factory in England for rework.[14]

After modifications and further testing, the F402-RR-408 was cleared for service deliveries. Rolls-Royce continued to develop and refine the -408 engine, and eventually all U.S. Marine Corps Harrier IIs, including the two-seat TAV-8Bs, were equipped with the higher-thrust -408 engines. This engine has also been fitted to RAF, Spanish, and Italian Harrier IIs.[15]

By the early 1990s, the impact of the end of the Cold War led to reductions in U.S. military numbers. One of the USMC's contributions to these cutbacks was elimination of the first Harrier II squadron activated, VMA-331, located at MCAS Cherry Point. The squadron was deactivated on September 30, 1992, leaving seven operational USMC "gun" squadrons with twenty AV-8Bs each and one large Harrier II training squadron with more than thirty AV-8Bs/TAV-8Bs in service. A small number of AV-8Bs also served with the Naval Air Test and Evaluation Squadrons at China Lake and Patuxent River, Maryland.

The bulk of the Harrier II force in the early 1990s was composed of the AV-8B day-attack Harrier IIs delivered (166 total plus the four FSD aircraft) during the first six years of production (FY1982–88). The first of sixty-six production configuration AV-8B Night Attack aircraft was delivered for testing on September 15, 1989 (aircraft 163,853, the 167th Harrier II).

A major industrial lobbying campaign on both sides of the Atlantic led to the procurement of seventy-two Harrier II aircraft, starting in the U.S. fiscal year 1989. Harrier II production deliveries included aircraft ordered in FY1989, FY1990, and the first part of FY1991. Aircraft 163,873, the 181st Harrier II, incorporated the higher-thrust Rolls-Royce F402-RR-408 Pegasus engine. Night-attack aircraft were delivered from late 1989 to 1993, and these went to Marine Air Group 13 at Yuma, to squadrons VMA-214, VMA-211, and VMA-311.[16]

Lt. Col. Russ Stromberg, USMC (Ret.), commanded VMA-214, the first USMC night-attack squadron.

> When we first got the night-attack jets they were brand-new airplanes. They had the -406 (Rolls-Royce Pegasus), which was a pretty reliable engine. And the other thing was [that] MAG-13, which was the last air group to expand, had four Harrier II squadrons at the time (VMA-513, VMA-311, VMA-214, and VMA-211). I had VMA-513 first and then I transferred to VMA-214. There were two squadrons behind me, so the way we were building up the

squadrons was they were force-feeding extra people in, training them, and buying spare parts in advance. We had brand-new aircraft, lots of spare parts, and trained people—how could you go wrong? We had about the right number of pilots . . . so we were each flying thirty to thirty-five hours per month per pilot. But we did not have extra pilots; they were more difficult to get than the enlisted troops, because both the AV-8B and F/A-18 communities were expanding and were barely able to meet the demand. Times were good! We were running 85 percent availability for aircraft, I could muster 100 percent of my maintenance personnel on deck, and I could pick the guys coming to my squadron! The biggest challenge was figuring out how to manage aircrew body cycles while chasing the moon for night-attack operations. . . .

Night-attack gave us a lot more combat capability—it gave us the moving map, the FLIR, and the ability to fly and strike at night. The biggest challenge we had was figuring out to safely manage circadian rhythm and aircrew fatigue in single-seat aircraft flying at night. You take a guy whose body is accustomed to coming to work at 7:30 AM in the morning and going home at 5:00 PM at night one week. And the next week he launches at 10:00 PM at night and he is flying at 200 feet at 450 knots, attacking at 500 knots, and [must] be alert and not kill himself. Managing pilot body cycles was a greater challenge than adjusting to the new combat capabilities. We sold the Office of Personnel Management on a study to develop a plan for both pilots and support personnel to face the challenge of getting enough rest to be able to do the job when going from day ops to night ops and chasing the moon . . . that was the hard part of our job.

There were two key things we added to the day-attack AV-8Bs and when you leveraged these with night-attack capability, the ground commander said, "Whoa, what an airplane!" The biggest advocates for the AV-8B were not aviators but the ground commanders. Bill Frailey [McDonnell Douglas chief of avionics for the Harrier II program] and his team figured out how the ground commanders and grunts thought. Ground forces and FACs give the target coordinates in Universal Transverse Mercanian (UTM) coordinates, which are the map systems [that] ground commanders use. They put this into the aircraft by coming up with the capability to send a nine-line brief (which included UTM coordinates) to the airplane (via the Automatic Target Handoff System [ATHS]). When you added the improved performance and accuracy of the AV-8B day-attack aircraft, and the ability to strike at night with the FLIR and NVGs and communicate (via ATHS) for air support in the same language, it really sold the ground combat element on the Harrier II.[17]

RAF Night-Attack Harrier IIs

In the early 1990s, the RAF was still introducing the Harrier II into service. The No. 1 squadron and the No. 233 Operational Conversion Unit were based at RAF Wittering in the United Kingdom. The first forty-three RAF Harrier IIs were

GR Mk. 5s, and aircraft numbered 44–60 were an interim configuration known as the GR Mk. 5A, built with the capability to more easily retrofit night-attack systems. British Aerospace began converting GR Mk. 5 day-attack aircraft to the GR Mk. 7 Night Attack configuration starting in late 1989. This was a significant upgrade, which involved the addition of a new nose, incorporating the FLIR, a rework of the crew station, and many other systems. RAF GR Mk. 5As were the last to be converted to full night-attack configuration.

The first of thirty-four new-production GR Mk. 7 Harrier IIs built with night-attack capability, similar to USMC aircraft, was delivered from the British Aerospace production line in May 1990, and the last in June 1992. RAF squadrons No. 3 and No. IV, located in Germany, received GR Mk. 7s with night-attack capability beginning in late 1990.[18]

By 1993 the RAF had three operational Harrier II squadrons and an Operational Conversion Unit (OCU) in service. The training unit formed a reserve squadron that could be deployed in an emergency. The forward-based Harrier II units in Germany, the No. 3 and No. IV squadrons, had moved from RAF Gutersloh to RAF Laabruch in 1992. Even while moving and converting to the GR Mk. 7s, these forward-deployed squadrons were actively training. In September 1992 No. 3 squadron sent a flight of Harrier IIs to Kuantan, Malaysia, to participate in multinational exercises.

No. 1 squadron, located at RAF Wittering, gradually replaced its GR Mk. 5 day-attack aircraft with GR Mk. 7s. In 1993 the Harrier II OCU was redesignated No. 20 (reserve) squadron located at RAF Wittering. The training squadron operated GR Mk. 7s. Starting in 1994 the two-seat Harrier trainers were replaced by T Mk. 10 two-seat night-attack trainers. Thirteen of these were delivered. Unlike the USMC TAV-8Bs, the RAF two-seat T 10s are combat-capable aircraft, fitted with a full suite of sensors, weapons delivery, and self-defense systems.[19]

After the end of the Cold War, the RAF Harrier II in Germany was withdrawn back to Britain. In 1999 No. 3 and No. IV Harrier II squadrons were moved to RAF Cottesmore. Even more changes were to come: the RAF and Royal Navy (RN) Harrier forces were combined into Joint Force Harrier in 2000, and the decision was made to retire the RN Sea Harriers by 2006. The Sea Harrier and Harrier II are slated for retirement, to be replaced by the JSF by 2015. A related decision was to embark Harrier II squadrons on RN *Invincible*-class aircraft carriers. In addition, the RAF GR Mk. 7 was improved and upgraded to the improved GR Mk. 9A and GR Mk. 9 configurations.[20]

CHAPTER 9

AV-8B Harrier II Plus:
Adding the Radar

McDonnell Douglas Company (now Boeing), British Aerospace (now BAe Systems), and Smiths Industries agreed to invest their own internal funds to begin development of a new version of the Harrier II equipped with a radar, and announced this decision at the 1987 Paris Air Show. The team initiated an engineering review and preliminary design studies to integrate several different radars. At the same time, a joint marketing committee of representatives from McDonnell Douglas and BAe reviewed the market potential for the radar-equipped Harrier II and identified several candidate customers, including the USMC, Spanish navy, Italian navy, and others.

Early in 1988, the U.S. Marine Corps identified an operational requirement for eighty-five radar-equipped Harrier II aircraft. Roger Mathews, McDonnell Douglas's Harrier II program manager, recalls the unique teamwork involved, the "cooperation and shared risk taking by all in the Harrier II community." In one meeting, McDonnell Aircraft Company president Bill Ross suggested to Colonel Priest that the savings of a multiyear contract would probably pay for the integration of a radar into the Harrier II. "Of course the bookkeeping would be hard pressed to prove this," notes Mathews, "but without the burden of the annual 'save the program' by industry and the Marine Corps, more time was available to focus on long-term issues to improve the Harrier II's capabilities for the end users."

After considerable effort, the U.S. Navy and DoD submitted a multiyear procurement contract for 72 Harrier IIs in the FY1989 budget, and it was eventually approved by the U.S. Congress.[1]

Spain was pleased with its fleet of AV-8S and EAV-8B aircraft, but operational experience in the naval environment pointed to the need for a radar, as the Spanish navy's primary mission was air defense and sea surveillance. Italy and several other nations were evaluating options for new naval fighters. For some time Italy had been working closely with Spain to learn about the EAV-8B and its operational utility in support of the Spanish fleet. Dick Wise was the BAe Harrier II program manager. "The birth of the Harrier II Plus was a classic example of two industrial companies working together toward a single vision," he says. "We held our first Harrier II Plus business working group meeting at Kingston, UK, in May 1988, at which time the issue of launch funds for this new program was high on the agenda. I think it was a tribute to management that McDonnell Douglas and British Aerospace decided to launch the program with company investment."[2]

Roger Mathews adds: "Jackie Jackson ferried a TAV-8B to the UK before the 1988 Farnborough Air Show. We briefed a few RAF Harrier pilots and senior leaders to help them decide on the purchase of the T Mk. 10. During the days of the actual air show, Jackie Jackson briefed several Italian naval officers and an Italian journalist and gave them rides in the TAV-8B, which helped develop support for the program. Hank Cole did a great job of planning these visits and securing approvals for the flights."[3]

Italy built and put into service the *Guiseppe Garibaldi*, a modern ten-thousand-ton aircraft carrier that needed a V/STOL tactical fighter to achieve its full promise. However, a law enacted in the 1920s prevented the Italian navy from operating large fixed-wing aircraft. This law was overturned by the Italian parliament in 1989, paving the way for the Italian navy to buy a V/STOL tactical aircraft.[4]

After considerable discussions the Italian navy and Spanish navy developed a common requirement for the radar-equipped Harrier II Plus to provide air defense for their fleets. McDonnell Douglas decided to integrate the proven Hughes (later Raytheon) APG-65 radar into the Harrier II. Commonality between the Harrier II and the F/A-18 Hornet, which was also in service with the U.S. Marine Corps and with Spain, was an important element of the decision.

The interest of Spain, Italy, and the U.S. Marine Corps in a radar-equipped Harrier II prompted the three countries to discuss ways to start this program. None of the three countries alone was able to fund the development, testing and production tooling necessary to upgrade the AV-8B; by working together, they could achieve this common goal. Another factor in favor of the Harrier II program was U.S. legislation known as the Nunn Amendment, which was passed as part of the 1985 U.S. Congressional defense bill. Sponsored by Georgia senator Sam Nunn, this amendment identified a mechanism to fund collaborative research and development programs that would benefit the United States and NATO countries.

Patrick J. Finneran, McDonnell Harrier II deputy program manager at the time, elaborates:

We had to work very hard as a team to craft an agreement to meet the aircraft requirements of the U.S. Marine Corps, the Spanish navy, plus the Italian navy, and fund profiles of the three nations, and develop an MOU [memorandum of understanding] all three parties could sign. Also we had to accommodate the needs of MACAIR, BAe, and the industries of Spain and Italy. A lot of credit must go to the U.S. Marine Corps and Spanish government representatives who secured a requirement for the Harrier II Plus long-term funding, brought Italy into the program, and sold the concept of the Joint Program Office where all the parties had a voice.[5]

In September 1990, after almost a year's worth of negotiations and review, the United States, Spain, and Italy signed an MOU concerning AV-8B Harrier II Plus development. This MOU established guidelines for sharing the costs of the integration effort and established a Joint Program Office (JPO) with representatives from the three governments to manage the program. The MOU also called for sharing of production for the Harrier II Plus program by industries of the United States, Britain, Spain, and Italy.

Integration of the APG-65 radar into the Harrier II began on September 28, 1990, with the agreement by the United States, Spain, and Italy to invest $55 million each in the program. On November 30, 1990, the U.S. Navy, acting as the agent for the allied participants, awarded McDonnell a contract for the Harrier II Plus, including an initial order for twenty-four aircraft.

This new AV-8B Harrier II Plus combined the Night-Attack upgrades, higher-thrust Rolls-Royce F402-408 engine, and APG-65 radar, giving the Harrier II the capability to perform air defense, fighter, and strike and reconnaissance missions. The Harrier II Plus aircraft was seventeen inches longer than the AV-8B day-attack aircraft, due to the enlarged nose, which accommodates the APG-65 radar antenna and the transmitter receiver. The radar data processor, power supply, and display computer are located in the aft fuselage in order to meet weight and balance requirements, which are critical in a V/STOL aircraft.

Robert White, business development director for Hughes (later Raytheon), says adding the APG-65 radar to the Harrier II Plus was a complex program.

The U.S. Marine Corps wanted to remove APG-65 radars from F/A-18C/Ds, modify and install them in the Harrier II Plus, and then buy new APG-73 radars for the Hornets. We had the goal of maintaining commonality between the existing Hornet radar and the one in the Harrier II Plus to take advantage of existing software, hardware, and support equipment. Also we had to develop a slightly smaller antenna in order to fit in to the radome and modified the environmental control system to provide cooling for the radar. The radar software had to be adjusted [because] the radar processors were located in the aft fuselage and power source in the nose to maintain weight and balance.[6]

The resulting AV-8B Harrier II Plus provided the basing flexibility previously only offered by the vectored-lift Harrier, and advanced avionics necessary for optimum performance in the modern air environment. This program demonstrated that several military forces in different countries can benefit when they harmonize new aircraft requirements and cooperatively develop, produce, and deploy the same aircraft.

In 1992 the production MOU was signed, calling for the assembly of Harrier II aircraft at the McDonnell Douglas plant in St. Louis; the CASA plant at Seville, Spain; and the Alenia factory in Turin, Italy. As part of the Harrier II Plus program, Spanish and Italian industries joined the U.S. and UK suppliers that have supported the AV-8B/GR Mk. 5/7 effort since its inception.

Negotiations concerning the division of responsibility for the production and support of Harrier II Plus aircraft concluded, and a production MOU was signed in December 1992. The Italian navy contracted for eighteen aircraft (sixteen Harrier II Plus aircrafts and two TAV-8B trainers), thirteen of which were assembled by the Italian aerospace firm Alenia. Fiat Avio, FIAR, and many other Italian companies were involved in production and support of the Harrier II Plus. The eight Harrier II Plus aircraft ordered by the Spanish navy were assembled by CASA in Spain and CESELSA-INISEL, Iberia, and a number of other Spanish firms were involved in Harrier II Plus production and maintenance. The USMC funded a share of the development and ordered twenty-seven new AV-8B Harrier II Plus aircraft.[7]

Colonel Priest recalls his exciting time as the program manager of the JPO, with the collaboration of the countries and their industries.

> It was encouraging to see officers from the three countries with a common goal working in my office to secure a radar-capable aircraft for all the countries. At times, however, it was discouraging and frustrating, because the acquisition community is much more accustomed to work with foreign military sales [FMS] than with collaborative programs. Few had experience with a collaborative program and the need for Spain and Italy as our equal partners to share in the work. With the low production rate of six aircraft per year, carving out work share for Spanish and Italian industry was extremely difficult. This put my office in the middle of industries from three countries as if they were industries trying to negotiate a win-win solution. To overcome this, the JPO worked hard to educate those we worked with as to the differences between an FMS program and a collaborative program and to introduce them to the various collaborative aspects of the program.[8]

On June 3, 1992, the U.S. Navy authorized the production of the Harrier II Plus. The prototype, aircraft 164129, first flew with Jackie Jackson at the controls on September 22, 1992. With its radar and FLIR, he says, it brought a huge increase in combat capability. "It had a slight increase in drag and a bit of additional weight, but there really was not much difference in performance between the [-408-powered] Night Attack and radar Harrier II Plus aircraft. Where you saw a little difference was in turning, but we made up most of that with the bigger LERX. The V-max [maximum speed] was nearly the same; perhaps only a five- to eight-knot difference." [9]

The first production Harrier II Plus was delivered in St. Louis, and the aircraft first flew on March 17, 1993. Radar integration tests were completed successfully, and the early aircraft were sent for testing to the Naval Air Test Center and VX-9, a VSN test squadron. Marine Attack Squadron VMA-542, located at MCAS Cherry Point, received the first production Harrier II Plus in June 1993. Delivery of twenty-seven new production Harrier II Plus aircraft ordered by the United States continued to USMC gun squadrons at MCAS Cherry Point until late 1995.

On August 23, 1991, two TAV-8B Harrier IIs landed on the Italian navy aircraft carrier *Giuseppe Garibaldi* at Norfolk, Virginia. The official delivery of two TAV-8B aircraft to the Gruppo Aerei Imbarcati marked a significant milestone for the Italian navy and a fourth customer for Harrier II program. It took a lot of work and effort to achieve this goal.

At first the Italian navy was restricted by a 1937 law to flying only light aircraft and helicopters. Until this law was overturned in 1989, there was no way to arm the *Giuseppe Garibaldi* with a new fighter. Then a new fighter had to be selected. Italy evaluated the Sea Harrier as well as the AV-8B, which at that time did not incorporate radar. In June 1990 the Italian minister of defense detailed plans to buy two TAV-8Bs and sixteen Harrier II Plus aircraft. The Harrier II Plus also involved a collaborative program with the United States, Spanish, and Italian industry.

After the 1990 agreement for Harrier II Plus cooperative development, a select team of ten Italian navy pilots and eighteen experienced support personnel arrived in the United States for training. Pilots went through the U.S. Navy/Marine Corps training program at NAS Meridian, Mississippi, and then to VMAT-203 at MCAS Cherry Point for instruction on the AV-8B Harrier II. Italian navy support personnel went through English language training at Shepard AFB in Texas. Then they went to MCAS Cherry Point where they went through training on Harrier II systems and support. All this hard work led to the creation of the Wolf Squadron, with the first two Italian navy Harrier IIs, in August 1991, and their arrival at their home base at Maristaeli (Naval Air Station) Grottaglie near Taranto, Italy.[10]

In February and March 1994 three Harrier II Plus aircraft for the Italian navy were completed at the McDonnell Douglas plant in St. Louis. These three aircraft were flown to MCAS Cherry Point, where Italian navy pilots and support crews received advanced training on these new aircraft. On November 21, 1994, the *Giuseppe Garibaldi* left Norfolk with its cargo of the new Harrier II Plus aircraft and squadron personnel.

The Italian navy's air arm did not have to wait long to see action. On January 20, 1995, three Harrier II Plus aircraft, five pilots, and a support crew embarked on the *Giuseppe Garibaldi*. The aircraft carrier patrolled off the coast of Somalia until March 22, 1995. The five Italian pilots flew more than one hundred hours, providing air support alongside USMC Harrier IIs for UN forces as they withdrew from the war-torn nation.[11]

The first Italian-built Harrier II Plus was delivered in mid-1996, and the final aircraft in late 1997. The team of Italian firms, led by Alenia as a subcontractor to McDonnell Douglas, included FIAR (which produced radar components), FIAT Avia (elements of the engine), Breda (cannon system), Aerea (wing pylons), and Magnaghi (hydraulic components). Alenia was responsible for assembling thirteen Harrier II Plus aircraft. Italian navy personnel provide first- and second-level support for its fleet of Harrier II Plus aircraft, and depot-level assistance is provided by Alenia, with assistance from the prime contractor and other firms.[12]

The Spanish navy air arm has flown the Harrier II since October 1987 when the first of a dozen AV-8B day-attack aircraft were delivered. In March 1993 Spain ordered eight Harrier II Plus aircraft and a single TAV-8B two-seat trainer. All of the Harrier II Plus aircraft were assembled by CASA at its Seville factory. The eight aircraft were delivered from January 1996 until July 1997. Spanish companies—including CASA, Iberia, and Inisel—were involved in producing trainers, components, and support.[13]

AV-8B Remanufacture Program

One of the more interesting aspects of the Harrier II Plus program is its encompassing of both new production and the upgrade and remanufacture of older day-attack AV-8B aircraft into the radar-equipped Harrier II Plus configuration. Pat Finneran was the Harrier II program manager at the time when the Marine Corps wanted more than the twenty-seven new radar aircraft it had ordered as a part of the three-nation Harrier II Plus program.

> Our team at MacAir developed and delivered to the U.S. Marine Corps a proposal called "remanufacture" that would convert older, less capable day-attack AV-8B aircraft into the more advanced Harrier II Plus configuration. Col. Mike Ryan and Lt. Col. Joe Anderson at HQMC [Headquarters Marine Corps] APW [Aviation Weapon Branch] liked the idea and recommended it to Lt. Gen. Rich Hearney, who was DCS (Aviation) [Deputy Chief of Staff, Aviation] at the time. He secured support to include this concept in the Marine Corps aviation budget. A partnership was formed among McDonnell Aircraft Company, British Aerospace, the Naval Air Depot at MCAS Cherry Point, North Carolina, and Rolls-Royce to perform the overhaul and upgrade.[14]

The purpose of this program was to extend the life and increase the capability of the USMC Harrier II fleet without expanding the total inventory of aircraft. In 1992 the Harrier II industry team submitted an unsolicited proposal for remanufacture, and a formal proposal was delivered in late 1993. The program was approved by the Defense Acquisition Board on March 11, 1994, and the U.S. Congress approved the remanufacture program for inclusion in the FY1994 budget.

The remanufacture program involved the addition of a new Rolls-Royce -408 engine, APG-65 radar, night-vision equipment, and other systems that increased the aircraft's combat capabilities, safety, and effectiveness. The wings, tail planes, horizontal stabilators, landing gear, and some avionics of older AV-8B aircraft were inspected, overhauled, and then mated with new fuselage, which included the radar, upgraded cooling, and wiring necessary to utilize the new avionics effectively.[15]

A remanufactured Harrier II Plus is nearly identical to newly built aircraft. The upgraded aircraft has a full 6,000-hour service life but costs considerably less than a new Harrier II Plus. The Marine Corps supported this concept as an economical way to upgrade their Harrier II V/STOL force and achieve the operational requirement for 72 radar-equipped AV-8Bs. Deliveries of remanufactured Harrier II Plus aircraft continued from 1996 to 2003.[16]

On May 11, 2000, a contract was signed between Boeing and the U.S. Navy for the remanufacture of the Spanish navy's EAV-8Bs into the Harrier II Plus configuration. The last remanufactured AV-8B Harrier II Plus was delivered to the Spanish navy in December 2003. This was the end of the production of the Harrier II family of aircraft.[17]

Harrier II Plus Operational Utility

The Harrier II Plus was the last and most advanced version of the Harrier V/STOL family. Addition of the APG-65 multimode radar integrated with night-vision sensors, a computer-controlled navigation/attack system, and a modern crew station allows Harrier II pilots to find and attack air and surface targets at night and in poor weather conditions.

Combat in the Falklands demonstrated the British Harrier's effectiveness as a fighter. Integration of the APG-65 radar and beyond-visual-range AIM-120 AMRAAM air-to-air missiles dramatically improved the air defense potential of Harrier II Plus. For navigation and air-to-surface attack, the APG-65 provides long-range surface mapping to improve target location and identification, and adds a complete set of modes for accurate weapons delivery in adverse weather conditions. This new capability, coupled with the aircraft's unmatched basing flexibility, made the Harrier II Plus highly versatile. Operating from amphibious assault ships, small aircraft carriers, or short strips on land, the Harrier II Plus could perform air defense, sea surveillance, and surface attack missions. The aircraft's radar and FLIR can be used to find and strike fixed and mobile targets, including even small patrol boats in high sea.

This multimission aircraft has been in service since the mid-1990s with USMC and naval air arms of Italy and Spain. Capable of operating from ships and bases where no other tactical aircraft can, the Harrier II Plus has demonstrated itself to be the ideal aircraft to deploy to trouble spots around the world and to defend the interests of the United States and NATO nations. The Harrier II program has been highly successful in international collaborative effort, and the Harrier II Plus broadened the scope of this program to include Italy and Spain.

CHAPTER 10

Harrier II Support of NATO Peacekeeping

arrier IIs of the RAF and USMC participated in combat operations in support of United Nations peacekeeping efforts in the former Yugoslavia. The Balkans has long been an area of instability. Following the death of Tito in 1980, the power of the Yugoslavian central government declined, and economic and political problems intensified. A civil war began in the late 1980s and broke out full-scale in 1991.

From the late 1980s until 2000, civil war continued in the territory of the former Yugoslavia. More than forty Yugoslav and Serbian aircraft, plus several Croatian and Muslim aircraft and helicopters, were shot down (mostly by ground fire) during the civil war. This conflict included at least four significant phases: the 1991–92 Slovenian, Croatian, and Serbian war of independence; the 1992–95 Bosnia-Herzegovina conflict; and the 1998–99 Kosovo conflict and peacekeeping phase from 1999 to the present.

NATO air power, operating in support of the United Nations, was involved in the region starting in 1992. From 1992 to 1995, NATO and other coalition aircraft flew more than a hundred thousand sorties, performing humanitarian airlift assistance for peacekeeping forces, air defense operations, and reconnaissance and attack missions.

RAF Harrier II Operations

Fighting between the Croats and Serbs intensified in the summer of 1995, and additional NATO airpower was brought to the region to encourage peace. The RAF sent GR Mk. 7 Harrier IIs from No. IV squadron at RAF Laarbruch in Germany to the Gioia del Colle air base in Italy on July 28, 1995, to relieve a detachment of RAF Jaguar aircraft.

Map showing former Yugoslavia. RAF and U.S. Marine Corps Harrier IIs supported
United Nations Peacekeeping Operations in Bosnia/Kosovo (the former Yugoslavia)
1995–99, flying from airbases in Italy and from U.S. Navy amphibious assault ships
operating in the Adriatic Sea. *Steve Karp*

These GR Mk. 7s were configured to perform both attack and reconnaissance missions in support of Balkan operations. RAF GR Mk. 7 aircraft assigned to Bosnian operations carried either the three-camera, vinten 18-63 LOROP (long-range optical reconnaissance pod) or the Vicon 57 multi-sensor reconnaissance pods. RAF GR Mk. 7s flown in Bosnia/Kosovo operations included gray camouflage, capability to carry reconnaissance pods, BOL chaff dispensers, and software modifications that included integrated GPS within the inertial navigation system.[1]

The GR Mk. 7s were sent initially just to replace the Jaguars, and only eight aircraft were deployed. In late August 1995 the detachment was increased to twelve GR Mk. 7 aircraft and two Jaguars equipped with Thermal Imaging and Laser Designation (TIALD) FLIR/laser pods for cooperative delivery of laser-guided thousand-pound bombs. NATO air strikes were initiated on August 30, 1995, in Operation Deliberate Force.

NATO air strikes and reconnaissance efforts continued on and off along with diplomatic efforts until late 1995. NATO air strikes plus the changing situation on the ground helped bring the Serbs, the Croats, and the Bosnians to the negotiating table, resulting in the December 1995 Dayton Accords.

Bosnia was not a low-threat environment. A Royal Navy Sea Harrier FRS1 was downed by an SA-7 while flying over Gorazde in April 1994, a USAF F-16C was shot down by a radar-guided SA-6 in February 1995, and a French air force Mirage 2000K was shot down by a shoulder-fired IR SAM (probably an SA-14 SAM) and its two crew members captured in September 1995. RAF Harrier II pilots flew most of their missions above the threats and were briefed to be very careful about delivering weapons accurately to minimize military and civilian casualties.

RAF GR Mk. 7 crews flew more than 126 strike sorties and delivered 32 free-fall bombs and 48 thousand-pound Paveway II laser-guided bombs working in conjunction with FLIR and laser pod–equipped Jaguar strike aircraft. Reconnaissance GR Mk. 7s conducted 49 sorties during Operation Deliberate Force. RAF GR Mk. 7s remained in Italy as a part of the NATO Rapid Reaction Force during 1996. Pilots and support crews from the RAF's No. 1, No. 3, and No. IV squadrons maintained reconnaissance operations over Bosnia.[2]

USMC Maj. Michael Hile was on exchange with No. IV (Army Cooperation), a Royal Air Force squadron based out of Laarbruch, Germany. "With my British counterparts," he says, "I experienced their perspective of combat operations and learned a great deal concerning precision strike operations. At the time I flew the GR Mk. 7, an aircraft comparable with the USMC Harrier II Night Attack aircraft."[3]

In Bosnia RAF GR Mk. 7 crews developed cooperative laser designation procedures between formations of different types of aircraft. Harrier IIs also demonstrated the flexibility of operating as a multirole intelligence strike reconnaissance (ISR) platform. With their reconnaissance pods and strike weapons, flights of GR Mk. 7s could conduct tactical reconnaissance, bomb targets, and also provide post-strike bomb damage assessment.

In the spring of 1998 violence intensified in the central province of Kosovo, an area that saw only minor fighting during the early part of the Yugoslav civil war. No-flying patrols, reconnaissance efforts, and support for NATO peacekeeping forces continued over the region. The RAF detachment of GR Mk. 7s flying from the Gioia del Colle air base was expanded from four to eight aircraft in late 1998, supported by Tri-Star air refueling tankers.

In February 1999 additional NATO airpower was deployed in preparation for an air offensive. Three weeks of peace talks with Serbian leaders in France during early March 1999 failed to make progress. While NATO and the Serbs talked, the fighting in Kosovo intensified.

Continuing conflict in Kosovo led to NATO air intervention, which began on the evening of March 24, 1999, and continued until June 10, 1999. RAF GR Mk. 7 pilots flew strike sorties on the first night of Operation Allied Force. On March 28, 1999, four more GR Mk. 7 aircraft and additional pilots and support personnel were deployed to Italy.

The RAF Harrier II force was later expanded to a total of sixteen GR Mk. 7s. In addition, the RAF sent Tornado strike aircraft to Solenzara, Corsica, and several VC-10 tankers to the region to support NATO operations. The RN aircraft carrier HMS *Invincible* with its escort ships and air wing of F/A-2 Sea Harriers of Royal Navy 800 Squadron arrived in the Adriatic in early April. The Sea Harriers began flying CAP missions on April 17, 1999.[4]

RAF Harrier II pilots and support crews under the banner of No. 1 Squadron maintained a high level of strike sorties despite poor weather and strong air defenses. Only about twenty-five days of the seventy-eight-day air campaign featured good weather, and Serbian forces made effective use of camouflage, decoys, and night cover to counter NATO air operations. However, intense reconnaissance and strikes by up to seven air packages per day around the clock against the 350 targets maintained the pressure.[5]

Group Capt. Travers Smith, an RAF spokesman, commented on April 4, 1999, regarding GR Mk. 7 operations, "This is yet another form of frustration. Now that the weather has cleared they have taken off, but there is nothing for them to hit. This was the first of the daytime operations for the GR 7s that have managed to get airborne (without weather problems). Their prime purpose today would have been to hit mobile targets that would have been identified by other means. During the period the GR 7s were airborne, no such opportunities presented themselves, so the Harriers returned with their bombs."

This same day, No. 1 Squadron Wing Cdr. Andy Golledge remarked, "This is a new phase, [so] tensions are there because the pilots are facing something they have not done yet. This is actually a new experience in this operation for them. They will be tense about doing anything new." The squadron commanding officer added that after their return, the Harrier pilots went through an extensive debriefing, up to four hours in duration, to ensure that all the lessons from the missions were documented.[6]

The Italian navy also supported Operation Allied Force, flying Harrier II Plus aircraft from the aircraft carrier *Giuseppi Garibaldi* in the Adriatic Sea between Italy and the Yugoslav coast. The Italian navy pilots flew about sixty sorties, delivering conventional and laser-guided bombs, with guidance for the latter provided by U.S. aircraft. Lt. Cdr. Massimo Russo operated many close air support missions over Kosovo.

"I remember we always flew in pairs," he says, "one aircraft flew at altitude controlling the situation, while the other moved to hit the target or identify suspected movement; the Harriers would then change roles by alternating altitude. In Kosovo . . . the Italian navy pilots trained and prepared by the U.S. Navy had no problems integrating with the allied air command, interoperating immediately with aircraft from other nations."[7]

During Operation Allied Force, NATO forces flew 38,004 sorties, including 10,484 attack missions in seventy-eight days (fifty-seven of which included air attacks) with the loss of only two aircraft, despite the firing of nearly seven hundred SAMs. NATO air attacks deterred efforts in Kosovo; damaged Yugoslav infrastructure, army, and paramilitary force; and brought an end to the fighting.[8]

RAF GR Mk. 7 pilots flew about eight hundred strike and reconnaissance sorties during Operation Allied Force and dropped several hundred bombs. A typical load for the Harrier II was two thousand-pound Paveway II laser-guided bombs and a TIALD pod or a mix of one thousand general-purpose or up to four BL755 cluster bombs, plus a pair of external fuel tanks. The GR Mk. 7s frequently carried the SR603 reconnaissance pod.[9]

The UK government identified a significant shortfall in air-delivered precision-guided munitions appropriate for use in poor weather. The GR Mk. 7 carried the TIALD pod and laser-guided bombs for precision attack, but these required a clear line of sight to the target. General-purpose thousand-pound bombs and BL755 cluster bombs were employed against area targets where the threat of civilian casualties was low. As a result of their integrated GPS/INS, the RAF GR Mk. 7s were approved to release weapons through the clouds against predesignated targets where the risk of collateral damage was low.

The self-designation capability of GR Mk. 7s with the TIALD pod for effective delivery of laser-guided bombs proved successful, though better fidelity of the image on the screen in the cockpit was desired by most pilots. After the conflict the United Kingdom quickly allocated funds to integrate the AGM-65G2 IR Maverick with the GR Mk. 7 for the effective engagement of point targets such as armored vehicles. In addition, the United Kingdom elected to purchase the EGBU-10 enhanced Paveway II thousand-pound bomb with both laser and GPS guidance.[10]

Improved intelligence, reconnaissance, and surveillance capability was another shortfall. RAF GR Mk. 7s often flew reconnaissance missions. Once the film was developed and image analysts had identified targets, this information was passed on to NATO mission planners for air strikes. Harrier II reconnaissance imagery was used by the RAF detachment and the U.S. Air Force A-10 unit colocated at Gioia del Colle for targeting. Some pilots were able to take off with imagery just two hours old.

UK defense planners made a commitment to field a standoff radar platform and additional unmanned aerial vehicles to identify targets. Improved sensor-to-shooter data links to send targeting information rapidly to pilots over the battlefield was another need to be addressed.

USMC Harrier II Operations in Bosnia/Kosovo

From July 1992 to March 1996 four Marine Amphibious Ready Groups—which included AV-8Bs deployed on U.S. Navy amphibious assault ships (USS *Wasp,* USS *Guam,* USS *Kearsarge,* and USS *Saipan*)—supported NATO air operations over Bosnia to protect UN forces. In May 1995 the 24th MEU (SOC) moved into the Adriatic, ready to perform a variety of missions. Maritime interdiction was the primary mission of the force, but rescue for NATO aircrews was also on the list of assignments.[11]

On June 2, 1995, USAF F-16C pilot Capt. Scott O'Grady was shot down by a Bosnian SA-6 SAM. The Harrier II and helicopter crews on the USS *Kearsarge* prepared plans for rescue operations. On June 5 radio communication was established with Captain Grady, but confirmation of his identity and location did not come until early on June 8.

Shortly after this, CH-53Es, AH-1Ws, and four AV-8Bs launched from the USS *Kearsarge.* Two CH-53 crews, escorted by AV-8Bs and Cobra attack helicopters from the 24th MEU, conducted a successful rescue. The return to the ship was challenging, as several aircraft were hit by antiaircraft fire and several SA-7 SAMs fired (which were successfully evaded).[12]

Harrier IIs from the 26th MEU flew top cover for the March 1997 emergency evacuation from Albania. A year later the 24th MEU and (after May 1, 1999) the 26th MEU sent Harrier IIs over the former Yugoslavia in support of NATO operations. During Operation Allied Force over Kosovo (April–May 1999), USMC Harrier II pilots operating from ships in the Adriatic flew numerous sorties in support of NATO strikes, which led to a ceasefire and deployment of peacekeeping forces.

When the province of Kosovo was threatened NATO unleashed its airpower, in Operation Allied Force, to force a political solution. USMC Harrier IIs participated in this campaign. The true value of the AV-8B's V/STOVL capability was again demonstrated during Operation Allied Force and Operation Joint Guardian, when AV-8Bs already deployed in the Adriatic prepared to conduct combat operations. The AV-8Bs were assigned to the forward deployed 24th and 26th MEU (SOC)s and integrated into the joint NATO air campaign.

The dozen AV-8Bs that participated in this NATO air operation were assigned (a six-aircraft detachment with each MEU) to the 24th and 26th MEVs. AV-8Bs assigned to the MEU flew offensive air support missions for NATO over Kosovo, and the MEU's helicopter, ground, and logistics BLTs (Battalion Landing Teams) provided humanitarian assistance to Kosovo refugees in Albania (Operation Shining Hope).

During Operation Allied Force, the initial Marine contingent was provided by the 24th MEU (SOC), centered on the USS *Nassau*. They were replaced at the end of their normal six-month rotation (on April 28, 1999) by the 26th MEU (SOC). Harrier II Plus aircraft from the 24th MEU (SOC), operating from amphibious ship USS *Nassau*, flew their first allied force strike on April 14, 1999, and the detachment performed thirty-four combat sorties by the time the unit was released by the arrival of the 26th MEU (SOC).[13]

During the six-month deployment, 24th MEU AV-8B aircraft readiness rates were extremely high, averaging 91.8 percent mission-capable and 88 percent full mission-capable. At the onset of Operation Allied Force (OAF), the Amphibious Ready Group (ARG) supporting 24th MEU had on store only twenty-seven laser-guided bombs (LGBs). In a high-intensity conflict, the total numbers of PGMs (precision guided munitions) available were insufficient to sustain combat operations.[14]

The 26th MEU, which relieved the 24th MEU in the Adriatic on April 28, 1999, included HMM-365 based on the USS *Kearsarge*. The composite squadron included six AV-8Bs from VMA-231. VMA-231 Det. "B" included ten pilots and ninety-nine support personnel.

On May 1, 1999, the Harrier detachment aboard the USS *Kearsarge* flew their first combat sorties. Unfortunately, on the same day, the squadron lost a Harrier II in a training mishap, leaving the detachment with only five AV-8Bs until a replacement aircraft could be delivered. AV-8Bs started combat operations in theater on May 1. Combat sorties continued until May 28, 1999, when the MEU was ordered to port in Brindisi, Italy.[15]

The AV-8B's combat configuration typically included strakes; drop tanks on stations 3 and 5; and the Defensive Electronic Countermeasure (DECM) pod on the centerline. Air-to-ground ordnance was carried on stations 1, 2, 6, and 7. The theater requirement to launch only with recoverable loads typically forced the AV-8Bs to carry two MK-82 five-hundred-pound bombs.

For combat missions, a section of AV-8Bs would launch with half-full drop tanks and go to a 26th MEU KC-130 air refueling tanker for premission tanking. They would then proceed to the orbit point for mission assignment. This gave the AV-8B from forty-five minutes to an hour on station. Targets were typically located and assigned by an FAC.

Rules of engagement, which changed daily, determined whether the AV-8Bs would drop on the secondary target "through the weather" (nonvisual bombing). The Harrier II was one of only two platforms that were allowed to drop through the weather, due to its high-order tightly coupled Global Positioning System (GPS). The AV-8Bs flew combat strike missions into Serbia as part of combined NATO integrated strike packages. The majority of combat missions were against "tactical" targets in Kosovo under FAC control.

The 26th MEU AV-8B detachment usually flew two combat sorties a day, due to the large number of aircraft participating in OAF. AV-8B missions assigned by the joint ATO in no way exercised the full combat sortie generation capability of the aircraft and amphibious assault ship team.

Initially the AV-8Bs dropped Mk-82 free-fall bombs until ship armament procedures were refined. Laser-guided bombs became the weapon of choice if laser designation could be coordinated, and the CBU-99 cluster bomb units (CBU) became the next best choice if laser designation was not available.

However, theater rules of engagement (ROE) banned the use of cluster bombs due to the danger to civilians early in the conflict. The AV-8Bs reverted to dropping Mk-82s and Mk-83s when laser designation was not available. Because the ROE stipulated weapons release at altitudes of fifteen thousand feet and higher, GAU 12 25mm guns were not carried. This practice allowed for better performance when returning to the ship with ordnance. On several occasions the AV-8B weapon load had to be quickly switched from general-purpose bombs to LGBs, because the primary target changed from an area target to a point target.

The 26th MEU AV-8Bs were directed by 6th Fleet to take off only with ordnance loads that were recoverable on the amphibious ship, an order that reduced the amount of ordnance that the AV-8Bs were able to carry on each combat mission. This ROE was instituted due to short notice in coordinating emergency jettison areas with regional neutral and friendly countries near the area of operations. To meet this restrictive ROE, standard load out of the AV-8B was either Mk. 82s or GBU-12s on stations 2 and 6, plus two three-hundred-gallon fuel tanks and the DECM pod.

During OAF (Operation Allied Force), all NATO tactical aircraft were required to carry a fully mission-capable defensive ECM capability against radar-guided surface-to-air missile threats. The AV-8B carried the ALQ-164 DECM pod, but demonstrated the need for upgrades to it because of the rapidly evolving capabilities of the threats.

Although the twenty-six MEU Harrier IIs were scheduled for fifty-eight combat sorties (67 percent of the sorties scheduled for May 1999), many of the sorties resulted in cancellations or in-flight aborts due to weather. Weather played a significant role in how many missions were successful in releasing ordnance on enemy targets, effectively canceling one-third of the sorties. Standard Operating Procedures (SOP) for flying over Kosovo set minimum altitudes and high weather minimums. If an alternative target were assigned, the Harriers were authorized to "GPS bomb" through the cloud deck.

In all, the AV-8Bs flew 71.5 combat flight hours (averaging 2.1 flight hours per combat sortie). Ordnance distribution on target was 30 percent MK 82s, 43 percent CBU-99s, and 27 percent GBU-12s. The need for laser self-designation capability (a "targeting pod") on the AV-8B stood out among the lessons learned following Desert Storm. The AV-8B trailed other TACAIR assets in the U.S. inventory in obtaining that capability.

Consequently the USMC AV-8B had to be worked into the ATO to hit area targets or work in cooperation with other aircraft with laser self-designation capability. Although the AV-8B was one of only two platforms in the operation allowed to drop "general purpose" bombs on GPS coordinates, the need for a targeting pod and the integration of the JDAM in the Harrier II was highlighted.[16]

While the AV-8B performed its missions, the amphibious ship deck space was shared with CH-53, CH-46, AH-1W, and UH-1N helicopters, which were simultaneously conducting humanitarian missions. In support of Operation Allied Force in the former Republic of Yugoslavia (FRY), the AV-8B's primary mission was Tactical Recovery of Aircraft and Personnel (TRAP). Its secondary mission was BAI. These BAI combat missions were not in direct support of MEU forces but part of a joint NATO air campaign.

The AV-8B combat deployment in Operation Allied Force accomplished several firsts: the first ever preplanned combat employment of MEU (SOC)–embarked AV-8s and the first time that AV-8Bs employed LGBs in combat. Laser designation for AV-8B LGBs was provided by USAF F-16s. The Harrier II was one of only two aircraft in Operation Allied Force that was authorized to release ordnance on GPS target coordinates.

Operation Allied Force also marked the first combat use of CBU-99, advanced cluster munitions by the AV-8B, and operational deployment of the then-new Harrier II Plus with the APG-65 multimode radar. The AV-8Bs based on forward-deployed amphibious ships were able to equal any of the other allied strike aircraft's "time on station" without aerial refueling. Because amphibious shipping was located in close proximity to Kosovo, the short distance did not require airborne refueling to strike preplanned targets.[17]

Although the employment of the AV-8B revalidated the many benefits of V/STOL, the strike capability of the AV-8B against time-critical targets in a dynamic environment remained modest. However, in OAF the AV-8B began scratching the surface of the sensor-to-shooter equation.

Another lesson learned was that all USMC strike aircraft must have secure, antijam voice communications, as well as datalink capability, in order to be fully interoperable with joint and combined operations.

CHAPTER 11

Harrier II
Operational Experience

USMC Harrier II squadrons have operated for months at a time deployed away from home at sites such as Japan. In addition, Harrier II squadrons have participated in exercises around the world in support of U.S. operations. Six-aircraft Harrier II detachments have made regular deployments aboard LHA and LHD amphibious assault ships in support of U.S. Navy and USMC amphibious task forces since the early 1980s.

USMC AV-8Bs regularly deployed as a part of the aviation combat element of an MEU on amphibious assault ships assigned to an ARG, which is usually composed of one forty-thousand-ton LHD/LHA (which carries most of the aircraft and more than half of the personnel and equipment of the MEU) and two smaller amphibious landing ships. Generally, six Harrier IIs, eight to ten pilots, and about 125 support personnel from a Marine Corps Harrier II squadron and intermediate maintenance support element are assigned to a composite squadron. This unit also includes a squadron of CH-46 medium-lift helicopters and a detachment of CH-53 heavy-lift helicopters, plus a smaller number of AH-1W Super Cobra attack helicopters, UH-1N liaison helicopters, and several hundred support personnel and flight crew personnel.

The aviation element provided support for the twelve hundred Marines assigned to combat units of the three ships of the amphibious ready group. In the 1980s the Marine Corps expanded the size, equipment, and training of infantry battalions slated for regular amphibious deployments (MEU) and made them special-operations-capable (SOC).[1]

Marine Corps Harrier II units have supported many contingency operations. In Operation Restore Hope in Somalia (December 1992–March 1994) USMC Harrier II crews provided fixed-wing tactical air cover and armed reconnaissance in support of humanitarian efforts. USMC Harrier IIs, again operating from amphibious assault ships, supported humanitarian missions in Rwanda Operation Distant Runner (April 1994) and Operation United Shield in Somalia (January 1995–March 1996). In these cases USMC Harrier IIs provided the only fixed-wing tactical aviation support available. Harrier IIs also have assisted in many other humanitarian operations in Liberia and the Central African Republic during Operation Assured Response (April–August 1996), Albania during Operation Silver Wolfe (March 1997), Zaire/Congo during Operation Guardian Retrieval, Sierra Leone during Operation Nobel-Obelisk (April–June 1997), and East Timor (2000–2002).[2]

The need for the AV-8B to have a FLIR laser self-designation capability (a targeting pod) and precision guided munitions (such as laser-guided bombs) was made apparent during Desert Storm and again in Operation Allied Force. The AV-8B trailed other tactical aircraft in the U.S. inventory (such as the F-14A/B/D, F-15E and F16C/D with LANTIRN, and F/A-18C/D with the AAS-38 Night Hawk pods) in obtaining this capability. Consequently the USMC AV-8B had to be worked into the ATO to hit area targets or work in cooperation with other aircraft with laser self-designation capability to strike accurately against point targets.

Although the AV-8B was one of only two platforms in OAF allowed to drop "general purpose" bombs on GPS coordinates, the need for a targeting pod was highlighted. Other aircraft also were also equipped much earlier than the Harrier II to deliver the JDAM near-precision guided weapon. In the late 1990s, the U.S. Marine Corps sought funding from Congress to purchase and integrate new systems into the Harrier II fleet. Lt. Col. Bob Claypool recalls:

> We knew that combat relevance was the key to permanently fixing the Harrier II platform problem, since people would want to have it there on the battlefield. For years the Harrier II community had pitched the need for a targeting pod. When it was my turn to show up at Marine Corps headquarters, my general officer and the DCS Aviation, Lt. Gen. Frederick McCorkle, was willing to sign a need letter [with which] we could get supplemental funds from the U.S. Congress. So we went out and looked at every targeting pod that was available. We found one that could be readily adapted to the Harrier II because of the work of one very bright guy who figured out that the LITENING II pod would work, since it cooled itself and could be bolted to a pylon under the wing of our airplane. With a million-dollar computer software rewrite, the airplane thought the pod was a Maverick missile, and now we had a state-of-the-art targeting pod we could use on the Harrier II. . . . [W]e did a great job of selling this requirement on Capitol Hill and Congress gave us the money to make it happen.[3]

Mounted on a wing pylon like a bomb or fuel tank, the Northrop Grumman LITENING II Pod allowed Harrier II pilots to detect and track tactical targets from above the range of antiaircraft fire and shoulder-fired IR-guided surface-to-air missiles like the SA-7 and SA-14, which proved lethal in the first Gulf War and the Bosnia and Kosovo conflicts. Once a potential target was detected, the pilot locked on with the pod's laser illuminator, which provided a spot for a laser-guided bomb to guide to.

Target acquisition, recognition, and designation ranges enabled AV-8B pilots to employ precision-guided munitions (PGMs) at maximum ranges. These tactics increase survivability and lethality, while reducing collateral damage. Because the pod is carried on a wing station, it can be rapidly loaded and unloaded, adding flexibility to the Harrier II's capabilities and weapons mix. The LITENING II pod entered the USMC Harrier II inventory in August 2000.[4]

The Marine Corps was also able to secure funds to continue the development of the Harrier II capabilities in the avionics and systems areas, including support for the retrofitting of GPS capability into the Harrier II. The ATHS provided for the exchange of targeting data between ground units and pilots to enhance strike effectiveness.

Jerry Dolvin was a Marine Corps Harrier II pilot and Boeing engineer. In his view, close air support is today the tactical aircraft's most important and challenging mission.

> The targets are lethal and fleeting and as close as a few hundred meters from friendly forces. The consequences of errors, anywhere in the process, risks blue-on-blue encounters, or fratricide. Conducting the mission from a tactical pilot's perspective is extremely difficult. Plainly speaking, the pilot must do a lot of detailed planning, very accurately, in a short period of time. Today, most of this planning is accomplished by the Forward Air Controller on the ground, and communicated to the pilot via voice radio. The pilot, [most often] right-handed, must fly the aircraft with his left hand while copying the brief with pen and paper on his right knee. If the pilot has not understood the FAC, he requests a retransmission of the information to be sure. Assuming the pilot has copied the information correctly, he proceeds to type the information into the aircraft's computer system via the Up Front Control. Obviously, any error in recording the brief or typing the information into the system can lead to disaster—not to mention the seveal minutes required to perform all the aforementioned steps.

> To speed up the process, reduce errors, and allow the pilot to fly with the correct hand were all benefits of the Automatic Target Handoff System. ATHS significantly lowers the pilot workload by receiving the CAS brief digitally and, with the push of one button, automatically enters the data into the aircraft's system. This allowed the pilot time to focus on other things, like survivability, general situational awareness, and safety of flight. For coalition operations, another advantage during initial ATHS operations was overcoming the "language barrier" between coalition partners for conducting mutual CAS. Digital data is typically written in English and very readable to a computer,

while broken English spoken by foreign allies is most problematic for relaying the CAS brief, if successful at all.[5]

Harrier II Support and Safety Issues

James Mason is a McDonnell Douglas/Boeing superintendent of prototype flight operations. He has more than thirty years' experience with the Harrier II.

> When McDonnell first started building the Harrier IIs for the USMC, it was a new experience for everyone involved—engineering, maintainers, and support folks. We soon found the aircraft looked more complicated than it was. Once the maintainers became more familiar with the aircraft, we found wing removal and engine changes were much easier and quicker than we thought it would be. Removal also gave us full access to the engine bay and airframe for maintenance. The more sorties we flew in the AV-8B, the better it performed its job. As the improvements were incorporated—night attack, radar, and other advances—the Harrier kept up with the technology that was needed to keep the Harrier II as a top-of-the-line weapons system.[6]

Col. Lee Buland (USMC) served as a maintenance officer and commanded two Harrier II squadrons and Marine Air Group 14. He adds:

> Maintenance is a challenge with an aircraft where you have to remove the wing in order to work on the engine and get at hydraulic lines and pneumatic ducting or to pull out a lost tool an eighteen-year-old mechanic dropped by accident when he was working at 2:30 in the morning while trying to put safety wire on the APU. It was difficult to maintain this aircraft because of the engine configuration. Now, having said that, there was no other way that they really could have installed the motor in order to have created V/STOL given the technology when the Harrier was developed in the late 1950s. . . .
>
> The fact that you have to remove a wing to do an engine change automatically puts more man-hours into the support equation for the Harrier. Most other aircraft did not suffer under this challenge, or if they did, it was not to the level the AV-8B was. The AV-8A and AV-8B have an engine with rotating nozzles, hot gas ducting, and reaction control nozzles for vertical takeoff and landing control and other systems. No other aircraft have water injection systems in order to generate the maximum thrust for the limited time in takeoff hover and landing to give you recovery capability in hot and high ambient conditions. These were things that made the Harrier very different, from a maintenance perspective, from conventional aircraft. These things resulted in an aircraft that was unique in its design, function, and operations and, as a fallout, unique in its maintenance requirements. . . .
>
> The other part of that maintenance issue we found with the Harrier was that once you lifted the wing and the motor and did whatever work you had to do,

replace the motor, perform maintenance on hydraulic lines, or whatever, if you were not properly trained, experienced, and careful, you were likely to damage the ducting lines, heat shielding, hydraulics, or other fragile components in the bottom portion of the fuselage. Not only did the design drive man-hour levels higher than you would see on other aircraft like an F/A-18, an F-16, or an A-4, now you had the additional risk of damage of special systems during maintenance. As you know from research, we created some mishaps and losses as a result of maintenance procedures and errors, such as a nick in the reaction control systems, or when they reinstalled the motor the fuel coupling was not put in correctly. It was a very complex and man-hour-consuming machine, and I do not believe the Marine Corps leadership, during the life of the AV-8A and well into the AV-8B, had an appreciation for the difficulty, man-hours required, and risk involved with a V/STOL aircraft. Therefore they tended to treat it as any other platform, except that it had the unique V/STOL capability, which we like. . . .

We had cycles of peaks and valleys with personnel. . . . For example, after the first Gulf War our leadership felt we had an excess of senior experienced maintenance personnel at a time when all the services were experiencing a reduction in total force structure. Efforts were made to try and manage the draw down to reduce the impact but we lost very skilled and experienced maintenance troops, and once we lost them it took a great deal of time and effort to train younger support personnel to develop these skills. This impacted our ability to maintain our aircraft. This was not unique to the Harrier; other aviation platforms also experienced this turbulence. However, I think these reductions had a greater impact on the Harrier community in terms of readiness and safety. . . .

We, the senior leadership, never really understood the AV-8B was unique and could not be treated the same as other aircraft platforms, which did not require the same level of maintenance man-hours. The argument was that the helicopter community also requires many man-hours per flight hour; their aircraft are complex, like the CH-53; and they also work very hard to keep their aircraft in service. However, look at the systems and the platform. Helicopters are always crewed by a pilot, copilot, and a full-time crew chief; it is always an aircraft that has more then one engine; the aircraft flies at speeds of about 120 knots or less; and there were a lot of redundancies with helicopters. The Harrier was single-pilot, single-engine, flew at 500 knots and in the V/TOL mode, and depended upon the engine performing at 100 percent. At operations around the ship, top performance was especially critical. And it took Marine Corps leadership a long time to realize the differences and address [them] to correct the problem.[7]

The technological advances of the second-generation V/STOL Harrier II significantly reduced the workload of the pilot and increased the reliability of the aircraft. Technology such as the composite supercritical wing, the maneuvering and positive circulation flaps, the stability augmentation and attitude hold system, the raised cockpit with an advanced heads-up display, and an improved engine were instrumental in decreasing the mishap rate of the AV-8B by more than 50 percent compared to the AV-8A.[8]

However, the loss rate of the Harrier II still averaged about twice that of similar single-engine fighters such as the F-16. The causes of Harrier II Class A accidents, which involve the loss of aircraft or damage in excess of $1 million, have been grouped into three areas: pilot error, maintenance error, and material failure. Through 2004 the average USMC Harrier II Class A loss rate has averaged 11.2 per hundred thousand flight hours.[9]

The Harrier II has a unique configuration with a vectored-thrust engine, which allows for V/STOL operations from ships, airfields, and roads. As a result of a number of factors—including the design of the aircraft, maintenance, support, training, and the challenging sea and land operational environment in which the aircraft flies—Harrier II aircraft losses have been higher than that of conventional or aircraft carrier–based tactical strike fighters.

In the fall of 1992, the Harrier community convened what became the annual V/STOL symposium. The purposes of the symposium are to identify root causes of accidents and unsafe practices, to institutionalize those causes such that the remedy becomes ingrained in operational and maintenance concepts, and to provide community-wide goals and standardization. Pat Finneran, former McDonnell Aircraft Company Harrier II program manager, says that safety of flight has always been the top concern for the Harrier II. "We constantly worked with the Marine Corps, our international partners, and the industry team to understand the root causes of problems. In 1993 together we performed an in-depth analysis of all Harrier II failures and identified some 'single point failures,' and we initiated emergency changes to correct these problem areas."[10]

The USMC, the U.S. Navy, and industry have worked together to identify Harrier II issues and to implement corrective actions. As a direct result of these symposiums, the combat-capable training syllabus was revamped to provide more training and flight time to replacement pilots; enlisted manning levels were brought to workable levels to meet mission requirements and needs; and material improvements were accelerated or received renewed emphasis. As a result of corrective actions and investments in training and support, over time the loss rate of the Harrier II was reduced significantly.

Although the Harrier II accident rate dropped initially, it later climbed. As a result of continuing Harrier II accidents, in November 1997 the commandant of the Marine Corps, Gen. Charles Krulak, established the Harrier Review Panel (HaRP) to analyze accident trends and develop corrective actions. The HaRP found that the single-engine Harrier II was challenging to fly and difficult to maintain, and that investments in its support and combat modernization lagged behind other aviation programs.

Chuck Allen, Harrier II program manager in the 1990s, appreciated seeing the community from a new perspective on active duty as an aviation colonel (non–Harrier II type).

My belief then and now is that there was empirical evidence that showed the Harrier II accident rate went down significantly whenever attention was focused on the problem. That says the aircraft itself is not inherently unsafe. When the attention waned, the accident rate went back up. A study I did for the commanding general, 2nd Marine Aircraft Wing, was intended to institutionalize those processes that caused the improvement so that they became less dependent on personality and more dependent on process. That was precisely what the HaRP was chartered to do, so my participation on the panel became a natural conclusion. . . .

SARA [Squadron Assistance/Risk Assessment—a software scheduling and planning tool] was developed to help squadron scheduling officers weigh the risks associated with a daily flight schedule. It took into account things like total flight time, time in model, days since last flight, days since last flight in mission area, and so on, and gave a numerical score of the risk associated with each flight and the schedule as a whole. The intent was that each squadron would establish graduated criteria that said the scheduler could approve events below some nominal risk level, the ops officer approval was required between that and some higher level, and only the commanding officer could approve above a certain level. SARA also gave the schedulers an automated tool to help them simplify the development of the flight schedule. We gave the SARA package to the Marine Corps without charge, since we thought it might be beneficial. . . .

Technical publications have always been a problem for the aviation community. By the time the publications get updated, printed, and distributed, the fleet had often changed and there was no easy, inexpensive way to get corrections made until the next update cycle. The real problem was in the cycle time associated with the printing (by law done by the government). Since our contractor technical publications always work with digital publications anyway, we simply cut the printing out of the process. We did this by establishing online availability through a help desk number. Marines being Marines, we found they did not have enough computer assets in all the maintenance shops to access the online publications, so we were able to outfit every maintenance shop with leased computer equipment (so it could be updated) and provide the help desk within the finances available during the first year within their existing contract.[11]

USMC programs were often a lower focus within Department of the Navy funding priorities. Changes suggested by the panel included adequate funding for Harrier II support activities (especially upgrades to the Pegasus engine and the reliability-centered maintenance program), implementation of state-of-the-art engine-monitoring technology, strengthening of the Harrier II pilot training program, modernization of maintenance personnel training, increasing the experience level in the squadrons, configuring the AV-8B adequately for its mission, and improving information management systems.[12]

Col. Lee Buland believes that one of the things NAVAIR did was to reduce PRE (engineering and development funds) and PRL (support and maintenance) funds.

> These were engineering and logistics funds. In the 1980s these support funds were reduced by more than 50 percent, and in some cases 80 percent. The importance of this was eventually brought out in the HaRP, where funding issues needed to be addressed. All the communities were forced to deal with the cuts. For example, we had a guy from NAVAIR come out and give us a brief and he bragged about how they had spent some $5 million doing upgrades and modifications to the Pegasus and that was the same amount we spent on the Hornet's engines. He was so proud, but I stopped him right there and said, "All right, I am glad you are doing what you think we need to, but there is an important piece you missed. You just told me you spent the same on the Pegasus as the F404 but what is different?" He still did not get it . . . "The Hornet has two engines and the Harrier only one, plus the Hornet is not a V/STOL aircraft and thus [does not] rely totally on the engine to make a vertical landing. Plus the engines do not operate at the same temperatures and pressures. The Harrier has a single-point failure system, while the Hornet with two engines does not. So what you just told me leads me to believe that you really do not understand the single-point failure element of the equation." We were trying to convince them we needed to spend more money on engineering analysis to get out in front of engine trends before we experienced them in the fleet. They were not bad people. They just did not understand the critical nature of the Harrier's engine. Also we in the Marine Corps may not have done an effective job of selling the need for extra support.[13]

Another result of the 1997 HaRP and post–Cold War military reductions was the decision to reduce the size of USMC Harrier II squadrons. USMC Harrier II VMA squadrons had a primary aircraft authorization (PAA) strength of twenty aircraft, unlike fighter squadrons, which were listed as twelve aircraft. In late 1997 HQMC decided to reduce the PAA for Harrier II squadrons to sixteen aircraft in order to match personnel and aircraft inventory requirements. Later the PAA for Marine Corps Harrier II squadrons was dropped to fourteen aircraft.[14]

Despite improvement efforts, the Harrier II community suffered additional challenges. In June 1999 Rear Adm. Craig Steidel, vice commander of Naval Air Systems Command, grounded all Harrier IIs in USMC service following the loss of two aircraft. Both of the aircraft lost were powered by the Rolls-Royce Pegasus -408A engine. This engine powered both Night Attack and Harrier II Plus aircraft in service with the U.S. Marine Corps and the Harrier II Plus aircraft flown by the Spanish navy and Italian navy. The grounding significantly affected

Harrier II operations and was maintained well into the year 2000. As the inventory of -408 engines was inspected and corrective actions initiated, the Harrier II fleet returned to its normal operating level.[15]

The HaRP study identified a number of areas that needed corrective action. HQMC ensured that funds were allocated to correction of these challenges, with special emphasis on the engine, flap controller, nose wheel steering, ejection systems, and training issues. An extensive engine-life management program was implemented for the -408 engine, which has since improved performance and reliability. The faulty flap controller has been replaced by a digital flap controller, lowering flap-related mishaps. The Harrier II nose wheel steering system has been redesigned and the new system has been retrofitted to Marine Corp and export Harrier IIs. New equipment has been added to the Harrier II's ejection systems. Intensified support training, spare parts investments, and process improvements have improved Harrier II readiness, allowing for more flight time, more deployments, and enhanced safety.[16]

Lieutenant Colonel Claypool says that the Harrier II's positive place today is the result of the vision and determination of a large team between 1997 and 1998. "This team included the commandant, General Krulak, Lieutenant General McCorkle, DCS Aviation, and many other individuals. Their vision and determination is why the Harrier II is where it is today and it all came together just in time to allow the Harrier II to successfully contribute to the conflicts in Afghanistan and Iraq."[17]

The intense focus on enhancing the Harrier II fleet came at the right time. First the Harrier II was ready and in prime shape to provide effective air support for combat actions in Afghanistan and Iraq. Second, in the late 1990s and early 2000s, the cost of the war on terrorism and budget pressures forced the U.S. Congress and the Department of Defense to examine ways to reduce military expenses and better integrate and modernize U.S. military forces. A multitude of options were evaluated to achieve this goal. Some of the options called for significant reduction in U.S. Marine Corps aviation force structure, including severe cuts in the Harrier II numbers.

In the end, the plan approved called for elimination of one U.S. Marine Corps F/A-18 squadron and integration of six more (in addition to the four currently deployed) F/A-18 squadrons assigned to naval aircraft carrier battle groups. In addition, both the size and manpower of U.S. Marine Corps and U.S. Navy squadrons were being reduced.

However, the Harrier II forces remained at the level of seven squadrons with fourteen aircraft each, plus a large training squadron. The Harrier II fleet was the youngest (in 2006) in the Marine Corps tactical aviation community, since the AV-8B day-attack aircraft was replaced with a mix of new and remanufactured Harrier II Plus and relatively new Night Attack aircraft. In addition, the V/STOL

Harrier II force was the only tactical aircraft that could operate from the large amphibious assault class ships and from forward austere bases. This force structure was to be maintained until the F35B V/STOL version of the JSF replaces both Marine Corps Hornets and Harrier IIs.

"As the AV-8B received incremental improvements to its avionics and weapon systems, the aircraft's mission and stores management computers became insufficient in both memory and processor speed," notes Maj. James Coppersmith, USMC AV-8B class desk officer.

> To accommodate further developments, a program called Open Core Avionics Requirement (OSCAR) was funded, providing the AV-8B with upgraded mission systems and warfare management computers. The new computers offered much-improved speed and memory, using a new and improved programming language. The OSCAR combination of hardware and software has greatly increased the AV-8B's capabilities through improved integration of communication, navigation, IFF, threat countermeasure dispenser, sensor (RADAR and Litening targeting pod), and weapon systems. Additionally, a weapons interface was added to the AV-8B's weapon pylons, giving the aircraft a smart-weapons capability. The 1,000-pound class JDAM, called the GBU-32, was the initial smart weapon integrated with the first OSCAR Operational Flight Program (OFP) released to the USMC Harrier Fleet in 2004. Two subsequent OFPs have been developed that continue to improve the aircraft's mission system and weapon integration/capability.
>
> The most noted improvements are the 500-pound class JDAM (GBU-38) and Litening pod upgrades and integration on the platform. The GBU-38 is a very desirable weapon for the AV-8B's current mission in the global war on terrorism (GWOT). First, the 500-pound weapon fits the V/STOL mission, providing multiple stores carriage without a substantial weight penalty against V/STOL operations both ship and shore-based. Additionally, the GBU-38 complements the current mission in support of the GWOT where weapons must be delivered with a high degree of precision and collateral damage from the weapon must be minimized. The 500-pound weapon is the right size and yield for the AV-8B and its current mission. The Litening targeting pod upgrades and pod integration with the AV-8B's navigation and weapon systems have given the aircraft the ability to determine very precise target location coordinates and a means to transfer these coordinates to the smart weapons all via Hands-on Throttle and Stick (HOTAS). JDAM guides inertially, with GPS assistance to these coordinates (a location defined by a latitude, longitude, and elevation). The AV-8B's Target Location Error (TLE), when using the Litening pod, is arguably the best (smallest error) in the DoD on a tactical aircraft. This target location capability, combined with the JDAM weapon system, make the AV-8B a very lethal and much-called-upon aircraft over the battlefield.

With the AV-8B's future roadmap projecting service life through 2024, the overall program, which includes the USMC Harrier Fleet, NAVAIR, and supporting industry, will have to strike a balance between capabilities growth and operational sustainability of the aircraft. Future capability upgrade efforts for the AV-8B are focused on continuing to increase its weapons flexibility (new and multiple weapons carriage) and communications upgrades (radio/data link capabilities that will allow the AV-8B to be interoperable over the future net-centric battlefield). Sustainability funding and efforts are targeting airframe and engine safety/reliability improvements, implementation of an integrated maintenance plan (depot-level scheduled maintenance activities), and procurement of replacement materials and components that will become obsolete during the aircraft's lifetime.[18]

The AV-8B is now out of production, and program funding is finite. The relatively expensive capability upgrades are fiscally in stark contrast with the operational sustainability requirements. It will be an interesting challenge for the program to maintain the AV-8B's war-fighting relevance and materiel operational readiness in order to fulfill our nation's and the U.S. Marine Corps' much-needed tactical strike aircraft V/STOL requirement.

CHAPTER 12

Ongoing Confrontation in Iraq

Following the 1991 Gulf War, the United Nations placed severe economic sanctions on Iraq and limitations on its military operations. The coalition led by the United States, supported by UN Resolution 687, maintained a policy of containment to prevent Iraq from developing weapons of mass destruction.

UN Resolution 688 created no-fly zones to prevent Iraqi military aircraft and helicopters from attacking the Kurds in the north and Shiites in the south, and to limit Iraqi air flexibility. Coalition operations included regular air patrol missions to restrict Iraqi flying—aircraft encountered could be shot down. This included Northern Watch air patrols flown above the 36th northern parallel and Southern Watch patrols for surveillance activities below the 32nd parallel. U.S., French, Turkish, and British aircraft flew hundreds of thousands of sorties during the next decade patrolling these no-fly zones. The first operational deployment of the RAF GR Mk. 7 Harrier II took place during the no-fly zone missions. USMC Harrier IIs also participated in these operations.[1]

After the end of the 1991 war, Iraq had repeatedly defied the United States and the United Nations flying restrictions and the U.S. and its allies increased our patrols to enforce the limits. On December 27, 1992, an Iraqi MiG-25 was shot down by a U.S. Air Force F-16 using an AIM-120 air-to-air missile. Iraqi forces moved surface-to-air missile batteries and hundreds of antiaircraft guns into the no-fly zones and continued to fly fighter missions against coalition patrols.[2]

With increasing frequency, Iraqi air defense units locked missile and gun fire control radars onto coalition aircraft and opened fire with radar and IR-guided surface-to-air missiles and guns. U.S. and NATO forces responded with continued air surveillance and reconnaissance sorties and struck back when fired upon. To protect against Iraqi missiles, guns, and interceptors, most patrol sorties over Iraqi territory received electronic support from EF-111A or EA-6B radar-jamming aircraft, while F-15 and F-16 fighters provided escort support, working with E-3A airborne warning and control aircraft (AWACS).

There were several periods of intensified combat activity over Iraq. Following an Iraqi attempt to assassinate former President George H. W. Bush during his visit to Kuwait in June 1993, the United States fired twenty-three cruise missiles at targets in Baghdad, including the headquarters of the Iraqi secret police. In June 1994 the United States sent additional forces to Kuwait as a result of a buildup of Iraqi units along the border. On September 3–4, 1996, the United States fired ALCM and Tomahawk cruise missiles against air defense targets in southern Iraq to remind Saddam Hussein to follow UN mandates.

RAF Harrier II Northern Watch No-Fly Zone Support

In early 1992 the RAF modified nine GR Mk. 7 aircraft from No. 3 squadron, based at RAF Laarbruch in Germany, and sent these aircraft with pilots and support crews to enforce the northern Iraqi no-fly zone. Because the mission was armed reconnaissance, these GR Mk. 7 aircraft were fitted to carry a modified Harrier GR Mk. 3 reconnaissance pod. The Vinten reconnaissance pod provided forward and horizon-to-horizon coverage with five cameras. These aircraft were also fitted with TACDS V-10 flare dispensers for improved self-defense against Iraqi threats.

The RAF deployed Harrier IIs to Incirlik Air Base in Turkey in early April 1993. This effort was named Operation Warden and involved air patrols over the Kurdish "safe areas" in northern Iraq. Pilots and support crews from all three RAF front-line Harrier II squadrons (No. 1, No. 3, and No. IV) served two-month rotating tours at Incirlik Air Base maintaining the no-fly zone detachment.[3]

On November 23, 1993, aircraft ZD 432 suffered an engine surge while refueling from a VC-10 tanker over Iraq. The RAF pilot successfully ejected near the village of Dahluk and was rescued by a U.S. helicopter. Kurdish villagers took care of the pilot and guarded the wreck of the GR Mk. 7 until it could be salvaged. The RAF rewarded the villagers for their support by the delivery of livestock and other gifts. Harrier II no-fly zone operations continued well into 1994.[4]

USMC Harrier II Southern Watch Support Operation

From 1992 to 2003 Marine Corps AV-8B Harrier II detachments assigned to amphibious ships patrolling in the Arabian Gulf have performed missions over Iraq in support of Operation Southern Watch. The first of these was performed on August 27, 1992, when AV-8Bs from the USS *Tarawa* joined twenty U.S.

Navy aircraft from CVW-5 off the USS *Independence* for the first naval aviation Southern Watch patrols.[5]

Marine Corps Harrier II Southern Watch sorties were usually flown as a part of U.S. Navy force packages, which included F-14s, F/A-18s, and E-2Cs for air defense; EA-6Bs with HARMs for electronic defense; and F/A-18s and Harrier IIs flying in the strike role. Some Harrier II missions were integrated into USAF-coordinated strike packages, which included a mix of sea-based and allied land-based aircraft.

Most of the time AV-8Bs flew from their ship, but sometimes they operated from forward bases such as Ali Al Salem Air Base in Kuwait. Harrier II pilots would usually fly one or two familiarization flights over the Kuwait-Iraq border area outside of the known Iraqi missile engagement zones to become familiar with mission rules and tactics. After that, Harrier II pilots were assigned air patrol missions along with USAF, U.S. Navy, and RAF aircraft flying as far as two hundred and fifty nautical miles into Iraq air space.

On a typical Operation Southern Watch air patrol mission, a flight of two or more AV-8Bs would take off from their amphibious assault ship, equipped with two external fuel tanks and a mix of air-to-ground bombs (typically two Mk-82 five-hundred-pound bombs or CBU-89 cluster bombs) and AIM-9M Sidewinder air-to-air missiles for self-defense. After takeoff the Harrier II pilots would link up with an aerial refueling tanker (USN S-3B, USAF KC-10, or other aircraft) and fill up before starting their patrol or air interdiction missions in concert with the other coalition aircraft.

Many Harrier II missions were flown over the Basra area of Iraq, which included many active air defense sites. Most Operation Southern Watch sorties were routine, but on other occasions the flights were engaged by radars or fired upon by missiles or antiaircraft fire, and life got more interesting. The Harrier II has a video recording system, and the six-times magnification power of the ARBS and HUD video imagery provided excellent intelligence imagery of Iraqi targets and points of interest. On the return flight Harrier II pilots would again meet refueling tankers for a top-off before the long flight back to the northern Persian Gulf and a vertical landing on the ship.

Pilots and support crews start to prepare for a Harrier II deployment well in advance. For example, in December 1997, nine pilots from VMA-513 located at MCAS Yuma were selected for a deployment with the 15th MEU (Special Operations Capable), assigned to the USS *Essex*. Six of the unit's AV-8B night-attack aircraft were assigned to the detachment.

Intense maintenance efforts were conducted on the aircraft and support equipment, and so was special training of maintenance personnel to prepare for the deployment. The flight crews trained for six months to qualify for flying from amphibious assault ships in daytime and nighttime and to perfect a wide variety of mission profiles. The VMA-513 detachment included the first Harrier IIs to deploy and fly operational missions with the third-generation AN/AVS-9 night-vision devices, which—along with the FLIR in the nose of AV-8B Night Attack Harrier IIs—provided excellent around-the-clock operating capability.

On June 22, 1998, the 15th MEU left San Diego and headed to Hawaii. Harrier II pilot flight training operations continued as the amphibious-ready group of three ships crossed the Pacific and made stops in Hong Kong, Singapore, Thailand, and Malaysia. The ships moved through the Indian Ocean, and by mid-August 1998 the *Essex* ARG was in the Arabian Gulf. VMA-513 pilots flying from the USS *Essex* started flying Operation Southern Watch missions in September 1998, working in conjunction with the aircraft of the USS *Abraham Lincoln*.

In late September and early October 1998 more than fifteen hundred Marines and sailors from this force conducted an amphibious training assault and live fire exercise into Kuwait. The Harrier II pilots of the VMA-513 detachment, led by Maj. Dale Willey, provided CAS for the exercise. Many of these missions were conducted at night, with sorties running three to four hours in length. These ground-attack missions were coordinated with artillery, AH-1W attack helicopters, and assaults by Marine ground forces. On November 1, 1998, the *Essex* ARG left the Arabian Gulf for home but was called back on November 5 due to rising tension in the region. On November 18 the 15th MEU (SOC) was released to return home to San Diego due to the arrival of the USS *Belleau Wood* and the 31st MEU (SOC).[6]

After the 1991 ceasefire, United Nations Special Commission (UNSCOM) inspectors operated in Iraq to ensure that weapons of mass destruction were not being developed. Several times in late 1997 and 1998 Iraq denied access to UNSCOM inspectors and challenged the United Nations and the United States. However, Russian diplomats and (later) the UN Secretary General Kofi Annan negotiated settlements, just barely avoiding a conflict. In October and November 1998 Iraq again refused to cooperate with the UN weapons inspectors, but then backed down on November 14 when the United States sent additional ships and aircraft to the Arabian Gulf region.

In reaction to continuing tension in Iraq, the United States maintained ground forces in Kuwait and two hundred aircraft in the Arabian Gulf region. The U.S. Navy and Marine Corps air units regularly flew in support of Operation Southern Watch. Additional air and ground forces were based in Turkey to support Northern Watch operations. In late 1989 the United States had 11,895 sailors and Marines and ninety-seven aircraft in the Arabian Gulf and surrounding area, on thirteen ships of the USS *Enterprise* carrier battle group and an amphibious task force. The nuclear-powered USS *Enterprise* had more than seventy aircraft embarked and was escorted by two cruisers, two destroyers, and a submarine capable of firing Tomahawk cruise missiles, plus a frigate and support ships. The three ships of the amphibious assault group carried seventeen hundred Marines of the 31st MEU. The air combat element of the 31st MEU included six AV-8B Harrier IIs plus Super Cobra attack helicopters and transport helicopters on the USS *Belleau Wood.*

Following a December 16, 1998, report by UN Chief Weapons Inspector Michael Butler, which stated that Iraq was again not cooperating, the United Nations pulled its inspectors out of the country. From December 16 to 20, American and British forces based in the Arabian Gulf region and aircraft from the USS *Enterprise* and USS *Carl Vinson* carrier battle groups struck at targets in Iraq to support the UN mandate in Operation Desert Fox.

More than three hundred U.S. and UK aircraft participated in the raids, and 415 cruise missiles were fired at more than eighty-five Iraqi targets. Helicopters from the USS *Belleau Wood* deployed troops on the ground in Kuwait, and Harrier IIs provided air cover during Operation Desert Fox. President Bill Clinton announced a halt to the attacks late on Saturday in Washington, D.C. (2:00 AM Sunday, December 20, Baghdad time), with the start of Ramadan, the Islamic holy month of fasting. This was the third major attack against targets in Iraq following the Gulf War.

The raids led to the expulsion of UN weapons inspectors and a continued high level of tension. The political cost of continuing strikes on Iraq was high. Russia, France, and many Arab nations questioned the need for continued attacks against Iraq and maintenance of the UN resolutions.

However, during 1999–2003 Iraqi air defense sites tracked and fired on U.S. and UK aircraft that were enforcing the no-fly zones more than fifteen hundred times, resulting in the firing of many HARM missiles against Iraqi radar and hundreds of bombing attacks on air defense sites throughout Iraq. This high level of confrontation continued until early 2003. Iraqi defenses have downed a number of unmanned reconnaissance aircraft, but no manned aircraft were shot down. However, during no-fly zone operations several U.S. and UK aircraft were lost due to malfunctions or accidents.

Throughout 2002 there was a public debate among the United States, the United Nations, and Europe concerning the threat posed by Iraqi weapons of mass destruction and the nation's support for terrorism. On November 8 the UN passed Resolution 1441, which called for immediate access to all sites in Iraq and stated that refusal could lead to a military confrontation. Even though France, Germany, and Russia voted for Resolution 1441, they blocked every effort the United States made to enforce the resolution. This situation led to the decision by the U.S. government, with support from the United Kingdom, Spain, and several other nations, to change the political situation in Iraq.

In 2002 U.S. and UK leadership decided that there was a high probability of war with Iraq. Military leaders quietly began training, preparing forces, and moving units into position for an invasion of Iraq. For Marine Corps and RAF Harrier II squadrons this meant intensified training for pilots and ground personnel and operational deployment planning for a conflict in Iraq.

By late 2002 all of the seven fleet Marine Corps Harrier II squadrons were equipped with ten to twelve radar-equipped Harrier II Plus aircraft and four to six Night Attack Harrier IIs. The Marine Corps investment in the higher-thrust Pegasus -408 engine, safety, support, and improved training was having a positive impact. Another plus was the procurement of six to eight LITENING II FLIR laser-designation pods for each Harrier II squadron. This second-generation FLIR laser targeting pod allowed pilots to identify tactical targets from medium altitudes. The LITENING II pod allowed Harrier II pilots to stay above most tactical threats, such as antiaircraft fire and shoulder-fired IR SAMs, and still deliver laser-guided bombs.

In January 2003 Harrier squadrons embarked on U.S. Navy amphibious assault ships, including the USS *Bataan*, USS *Bonhomme Richard*, USS *Tarawa*, and USS *Nassau,* to participate in Operation Iraqi Freedom. Elements from four USMC Harrier II squadrons—including VMA-211, VMA-223, VMA-311, and VMA-542—deployed on the ships and crossed the ocean, headed for the Arabian Gulf.

Approximately sixty Harrier IIs, more than 45 percent of the 3rd Marine Aircraft Wing's fixed-wing offensive air support aircraft, flew from amphibious assault ships that orbited in the Arabian Gulf. Harrier IIs from VMA-542 and VMA-223 were concentrated on the USS *Bataan* forming the East Task Force, and the West Task Force included the USS *Bonhomme Richard* with elements of VMA-311 and VMA-211. A six-aircraft detachment of Harrier IIs from the VMA-311 operated from the USS *Tarawa*, and a similar detachment from VMA-231 flew off the USS *Nassau*.[7]

The USMC V/STOL strike force was a much-appreciated capability, as airfields in the theater were limited by geographical and political aspects. According to postwar analysis, of the fifty-eight airports and air bases within range of tactical strike aircraft, political aspects limited coalition airpower to only three sites.

Sixteen USMC Harrier IIs from VMA-214 and support personnel flew to Ahmad al Jaber airbase in Kuwait in February 2003. Lt. Col. R. E. Claypool commanded VMA-214. "We flew Operation Southern Watch missions with two AIM-9L Sidewinders, two fuel tanks, and a LITENING targeting pod, plus a thousand-pound LGB or two five-hundred-pound LGBs on aircraft without the pod."[8] Marine Corps and RAF Harrier IIs operated alongside five squadrons of U.S. Marine corps F/A-18C/Ds and several squadrons of USAF A-10s and F-16Cs at Ahmad al Jaber, which made for limited space and intense operations.

Operation Iraqi Freedom

Harrier II mission assignment in Operation Iraqi Freedom (OIF) included attack of surface targets (day or night), escort for helicopters, and other air operations as assigned by the Marine Corps direct air support center, which managed air operations. Operations included CAS, armed reconnaissance, air interdiction, and helicopter air assault escort. Weapons load for Marine Corps Harrier IIs included GBU-12 Mk-82 five-hundred-pound, GBU-16 Mk-83 thousand-pound laser-guided bombs, AGM-65E/F Maverick air-to-surface missiles, CBU-99/ CBU-100 Rockeye cluster bombs, and AIM-9L/M air-to-air missiles.

Typically one or two aircraft in a flight of four carried the LITENING II FLIR pod, two external fuel tanks, and a GBU-16 laser-guided bomb, while the other aircraft of a flight of four had two GBU-12 laser-guided bombs, two external fuel tanks, and AIM-9L/M air-to-air missiles. For helicopter escort or strikes against area targets, general-purpose Mk-82/Mk-83 bombs and cluster bombs were carried. Land-based Harrier IIs could carry additional munitions on the outboard stations.[9]

The RAF also sent Harrier IIs to participate in Operation Iraqi Freedom. Eight RAF GR Mk. 7 aircraft from No. 3 squadron formed Detachment A, operating from an air base near Iraq. Led by Wing Cdr. Stuart Atha, these aircraft were in position to support special operations forces operating in western Iraq. The United Kingdom also deployed a force of ten RAF GR Mk. 7 Harrier II aircraft, support crews, and pilots to Ahmad al Jaber Air Base in Kuwait in February 2003. A mix of aircraft and crews from RAF No. 1 and No. IV squadrons formed this unit, known as Detachment B and commanded by Wing Cdr. Andrew Suddards.[10]

The GR Mk. 7 was similar to the Marine Corps Night Attack Harrier II with an internal FLIR and the night-vision goggles. RAF aircraft included an internal ECM suite. The RAF Harrier IIs were upgraded prior to deployment to OIF to enable the aircraft to perform both strike and reconnaissance missions. For reconnaissance, the GR Mk. 7 was equipped with the Joint Reconnaissance Pod employing digital information that had been developed for the Jaguar. In the strike role the Harrier II carried the TIALD pod to detect tactical targets and provide laser guidance for Paveway II. The RAF GR Mk. 7s deployed to the Middle East were modified to deliver the GPS/laser enhanced Paveway II bomb, the AGM-65 TV and IR-guided Maverick missiles, unguided bombs, BL-755 cluster bombs, and CRV-7 rockets.[11]

Despite the damaging 1991 Gulf War, UN oil embargo, weapons inspections, and twelve years of Northern and Southern Watch operations, Saddam Hussein still possessed a powerful military. This included the field army of twenty-four divisions, the powerful Republican guard with more than six divisions, and the thirty-thousand-man Fedayeen Saddam militia. Since there was no real element of surprise, given the intense U.S.-UN debate, Iraqi forces had time to develop fortifications around urban areas, especially Baghdad. In addition, Iraqi forces and air defense units were located in or near mosques, hospitals, schools, and other buildings, which would limit the use of airpower. Ground and air defenses around Basra and Baghdad were especially heavy. Large numbers of small arms were distributed to the militia and weapons stockpiled throughout the country.[12]

The campaign plan for the assault on Iraq focused on heavy application of airpower and rapid movement of armored forces supported by airborne units. Special forces from the United States, the United Kingdom, and Australia played a major role providing reconnaissance, fighting alongside Kurdish units in the north, and capturing airbases and facilities in western Iraq.

Airpower played a major role in Operation Iraqi Freedom. By achieving air superiority the coalition was able to understand the rapidly evolving military situation through information dominance. The coalition had almost total air superiority, which allowed systems like the TR-1, E-8A JSTARS, and RC-135 Rivet Joint; manned reconnaissance like the GR Mk. 7s; and similar systems, plus unmanned air vehicles, to provide surveillance, reconnaissance, and strike assessment.

Airpower shaped the battle zone through strategic attack and support for ground forces (battlefield air interdiction and BAI/CAS). Air power and ground operations were closely integrated. The coalition air component deployed in 2003 was smaller than that employed in the 1991 Gulf War, but most of these aircraft were equipped with FLIR/laser pods or laser-guided munitions, and many could deliver Precision Guided weapons like the laser-guided bombs of various sizes, JDAM, CBU-105, and Sensor Fused Weapon. Aircraft ranging from the B-52G and B-1B to the AV-8B and GR Mk. 7 could detect targets at nighttime or daytime and under conditions of limited visibility, and strike them with precision accuracy.

The strategic and battlefield-shaping element of the air campaign was much shorter in duration than that of the 1991 Gulf War. During the period from July 2002 to March 19, 2003, U.S. and UK aircraft flew 8,600 sorties over Iraq and made several hundred air strikes. The coalition stepped up its sorties over Iraq, enforcing the no-fly zones, and staged defense suppression strikes against all air defense sites. Coalition aircraft struck at known artillery, missile, and command and control positions seen to be a threat to the ground invasion.[13]

The air campaign plan for the conflict was developed over a period of months, using the massive amount of intelligence information collected over the past twelve years of air effort over Iraq. Thousands of potential targets in Iraq were identified as Desired Mean Points of Impact (DMPI) and attack plans created. As a result of technology improvements, during OIF most aircraft could attack one or more targets per sortie rather than sending out groups of aircraft to ensure destruction of a single target, as in previous conflicts. Assignments for U.S. Air Force, Navy, and Marine Corps and RAF and Australian air units were developed at the OIF Combined Air Operations center at Prince Sultan Air Base in Saudi Arabia and distributed to forces spread across thousands of miles, from the Mediterranean to Diego Garcia in the Indian Ocean.

During OIF, Marine Corps and RAF Harrier II aviation forces were integrated into the ATO to perform air interdiction and CAS. Marines played an active role in developing the daily ATO and contributed the assets of the 3rd Marine Air Wing to the air battle via the sophisticated Marine air command and control system. The direct air support center controlled its air assets available on amphibious ships, on the ground in Kuwait, or in the air, and assigned aircraft to support the advance of the 1st MEF or other targets from the ATO priority listing.[14]

Operation Iraqi Freedom began during the night of March 19, 2003, when USAF F-117s struck at a bunker suspected to house Saddam Hussein, and about forty Tomahawk cruise missiles impacted in and around Baghdad. The following morning coalition forces initiated three major advances into Iraq: the U.S. Army V corps thrust across the border of Kuwait into Iraq toward Baghdad from the southwest, the Marine Corps 1st MEF went north from the southeast, and the UK 1 armored division penetrated southern Iraq. Coalition aircraft, including Harrier IIs, intensified strikes against battlefield targets and provided CAS for these advancing ground forces.

On March 21, 2003, day one of the conflict, British forces approached Basra while U.S. forces started their move north toward Baghdad on two axes. Iraqi military targets came under a hail of bombs and missiles from coalition aircraft ranging from Marine Cobras, Harrier IIs, and F/A-18s to U.S. Army Apache attack helicopters and a wide range of U.S. Air Force and Navy and RAF aircraft. Harrier IIs from VMA-311, flying off the USS *Bonhomme Richard* and led by squadron commanding officer Lt. Col. Michael Hile and wingman Capt. Jason Duncan, flew a strike mission early on March 21. Their first sortie, flown in the dark, engaged no targets due to poor visibility. After returning to ship and refueling, the two pilots took off again for another mission. They damaged their assigned target, the Alamo bridge located thirty miles west of el Basra, with three laser-guided bombs.

Lieutenant Colonel Hile notes that the capabilities of the targeting pod in Operation Iraqi Freedom were immediately appreciated. "Soon after combat operations began, the Harrier II became the preferred aircraft for strikes because of its ability to confirm tactical-size targets from medium altitude. Again, stringent Rules of Engagement requirements would dictate weapon engagement parameters and the ability to do this by day or night at medium altitude."[15]

By March 22 elements of the U.S. 3rd Infantry division had penetrated more than 150 miles into Iraq, nearly halfway to Baghdad. UK forces surrounded Basra and U.S. Marines continued their advance, meeting increasing resistance. Deteriorating weather affected the effective application of CAS and forced the cancellation of many planned interdiction missions.[16]

Lieutenant Colonel Claypool was CO of VMA-214, based in Kuwait. "We are going after tank divisions, Republican Guard divisions, and things traveling on the roads," he says. "At the start, we flew with Sidewinders for the air-to-air threat. There were many Roland and SA-8 mobile SAMs unaccounted for, so we also carried the DECM [defense electronic countermeasures pod]. All our RWR gear was good. We had all six buckets of chaff and flares, 180 expendables in all. Some aircraft had two 25mm gun pods."[17]

On March 23, U.S. Marine units fought a series of intense battles around the city of Nasiriyah. Aircraft provided CAS for the battle and punished Iraqi forces, but a misdirected air strike hit friendly troops, causing casualties. A Patriot missile battery mistakenly shot down an RAF Tornado, killing the crew of two, when the computer identified it to be an antiradiation missile. American troops of the V Corps moved north toward Baghdad, and coalition airpower pounded the four Republican Guard divisions in position to defend the capital from the south. An attack by U.S. Army AH-64D Apache attack helicopters on the Medina division ran into an air defense ambush, with one helicopter shot down and its crew captured and many others damaged. On this day a convoy from the 507th Maintenance unit was ambushed, resulting in heavy casualties and seven captured.

Lieutenant Colonel Hile notes, "Another overlooked contributor to the Harrier II success were the airfields from which they mostly operated—the amphibious assault ships in the Northern Arabian Gulf, which were referred to as Harrier Carriers. An aircraft carrier is a ready-to-deploy 'airfield' with communications links, maintenance, berthing, and messing facilities inherent."[18]

On March 24, more than fifteen hundred sorties were flown in support of the coalition ground advance and raids around Baghdad and Mosul. Air and ground operations were affected by storms and blowing sand. Despite poor weather in central and southern Iraq, the lead elements of the U.S. Army V Corps reached a point fifty miles south of Baghdad late on March 25. Coalition air units flew about fourteen hundred sorties during the day, including hundreds of strikes against the Republican Guard division holding positions south of Baghdad.

Lieutenant Colonel Claypool says that the LITENING pod, which became the cornerstone of Coalition tactics, was generally thought of as a lethality enhancement. But "it also had a major survivability enhancement. We could operate in the high teens (16–20,000 feet) and point seven Mach, we didn't have to expose ourselves to the majority of the defenses. Most of the active threats couldn't reach us at the speed and altitudes we were working. We saw antiaircraft fire, and I am sure we were shot at by Rolands, SA-8s, and SA-7s, at least ballistically, on the first days."[19]

After the first week of the war, they dropped the Sidewinders and DECM pod. The air and radar SAM threat had not yet materialized, and "we had standing orders not to operate below 10,000 feet, unless there was a very good reason. I decided to download the gun pods since we couldn't use them effectively from that altitude. Removing the DECM pod and guns increased our range and endurance, which helped as the war moved north."[20]

On March 26, American forces encircled Najaf while the 1 MEF continued their northern advance supported by heavy CAS. U.S. Army paratroopers dropped in northern Iraq linked up with Kurdish fighters to start a northern front. Coalition aircraft flew hundreds of interdiction missions and provided CAS for the ground assault driving north toward Baghdad and south on Mosul.

Weather was still a challenge on March 27 (day seven of the conflict). Toward the end of the day it improved, and air and ground operation in Iraq intensified. The following day, March 28, U.S. forces converged on Baghdad with the U.S. Army V Corps approaching from the southwest and the Marines from the southeast. Coalition aircraft and missiles continued their efforts on March 29, with targets around Baghdad receiving the most attention. Two AH-64D Apache attack helicopters from the U.S. Army's 101st Airborne division were lost to ground fire during attack operations, but the crews were recovered.

During March 28–30, the 3rd Infantry Division and 1st Marine Division slowed their advance to allow for resupply and rest. Advancing units bypassed urban concentrations and received CAS when called for, but the bulk of airpower focused on pounding Iraqi mechanized units and artillery surrounding Baghdad. The goal was to cause attrition and hold them in place to be surrounded or overrun. British Royal Marines initiated Operation James, an assault into Basra, on March 30. Harrier IIs and other coalition aircraft provided CAS and struck at battlefield targets. A Marine Corps AV-8B assigned to VMA-231 crashed while attempting to land on the USS *Nassau*, but the pilot safely ejected and the aircraft floated and was recovered.[21]

Lt. Col. P. Rupp was MAG-13 OPS officer during the conflict. "I think the Harriers were well trusted by the ground folks in the theater of operations," he

says. "Not only are they extremely effective in combat, but also extremely effi-
cient. Our airplanes had tremendous tactical aircraft readiness availability—our
planes were always ready to go."[22]

More than a thousand sorties were flown on April 1 (day twelve of the
conflict). Again, interdiction strikes on the Iraqi Republican Guard Divisions
forming the ring south of Baghdad were the primary focus. The three Republican
Guard Divisions in position around Baghdad included the Medina armored division south of the city, the Al Nida armored division to the east, and the Baghdad
motorized division located near the city of Kut.

As the Marines advanced, USMC Harriers used a road for poststrike refueling just sixty miles south of Baghdad. Lieutenant Colonel Claypool notes that
General Amos, commander of the 3rd Marine Aircraft Wing, gave them every
opportunity to be in this fight.

> He did not hold us back. Our ready room tent was almost next door to his
> CP at our base; on occasion he would visit, have a cup of coffee, and watch
> our tapes from the day's missions. One day he walked in, and I was in the
> middle of a flight brief. The general stated: 'I want you guys to land on a road
> south of Baghdad. See if it can be used as a Harrier FARP, can you do it?'
> My MAG CO remarked that there were risks involved. General Amos said,
> "The risk is on me." So we went there for postmission refueling, the first use
> of a road for combat ops by USMC Harriers, maybe anybody's Harriers.
> The road was rocketed shortly after we took off, so we didn't go back. When
> we captured an enemy airfield we would move in fuel, security, and an Air
> Boss and use it for refueling rather than go to an airborn tanker. There sim-
> ply weren't enough tankers, and this went a long way toward reducing
> the load.[23]

Often Marine Harrier II pilots would fly from their ship, strike a target, land
at the forward operating base to rearm and refuel, and then attack other positions
before flying back to their ship. This process again underscored the benefits of
USMC concept expeditionary planning and the multiple tocair basing options of
the Harrier II.

On April 2 the 1st Marine Division engaged elements of the Iraqi Baghdad
division as they continued their push north on Highway 7 toward the Tigris River
on Highway 27. U.S. Army units penetrated around the city of Karbala, established a bridge across the Euphrates River, and headed toward Baghdad. A U.S.
Navy F/A-18C flying off the USS *Kitty Hawk* was shot down and the pilot killed
while flying near Karbala by a U.S. Army Patriot SAM.

Heavy fighting continued on April 3, as elements of the 3rd Infantry Division
assaulted Baghdad International Airport and the 1st Marine Division engaged
entrenched Republican Guard units. UK forces continued their advance around
Basra. On this fourteenth day of fighting, heavy air support was provided for

these attacks, and interdiction strikes continued around Baghdad, around Basra, and in the north.

Baghdad Fedayeen launched a counterattack against U.S. forces at the airport on April 4 and suffered heavy losses. The 1st Marine Division fought with elements of the Al Nida division as it pushed up Highway 6 southeast of Baghdad. Coalition air strikes continued to support advancing units and punish Iraqi forces. Lieutenant Colonel Hile and Captain Duncan flew an early morning strike against the Al Nida Republican Guard armored division, which was located fifteen miles to the east of Baghdad. In a period of ten minutes the two pilots destroyed two .T-72 tanks and a fuel truck with laser-guided bombs. The pilots could see antiaircraft fire and surface-to-air missiles fired at them from defensive positions during the attack.[24]

The 2nd Brigade, 3rd Infantry Division, conducted a "Thunder Run" armored attack up Highway 8 on the morning of April 5 with dozens of M1 tanks and M2 Bradleys through the suburbs of Baghdad. Moving at a fast pace, the vehicles took heavy fire from small arms and rocket-propelled grenades, but also inflicted serious damage and caused panic among the defenders. The 1st Marine Division fought to within twelve miles of the center of Baghdad under CAS.

On April 6 British forces completed their assault into Basra and found that the Iraqi government had pulled out and the situation had quickly deteriorated into chaos. U.S. Army and Marine units linked up southeast of Baghdad. Iraqi military units retreated into the city under serious air and ground attacks.

The U.S. Army 3rd Infantry Division made another Thunder Run with armored vehicles into Baghdad on April 7, and this time the troops and vehicles remained to control several intersections and one of Saddam Hussein's palaces. Baghdad International Airport was cleared, the runways opened, and C-17s and C-130s started flying in troops and supplies. U.S. Marines crossed the Diyala Bridge under fire and pressed into Baghdad. During continuing air operations an F-15E and its crew were lost near Tikrit with the loss of its crew.

American forces poured into Baghdad, and there was heavy fighting with Fedayeen and militia units in urban terrain on April 8. Coalition aircraft intensified their attacks on targets in and around Baghdad, and during the day one A-10 was shot down and another seriously damaged.

Harrier II pilot Captain Kaczorowski flew a mission on April 8, 2003, with Major Musser.

> Concern was raised again over forces moving from the eastern side of the country to harass coalition forces and supply lines in central Iraq. After about ten minutes of searching with no indication of mass movements, we spotted a revetted vehicle that was positioned to engage traffic along the highway. After reporting its position and condition, we received permission to engage and destroy it with a single GBU-16 [one-thousand-pound laser-guided bomb].

On returning to the area to assess the damage and look for additional targets, I was locked and received missile launch indications from several ground threats. I maneuvered and expended chaff in an attempt to defeat the radar, but after a few seconds I received indications of a second launch. We were at altitude outside of the range of most smaller systems. I lowered the nose to preserve energy and then began a climb to regain altitude while continuing to expend chaff. The track lasted for about twelve to fifteen seconds, after which it dropped and we left the area.[25]

On April 9 Marines pulled down the statue of Saddam Hussein in Firdos Square, and this image—covered live on television and later in the newspapers worldwide—came to symbolize the defeat of the Saddam Hussein regime. Sporadic fighting continued in several areas of Baghdad until April 10, as the U.S. Army and Marines overran the final pockets of resistance. Coalition air strikes continued against the defenders.

Kirkuk, a town in the north, fell to Kurdish fighters assisted by special forces on April 11, and Mosul was also taken over by coalition forces on the same day. Marine Task Force Tripoli, with heavy air support, rushed ninety miles north to Tikrit. On April 14 the force took control of Saddam Hussein's hometown and the core of the Ba'ath party. By April 15, 2003, Operation Iraqi Freedom was complete, with Iraq under coalition control and most major fighting ended.

On an average day the 3rd Marine Aircraft wing provided 120 to 150 Harrier II and Hornet strike sorties, and about a hundred Cobra attack helicopter sorties were also flown to pave the way for advancing Marine units. Harrier II, Hornet, and Cobra attack helicopter missions were assigned each day by the Tactical Air Operations Center at 1 MEF. To protect U.S. Marine and Army units, a no-bomb line was established ten or more miles ahead of advancing columns. Marine strike aircraft were frequently assigned to patrol "kill boxes" where any Iraqi forces located could be attacked.

Intense air strikes were directed against the Iraqi divisions encountered on the Marine advance, and hundreds of vehicles and other targets were destroyed. Frequently Iraqis abandoned tanks, armored personnel carriers, artillery, and vehicles when they came under air attack. As a result, the combat effectiveness of an Iraqi unit was disrupted even if its equipment was not all damaged. Harrier IIs with the LITENING II pods were also frequently given the task of attacking point targets such as vehicles in kill boxes, command centers, bridges, or others, as they could effectively detect tactical targets from medium altitudes.[26]

FACs in armored vehicles or aircraft such as the F/A-18Ds or OA-10s often assisted in kill box strike efforts, and always were involved in coordinating strike aircraft and attack helicopter CAS attacks for advancing units. CAS intensified in the later stages of the campaign, as the U.S. Army and Marines approached Baghdad.

Offensive operation began on March 19, 2003, with the attacks on Iraqi leadership targets. After twenty-seven days of combat, by April 15 coalition forces were in general control of the major cities of Baghdad, Basra, Mosul, Kirkuk, and Tikrit. On May 1 President Bush declared an end of major combat activities.

During Operation Iraqi Freedom the coalition fielded 1,801 aircraft, of which 1,356 were fighters or bombers capable of delivering weapons. These strike aircraft flew about 20,700 sorties which targeted 19,900 DMPIs, delivering 29,900 munitions, of which 19,948 were precision-guided munitions and 9,251 were unguided bombs. About 60 percent of the strikes (twelve thousand DMPIs) were directed against Iraqi ground forces, which included Republican Guard and regular Iraqi army units. The rest of the strike sorties were directed at strategic targets and CAS. The Harrier IIs of the U.S. Marine Corps and RAF thus contributed nearly 8 percent of the total coalition sorties of the OIF air offensive.[27]

The twenty RAF Harrier IIs deployed to the region during OIF played an important role in supporting coalition operations, flying 720 sorties and 2,147 combat hours. RAF GR Mk. 7 pilot Flight Lt. Paul Francis of No. 1 squadron flew from Kuwait. "I flew mainly CAS missions and 'kill box' interdiction. We used image stabilized binoculars to PID [positively identify] targets from altitude. We worked heavily with U.S. Marine Corps ground FACs and also with U.S. Air Force F-15Es, who provided SCAR [strike control reconnaissance]. Some missions would involve us getting airborne with E-Paveway [enhanced Paveway laser-guided bombs] to attack a preplanned target, but many of our missions involved us getting tasked once we were airborne."[28]

Mission assignments for RAF Harrier II pilots came via the ATO from the Coalition Forces Air Component Command. Most of the RAF Harrier II missions involved attacking targets in assigned kill boxes or interdiction. However, about 30 percent of the missions assigned to RAF GR Mk. 7 pilots were CAS for British forces, the U.S. Army V Corps, and Marine ground forces advancing on Baghdad.

During OIF (March 19–April 13, 2003) USMC Harrier II pilots flew seven days a week and twenty-four hours a day. Col. Mark Savarese, commanding officer of Marine Air Group 13, describes the beauty of the Harrier II as its flexibility. "It is a unique airplane that can go anywhere, operate from anywhere, which is what allowed them to operate from what I like to call an attack carrier. During twenty-six days of combat operations, we flew more than two thousand sorties and logged more than three thousand combat flight hours. Harrier IIs expended more than 750 thousand pounds of ordnance in support of the 1st Marine Expeditionary Force, dropping thousand-pound and five-hundred-pound bombs." Colonel Savarese also notes that Harrier IIs with the LITENING II pod were able to achieve a kill rate of 75 percent with laser-guided bombs. One strike destroyed a tank battalion of the Republican Guard division that blocked the 1st MEF advance toward Al Kut. During the conflict, Marine Harrier IIs delivered more than nine hundred laser-guided bombs. A number of LITENING II pods were modified with video downlink capability from the Pioneer unmanned aerial vehicle and deployed with VMA-214. This feature enabled ground FAC to review imagery and identify potential targets in real time. [29]

After the end of Operation Iraqi Freedom, U.S. Marine units transitioned from combat to peacekeeping activities. By summer 2003 both the Marine and RAF Harrier IIs had left Iraq. There was a general perception that fighter aircraft were not needed for the rebuilding and peacekeeping role projected. Marine forces of the 1st MEF were gradually withdrawn as other coalition units arrived in country, so by late September 2003 most of the force was on its way back to the United States.

However, there was widespread looting in many cities and towns, and with the collapse of Iraqi governmental authority, factional violence erupted. The loss of order led to widespread looting and civil disorder, which required the presence of a significant military force to stabilize the situation until a new Iraqi police force and army could be trained. By the end of 2003, coalition peacekeeping forces in Iraq included more than 120,000 U.S. Army, 12,000 British forces, and 13,000 soldiers from Poland, the Netherlands, Italy, Spain, the Ukraine, and twenty-five other nations.

As coalition forces seemed to garrison Iraq, a violent insurgency began to develop. In expectation of an American assault, Saddam Hussein ordered distribution of arms, ammunition, funds, and trained militia forces to all of the major population areas of Iraq to continue a guerrilla-type campaign. Insurgent operations gradually expanded, with attacks concentrating first in central Iraq and later expanding to southern and northern Iraq. Expanding attacks disrupted efforts to restore normal services such as electricity, water, and sewage, which eroded popular support for coalition efforts.

In March 2004 the 1st MEU returned to western Iraq to take over for U.S. Army 82nd Airborne division, which had served a year's tour fighting OIF and then keeping the peace. The Marine assignment known as OIF II included much of the Iraq-Syria border and the Sunni triangle, an area of concentration of Sunni religious groups, including the city of Fallujah. The MEU deployment included Marine Air Group 16 from the 3rd Marine Air Wing, which included dozens of transport and attack helicopters and C-130 transports to support Marine operations. When insurgent operations intensified and tested the capabilities of Cobra attack helicopters, Marine commanders called for increased air support.

In May 2004, Harrier IIs from VMA-214 and VMA-542 assigned to the 3rd Marine Aircraft Wing deployed to Iraq to provide air support for the 1st MEU.

The jets operated from a former Iraqi airbase near Al Asad. Harrier II pilots flew a variety of missions, from armed reconnaissance and convoy escort to CAS.

Capt. Ryan P. Hough was a Harrier II pilot with VMA-542. "You have to always keep your guard up during these sorties," he says, "because in an instant the troops can be in contact with the enemy and need immediate attack. As a single-seat pilot in the Harrier II, you are always juggling many tasks, such as navigation and the LITENING II Pod all at one time, and you are expected to do all of these things perfectly."[30]

The Marines found the experience in western Iraq to be quite different than peacekeeping in the south. In the south the Shia tribes welcomed coalition forces, yet the Sunni tribes in the west were openly hostile. The Marines were involved in many serious combat operations. On March 31, 2004, four American contactors were killed and their bodies mutilated in Fallujah. In Operation Valiant Resolve, which began on April 5, a battalion of Marines, with a U.S. Army unit and USAF special operation force, entered Fallujah. The forces fought until May 1, but with limited results due to concerns about civilian casualties. Air support was provided by Cobra attack helicopters, AC-130 gunships operating at night, and a limited number of Harrier II strikes.

Over the next several months Fallujah grew to an insurgent stronghold from which many attacks were launched. By late 2004 many civilians had left the city, which formerly had a population of three hundred thousand, and insurgents had fortified their positions. A combined Marine-Army-Iraqi force of fifteen thousand troops launched Operaton al-Fajr on November 8. The assault force received air support from Harrier IIs and also Marine artillery. About twenty-four sorties were flown over the city on the first day of the assault, and four Mk-82 five-hundred-pound bombs were dropped. The fighting continued until December, when the city was overrun and insurgents forced out after suffering heavy casualties.[31]

Fallujah was particularly challenging, notes Captain Hough, because of the congested airspace.

> You have to be able to find the specific target in the urban environment, close to Marines, with only a short time you are allotted in order to enter the area you are sharing with other aircraft. . . . All of this is possible because of the hard work and dedication of our maintenance Marines. They have worked tirelessly, seven days a week, twelve hours a day for six months. . . . We have flown over the skies of Iraq for six months, and in that time we have fulfilled joint tactical air requests for every kind of ground unit. The tasks have varied, including convoy escort at night, supporting recon teams during raids, and providing on-call CAS for the troops on the ground . . . and even though there were many sorties where no ordnance was expended, we still used or LITENING II pods for reconnaissance.[32]

CHAPTER 13

Operation Enduring Freedom: Harrier IIs in Afghanistan

Following the September 11, 2001, terrorist attacks, the U.S. government accused Ousama bin Laden and his alliance of terrorist organizations of organizing the attacks. NATO invoked Article 5 of its charter and supported the U.S. call for action against the terrorist threat. Many nations, including Russia, called for efforts to fight this international threat. Ousama bin Laden congratulated those who made the attacks for striking a blow against the United States but denied that he was involved. President Bush announced the start of a war against terrorism and demanded that the Taliban turn over bin Laden and his lieutenants for trial. The Taliban leaders refused to comply, demanded proof of the U.S. allegations, and prepared for war.

The Islamic fundamentalist Taliban government assumed control of Kabul and much of Afghanistan after the civil war that followed withdrawal of Russian forces in the early 1990s. Initially the Taliban victory was welcomed by the average Afghan, as it brought an end to the costly civil war. However, the Taliban imposed a strict Islamic code that alienated women and many of the Afghan tribal factions and disrupted the economy. The Taliban hosted Islamic revolutionaries and allowed terrorist training in Afghanistan for Ousama bin Laden's al-Qa'ida and other fundamentalist groups. By the late 1990s the Taliban held control of nearly 90 percent of the country, but the opposition Northern Alliance and other tribal groups continued to fight back.

The al-Qa'ida network was suspected to be behind a number of terrorist attacks including the 1992 bombing of the World Trade Center in New York City, the 1996 bomb attacks in Saudi Arabia, and the 1998 bombing of U.S. embassies in Kenya and Tanzania. In retaliation for these attacks, on August 20, 1998, the United States fired seventy-nine Tomahawk cruise missiles at bin Laden's training camp near Knowst, Afghanistan, and at a suspected chemical factory in Sudan.

The United States rapidly mobilized its forces and secured support from allies for diplomatic and military action against the Taliban government. The United Kingdom pledged military support, and Pakistan agreed to allow use of its airspace and limited facilities for operations against Afghanistan. Twenty-six days, three hours, and twelve minutes after the first hijacked airliner hit the World Trade Center, U.S. and British missiles and bombs were dropped on targets in Afghanistan. At 20:57 hours local time, October 7, the United States and the United Kingdom (with support from other nations, including Australia, Canada, France, and Germany) struck at thirty-one Taliban military and government targets. Tomahawk cruise missiles fired from two Royal Navy submarines and several U.S. ships, plus fifteen long-range bombers and twenty-five carrier-based strike aircraft, carried out the initial strikes. U.S. Secretary of Defense Donald H. Rumsfeld remarked that the strikes were intended to "create conditions for sustained antiterrorist and humanitarian relief operations in Afghanistan. That requires that among other things we first remove the threat of Taliban air defenses and aircraft. . . . We need the freedom to operate on the ground and in the air."[1]

The 2001 offensive, named Operation Enduring Freedom, saw continuous coalition air attacks, including strikes by U.S. Marine Corps and Italian navy Harrier IIs, which demolished strategic targets and Taliban defenses. The air campaign began with attacks that destroyed the small number of Taliban air defense batteries, fighter aircraft, and command and control systems. Precision-guided weapons including the SLAM-ER, the AGM-130/GBU-15, GPS satellite–guided JDAM, and laser-guided were employed, allowing aircraft to hit targets accurately from above the effective altitude of Taliban air defenses.

The pounding from the air weakened defenses and demoralized Taliban troops, opening the way for a successful ground assault by the Northern Alliance and allied ground forces. As this book went to press, the ground campaign and peacekeeping efforts with air support were continuing in Afghanistan. Signs of progress have been noted, including the election of a central government.

The Afghanistan conflict again underscored the importance of sea-based airpower, especially aircraft carrier battle groups and amphibious assault forces. Many nations in the region were unwilling to provide airbases or port facilities to support a massive U.S. and allied forces intervention, even after the evidence of connection to the September 11 attacks was demonstrated. Thus the only airpower with the mobility and firepower to wage a sustained campaign against Afghanistan was provided by the U.S. Navy's carrier battle groups, amphibious assault ships, and USAF long-range bombers.

The USS *Enterprise* and USS *Carl Vinson* were involved in hostilities from the start, but the USS *Theodore Roosevelt* later took over for the USS *Enterprise*.

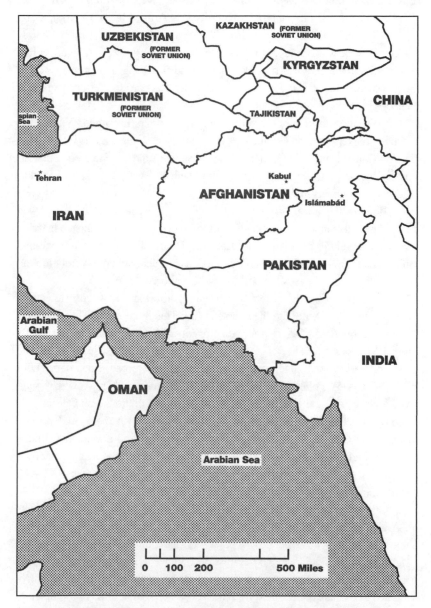

Map showing Afghanistan and the region. Harrier IIs flying from U.S. Navy and Italian ships in the Arabian Sea had to traverse Pakistan to perform their missions. *M. Monahan*

Each U.S. carrier was armed with a mix of seventy-five F-14s and F/A-18s and supporting aircraft. USMC AV-8B Harrier II and helicopters operated from the U.S. Navy amphibious assault ships USS *Pelileu* and USS *Bataan*. The USS *Kittyhawk* deployed carrying more than fifty U.S. Army, Marine Corps, and Air Force helicopters. The UK carrier HMS *Illustrious* and the French carrier *Charles De Gaulle* were also deployed to the region. The Royal Navy aircraft carrier had a mix of Sea Harriers, Harrier GR Mk. 7s, and Sea King helicopters, and the French carrier was armed with Rafael and Super Etendard fighter-bombers, and helicopters.

Again, the vital role of aerial refueling tanker aircraft is noted. Without the refueling tankers provided by the U.S. Air Force, Navy, and Marine Corps, UK, France, Canada, and other nations, strike aircraft would not have been able to sustain the long-range operations and carry the heavy weapons loads needed to effectively hit targets in Afghanistan.

The USMC Harrier II was among the first U.S. tacair units to be deployed to the region to support Operation Enduring Freedom over Afghanistan. Marine pilots flew hundreds of strike sorties from amphibious assault ships in the waters off Pakistan. This was a critical contribution, as political factors severely limited the availability of air bases for U.S. and coalition forces.

The 15th MEU (SOC) left San Diego, California, on August 13, 2001, for a planned deployment to the Arabian Gulf. This force included three ships, twenty-two hundred Marines, more than twenty helicopters, and six Harrier IIs from VMA-211. The Harrier IIs formed detachment "B," assigned to Marine Medium Helicopter Squadron-163 (HMM-163) (reinforced) aboard the USS *Peleliu* (LHA-5). Following the September 11 attacks on New York City and Washington, D.C., the 15th MEU (SOC) was diverted to the Indian Ocean.

In early October the three ships of the 15th MEU arrived off Pakistan. Secretly, on October 7 the unit inserted 350 Marines and several helicopters to Jacobabad Airbase in south-central Pakistan to serve as a staging area for search and rescue operations and as a base for Marine Corps KC-130 tanker transports.[2]

Marine Corps Harrier II pilots flew their first strike mission against targets in Afghanistan on November 3. Four Harrier IIs armed with Mk-82 five-hundred-pound bombs launched off the USS *Peleliu*, three of which hit targets in Afghanistan. "It felt like any other mission we have trained for," said one pilot, "nothing unusual."[3] During a normal six-month deployment, the Harrier II pilots assigned to a detachment would fly six to seven hundred hours. For the first two months of operations over Afghanistan, the 15th MEW Harrier II detachment launched two four-aircraft strikes per day and each pilot flew more than five hundred miles each way to the target, delivered their bombs, and had to refuel from tankers several times. The pilots and six aircraft of the detachment were flying more than five hundred hours each month.

By mid-November the 26th MEU (SOC) originating from Camp Lejeune, North Carolina, joined the 15th MEU (SOC) operating off Pakistan. The six Harrier IIs and nine pilots from VMA-223 were assigned to the 26th MEU air combat element under control of Medium Helicopter Squadron-365 operating from the USS *Bataan* (LHD-5). The Harrier II pilots began flying regular daily strike missions over Afghanistan in late November.[4]

Capt. Chris Raible flew off the USS *Bataan*. "The guys who really deserve the credit are the FACs [forward air controllers] sitting out in the desert," he said. "They often try to get us to perform reconnaissance of suspected targets."

Capt. Nathan Berryman was another pilot assigned to the 26th MEU. "I became the first VMA-223 pilot to drop a bomb in combat since 1969," he said. "It was near the end of a six-hour mission. We had twenty minutes left on station. . . . I was surprised to hear the FAC clear us weapons-free on a target."

Two F-14Ds with LANTIRN FLIR/lasers were in the air also and had detected targets and passed the information on to the ground FAC. Captain Berryman said, "The F-14s each made a pass destroying two vehicles in the convoy. We coordinated with them so they could laze the targets" (pinpoint a target with a laser beam for the Harrier's laser-guided bombs to guide on). Berryman's bomb hit the target, and he felt "proud that the Marine Corps can provide this kind of support hundreds of miles from the ship."[5]

Generally two missions were planned per day, each with four aircraft and a spare. One mission was flown in the morning and a second in the afternoon, extending into the night. After takeoff the USMC pilots met a USAF or RAF tanker to refuel; then they flew over Pakistan for a second tanking before flying strikes in support of coalition forces in Afghanistan. After about an hour in the combat zone delivering bombs, they would proceed back to the coast, meet another tanker and refuel, then fly back to their carrier for a vertical landing. Most of these missions lasted from five to five and a half hours and covered a distance of five to eight hundred miles.

USMC Harriers IIs flying off the USS *Peleliu* and USS *Bataan* also provided air support for the helicopter insertion of Marines into Afghanistan. On November 25 six CH-53s carrying a reinforced rifle company flew 441 miles from their ship and established Forward Operating Base (FOB) "Rhino" at a desert airstrip south of Kandahar, Afghanistan. Marine Corps CH-53 helicopters continued the inflow of troops and gear until the runway was repaired and lights were added to allow KC-130 aircraft filled with Marines and tactical vehicles to land. During the next week Marines from the 15th and 26th MEUs and supplies were deployed to FOB Rhino in KC-130s and USAF C-17s.

The expanded Marine force in Afghanistan began performing offensive operations under protective air cover from Marine Corps Harrier IIs, Cobras, and other coalition aircraft. In December the Marines deployed around Kandahar Airport near Kabul and returned to the former U.S. embassy. After flying a strike mission, two Harrier IIs forward-deployed to Kandahar overnight but returned to the ship the next day. At the end of December the 15th MEW pulled out of Afghanistan, and in January 2002 the 26th did the same, replaced by soldiers of the U.S. Army 101st Airborne Division.

In late November Italy assigned its aircraft carrier the *Giuseppe Garibaldi*, armed with eight Harrier II Plus aircraft, several helicopters, two frigates, and a tanker, to support Operation Enduring Freedom. This force performed operational mission during January and February 2002. Italian navy Harrier II Plus aircraft were the first Harrier IIs equipped and combat ready with the LITENING II FLIR pod for self-designation of laser-guided bombs. In less than two months, the Italian pilots flew 131 missions for a total of 647 flight hours.[6]

From January to March 2002, the 13th MEU (SOC) embarked on the USS *Bonhomme Richard* (LHD-5) with a six-aircraft detachment of Harrier IIs from VMA-211 assigned. The amphibious-ready group operated off the coast of Pakistan for several months, and Harrier II pilots flew many six-hour missions over Afghanistan in support of U.S. and coalition Operation Enduring Freedom activities. Several Harrier IIs and a contingent of support personnel forward-deployed to Kandahar and flew CAS missions.[7]

The 22nd MEU deployment on the USS *Wasp* (LHD-1) in mid-2002 included a six-aircraft Harrier II detachment assigned to HMM-261. This deployment was the first U.S. Marine Corps combat deployment with the LITENING II FLIR pod. The first combat sortie by Harrier II pilots with the LITENING II Pod and GBU-12 five-hundred-pound laser-guided bombs was flown in July 2002.

Maj. David A. Vorsteen was one of the Harrier II pilots assigned to the USS *Wasp* detachment. "We now have the ability to frag [plan] dedicated to obtaining and bringing tactical imagery back to the ship so it can be used for mission planning and execution. It [the LITENING II pod] also allowed us to stand off in an altitude sanctuary [above the effective altitude of antiaircraft fire and shoulder-fired IR SAMs] and deliver precision strikes on point targets, or mark these targets for others."

Capt. Michael J. Perez was also a pilot on the deployment. "It was good to be finally utilized in support of Operation Enduring Freedom," he says. "Having flown over Kosovo before, it was a familiar feeling. The hair stands up a little bit on the back of your neck when you realize that there are people underneath you that would love nothing better than to shoot you down; I would not call it fear, but a heightened sense of awareness."[8]

In October 2002, Marine Harrier IIs flew over Afghanistan. This time a detachment of six aircraft, a dozen pilots—plus more than two hundred support and security personnel from VMA-513 and Wing Support Squadron 373 (MWSS-373)—deployed from Yuma, Arizona, to Bagram, Afghanistan, and stayed there until September 2003.[9]

Commanding officer Col. Jim Dixon performed a site survey to see if the Harrier II could operate there.

It was Bagram, an old Russian base which they used during the Russian-Afghan War, located about 35 miles north of Kabul. My only concerns were an indirect fire threat on the base, land mines around the facility which could be a threat to our people, and the runway was pretty hideous. It reminded me of Highway I-10, where you go bump, bump. All the concrete blocks were not lined up just right. They were individual pieces, very age-worn, plus some had been hit by mortar, rocket, and artillery rounds and chipped or shattered and poorly repaired.

We sent an advance party there in September 2002 and I took all Night Attack Harrier IIs. The elevation in Afghanistan was nearly five thousand feet. Actually it was 4,900 feet elevation. I took all Night Attack Harrier IIs since they were lighter. The engine performance of the -408 motor at that altitude with the ordnance loads that we were expected to be bringing back, which was the pod [LITENING II FLIR] and a thousand-pound bomb [BGU-16 laser guided bomb], and our [25mm] gun and fuel tanks, was better with the night-attack. Plus our mission was ground attack, since there was no air-to-air threat which required the radar. . . .

We were told we were going there to provide air support for CJTF 180 and that air support included close air support, escort, and armed reconnaissance. When we got there with the LITENING II pods, we found that we made a shift toward doing reconnaissance, because we had the ability to see through the night very well. So we ended up with three major missions: close air support, escort for both helicopters, C-130s and ground convoys, and reconnaissance. . . .

We had six Harriers and there were also eight U.S. Air Force A-10s, and NATO F-16s left as we got there. I think initially the mission planners at Bagram did the scheduling and it was based on, "We need an airplane to fill the sky, so stick this jet in there." It took us a while before CJTF-180 planners figured out, "Why is it that the airplane with the pod that can see in the dark is flying in the day and the A-10 has to fly at night with Maverick and flares? Why don't you swap the mission assignment around?" So over the year I think we flew more than eighteen hundred hours of the total of thirty-seven hundred hours at night.

Operating alongside USAF A-10A strike aircraft, the Harrier IIs provided support for Task Force 180, a coalition force fighting terrorism and providing peacekeeping assistance.

Pilots in the AV-8B Night Attack Harrier IIs flying from the Bagram air base had the LITENING II FLIR pod plus night-vision goggles, which allowed them to operate safely at night. This system has received excellent reviews from pilots, SOFs, and commanders of the U.S. Army 82nd Airborne Division. At the time Colonel Dixon went to Afghanistan, the heavy fighting to take over the country was finished.

> It was sweeping up, mopping up and trying to root out evil wherever it went in the country. So the Army had different fire bases throughout the country. People maneuvered, there were ground convoys, helicopter missions, and so when something happened, our missions were mostly reactive. Someone got attacked and we were airborne, so we would dash over and help out. The three different times I dropped ordnance, all were reactive. I was flying and the next thing we knew a firebase in the south was getting shot at, so we went to their support. The second time I went out to drop was on an insert. The ground forces wanted to sweep a valley and we went in and bombed ahead of their sweep. Then the last time some naval SOF forces got engaged and again it was reactive. I came off the tanker and went to help them out. Ninety percent of the missions that we dropped on over there were reactive . . . most of our targets were troops; it was normally a gunfight. The friendlies were taking mortar fire, RPG [rocket-propelled grenade] fire, or small arms.

His pilots faced threats from small arms and early generation shoulder-fired SAMs, Dixon says, "the typical stuff you read about in the newspaper."

> We flew as if a missile would be engaged . . . anytime, you know from takeoff to landing. We always honored the fact that you know people are saying the missile's are out there. . . . I think the main threat was small arms fire, but it was very difficult to see if someone was firing at you or not, because typically they did not use tracers. If you go down in the weeds you are going to stand a chance of getting shot, so we tried to avoid that threat as best we could. I mean if you were going to go down on a gun run, you were a bit lower but mostly we tried to stay above 10,000 feet. . . .

> We flew our jets in two configurations—the hunter configuration carried the LITENING II pod, a GBU-16, thousand-pound LGB, the gun, and two external fuel tanks. The killer configuration had a GBU-12, five-hundred-pound LGB on one side, a pod of five-inch Zuni rockets on the other side, external fuel tanks, and the gun. We did have masking problems with the FLIR pod, fuel tanks, and gun pod so we had to work out interesting cooperative tactics, especially in mountainous terrain. We used the gun about 40 percent of the time. Early on we had some gun issues and we had two guns which failed to operate . . . but we fixed these. This is a pet peeve of mine—you get a lot of

commanders that want to pull the guns off the plane because it's extra weight, drag, and training evolutions, but as long as I sit at the head of the squadron we will always have a gun on the plane. Of course there were problems with the gun installations, butterfly valves, and things like that. But you cannot go out on a three-hour CAS mission with a single bomb. You drop the bomb and you are done, other than flying and scaring them. . . .

With the six Night Attack Harrier IIs, we flew in excess of 3,700 hours, all with six aircraft. Normally with six aircraft, you are going to fly 100 to 120 hours per month. You might be able to surge something over that, but in Afghanistan we had several months where we pushed close to 500 hours on the six planes. My belief when I went there, since I had grown up in this community, was [that] the airplane has the capability to perform. So long as you can find a way to organize turning wrenches and someone is willing to give you spare parts, you can keep on flying. Fortunately we took with us a sixteen-plane or full squadron parts supply, and we upgraded that a bit after our site survey with stuff like additional tires and some electronic systems. Our struts took a beating there due to the poor runway, and they were in short supply.[10]

In September 2003, the detachment from VMA-513 returned to Yuma. In April 2004, a detachment of Harrier IIs from the 22nd MEU (SOC) operating off the USS *Wasp* again deployed to Kandahar air base in Afghanistan. Lt. Col. Sean Blochberger led the Harrier II detachment that was assigned to HMM-266, Medium Helicopter Squadron (reinforced). The pilots and support personnel of the Harrier II unit were drawn from VMA-542, which was located at MCAS Cherry Point. "We have been flying a lot of aerial reconnaissance missions, helicopter and convoy escort, and close air support," remarked Lieutenant Colonel Blochberger, adding that the most important component of their success "has been the Marines who, day after day, have been able to deliver ready-to-fly aircraft when the MEU needed them. Having jets available for the mission is a key factor, as the most skilled pilots cannot do their job without jets to fly and weapons to employ on the enemy."[11]

The commander of the 22nd MEU (SOC), Col. Kenneth F. McKenze Jr., said of the Harrier IIs, "Their speed, lethality, and intelligence-gathering capabilities have made them invaluable to our operations here." In addition to the Harrier II detachment, the 22nd MEU deployed helicopters from Medium Helicopter Squadron 266, Battalion Landing Team 1st BN, 6th Marines, and MEU Service Support Squadron 22 into Afghanistan. The Marine force operated alongside elements of the U.S. Army 25th Infantry Division, conducting military and civil support operations.[12]

F/A-18 fighter weapon systems officer Capt. James Hunt served as a ground-based FAC assigned to BLT 1. "My job is to advise the company commander on the use of air-delivered weapons," he says, "and ensure that the ordnance hits the right target at the right time. There are basic differences in controlling fixed-wing or rotary aircraft. It's easier to control rotary-wing aircraft (helicopters), because they are closer to the fighting and see the battlefield similar to the way the guys on the ground do. Usually jets are higher, faster, and farther away, so it makes it a little harder to guide them onto the target, but they carry heavier ordnance, so it is a tradeoff."

Capt. James Hunt called in strikes by Marine Corps Harrier IIs, Super Cobra attack helicopters, U.S. Army Apache attack helicopters, USAF A-10s, B-1B bombers, and AC-130 gunships.[13] Capt. Andrew Miller, a Harrier II pilot also based in Afghanistan, flew in Operation Iraqi Freedom. "Providing CAS to the grunts is the most rewarding thing a pilot can do," he says. "During OIF most of our missions were deep-strike missions far ahead of the troops on the ground. . . . But here everything we have done has been in direct support of our troops in contact, so it's good to know we're having a tangible effect on these engagements."[14]

On August 25, 2004, the UK Secretary of State announced the deployment of six RAF GR Mk. 7 Harrier II aircraft to Kandahar. The initial deployment included support personnel from No. 3 Squadron based at RAF Cottesmore and commanded by Gp. Capt. Andy Golledge. In addition, 53 Field Squadron, Royal Engineers, also deployed to undertake construction and repairs at the Kandahar air base for a total of nearly three hundred UK military personnel. The GR Mk. 7 aircraft arrived on September 27 and commenced air support operation on September 30. After a period of construction to enhance airfield facilities and training, the engineers left and the RAF Harrier II force and supporting personnel settled at about two hundred personnel.[15]

The RAF unit maintained two aircraft armed and available for takeoff, with pilots and support personnel available for takeoff within thirty minutes. RAF Harrier IIs were responsible for providing air support for U.S. forces continuing Operation Enduring Freedom, hunting Taliban and al-Qaeda units in the southeastern region of Afghanistan. In addition, the Harrier II detachment was also assigned to provide assistance as required for the International Security Assistance Force (ISAF) maintaining peacekeeping efforts in Afghanistan. The United Kingdom sent an infantry regiment as a contribution to the eight-thousand-person force, made of units from more than forty nations, which provides security in Kabul and northern Afghanistan.

Capt. Harvey Smith led the squadron of RAF Harrier II pilots assigned to the detachment. "There was a lot of bombing in this region until 2003, and people who are here know what airpower can bring to the party . . . We can mount a graduated response. If we arrive on the scene and a show of force doesn't do the trick, then we may fire a warning shot with a single rocket into a piece of desert. If that does not do the job, we can salvo off up to thirty-eight rockets."[16]

Early in 2005, personnel from No. 1 Squadron assumed responsibility for the detachment of GR Mk. 7 aircraft assigned to Kandahar. In March 2005 a number of GR Mk. 7A Harrier II aircraft from No. IV (AC) Squadron Joint Force Harrier, operating from the HMS *Invincible* off Pakistan, flew to Kandahar. The pilots flew operations alongside their counterparts from No 1. Squadron and eventually returned to the HMS *Invincible*.[17] Personnel from No. IV (AC) squadron assumed responsibility for operations mid-2005.

On May 3 the RAF Harrier II detachment at Kandahar, under the command of Wing Cdr. Andy Offer, dropped Paveway II laser-guided bombs and fired CRV-7 rockets for the first time in support of ground combat between allied forces and Taliban forces. In a speech on May 25, 2005, at RAF Wittering, RAF Air Chief Marshal Sir Brian Burridge remarked that the Joint Force Harrier was "doing a great job."[18]

In mid-2005 RAF No. 3 Squadron took over the Harrier II detachment, and in late 2005 No. IV (AC) personnel assumed responsibility. RAF pilots flying Harrier IIs flew nearly every day weather permitting. Missions were flown by a pair of aircraft, one armed with a 540-pound bomb, CRV-7 rocket pod, and the Digital Joint Reconnaissance pod; while the other Harrier II generally carried a TIALD pod and a 1,000-pound Paveway II laser-guided bomb. RAF Harrier II pilots flew a large number of reconnaissance and cover missions and also many air strikes in late 2005 and 2006, as the fighting with remnants of the Taliban regime intensified while U.S. troops were largely replaced by a NATO-led force. Not all of the action was one-way; two Harrier IIs were damaged by Taliban rocket fire in October 2005. The UK Harrier II commitment in Afghanistan is planned into 2007.

CHAPTER 14

Conclusion

T he Harrier and Harrier II constitute the first and second generation of
the most successful fixed-wing jet V/STOL tactical aircraft to have been
developed and fielded with operational units. It has been a long, challenging path to field the capable Harrier II V/STOL force that serves with the
U.S. Marine Corps, the Royal Air Force, and the naval air arms of Spain and
Italy. Without the determination of military, industrial, and political leaders in the
United Kingdom and the United States to continue investment in technology and
innovative concepts, even in the face of aircraft and human losses, the Harrier
would have been just a historical footnote.

More than five decades have passed since the original concept of a small
tactical aircraft capable of V/STOL using a centrally mounted vectored-thrust
turbine engine. It took several years for the idea to take root at Bristol engines
and to lead to the BE53 engine, which was later central to the Hawker P1127
aircraft design. By 1960 the P1127 prototypes were flying, and in the mid-1960s
the first Kestrels were flying with the multinational evaluation squadron.

The RAF fielded first-generation GR Mk. 1 Harriers with Nos. 1, 3, and IV
squadrons in the United Kingdom and in Germany at the end of the 1960s and
the early 1970s. The leaders of these units and command personnel developed the
concept of remote-site operations. Harrier pilots demonstrated the unique strike
capabilities of the aircraft V/STOL flexibility. The support personnel of the RAF
units worked hard to maintain the unique systems of this aircraft. Eventually the
RAF Harrier force was upgraded to the GR Mk. 3 configuration, with a laser
rangefinder in the nose and an advanced Ferranti navigation and attack system.
The positive elements of the Harrier were noticed, which led to the development
of the radar-equipped Sea Harrier for the Royal Navy.

The V/STOL Harrier was evaluated by many air arms. The 1968 flight
evaluation by the U.S. Marine Corps led to the offshore procurement of 110 first-
generation Harriers during the early 1970s. The Marine Corps benefited from the

RAF experience, but the operational employment concepts for the AV-8A were quite different, including regular amphibious operations from ships and austere land bases. The focus of Marine Corps AV-8A operations was basing flexibility, deployment of independent detachments, and provision of air support for ground forces with rapid responsiveness. In addition, the Marine Corps equipped their AV-8As with AIM-9 Sidewinder air-to-air missiles and 30mm cannon pods for air-to-air combat. Marine Corps test pilots perfected unique tactics, often employing vectored thrust, for air combat either in the self-defense mode or offense in the event that other fighter aircraft were not available. The AV-8A was upgraded to the AV-8C configuration late in the Harrier's operational life to add ECM capability and other enhancements.

The Spanish navy bought thirteen AV-8A and TAV-8A Harriers via the U.S. Navy, since Spain and the United Kingdom were still experiencing political problems in the 1970s. Spanish navy Harriers operated from Rota Naval Air Station and the wooden-deck aircraft carrier *Dedalo* (the former USS *Cabot*, a 15,800-ton escort carrier). The Indian navy also saw the benefits of V/STOL aircraft for naval air defense and strike. In the early 1980s the Indian government bought twenty-seven radar-equipped Sea Harriers and two-seat trainers to equip a fighter squadron and a training unit. The aircraft embarked on Indian navy aircraft carriers from their base at Goa in southwest India.

Although the first-generation Harrier had range and payload performance limitations and challenging flight characteristics, this should not have come as a surprise, considering that it was the first operational V/STOL tactical aircraft to serve with front-line squadrons in significant numbers. However, the performance of the Harrier was equal to or better than the aircraft that it replaced in the strike role (first-generation A-4B, C, and E for the USMC and the Hawker Hunter for the RAF) and added a whole new dimension of operational utility with its V/STOL capability.

The Harrier suffered criticism for its high accident rate. When the facts were reviewed, the combined loss rate for U.S. Marine Corps and RAF Harriers (fifty losses at 213,000 flight hours) was lower than the rate of other single-engine strike aircraft such as the A-4 (sixty-four) and A-7 (seventy-three) and slightly more than the rate of the USN/USMC twin-engine F-4 (forty-four) experienced at 213,000 total flight hours. Many RAF, U.S. Marine Corps, and Spanish navy pilots have remarked that the Harrier was the most exciting fighter they have ever flown.[1]

The United States Marine Corps, Royal Air Force, Spanish navy, Royal Navy, and Indian navy demonstrated the utility of the first-generation Harrier and Sea Harrier and have built up considerable experience with this unique weapons system. The two air arms with the largest Harrier fleets—the RAF and the U.S. Marine Corps—were sold on the benefits of the V/STOL aircraft and convinced their respective governments to sponsor the development of the second-generation Harrier II.

Airframe, avionics, and propulsions advancements enabled McDonnell Aircraft Company, British Aerospace, Rolls-Royce, and the other aerospace firms on the Harrier II team to create a more capable V/STOL aircraft, known as the AV-8B by the USMC and the GR Mk. 5 by the RAF. Planned enhancements led to the fielding of the TAV-8B two-seat trainer with the U.S. Marine Corps and the combat-capable T Mk. 10 with the RAF. The second-generation Harrier II entered service in 1982 as a day-attack strike aircraft. Its major advances were significantly improved handling qualities, a much more advanced computer controlled avionics suite, and greater range and payload.

The AV-8B day-attack jet has been replaced by improved versions of the Harrier IIs with enhanced capabilities. First the United States and the United Kingdom developed and fielded the AV-8B Night Attack aircraft. This new aircraft did not attract a lot of attention, but it was the first U.S. and UK tactical aircraft to incorporate an integrated forward infrared system that projected imagery on the HUD, as well as NVGs, which allowed effective operations at night. RAF aircraft also incorporated a moving map system and internal ECM suite. The U.S. Marine Corps (and later the RAF) added the higher-thrust F402-RR-408 Pegasus engine and increased countermeasure dispensers. Finally, in the 1990s the United States, Spain, and Italy funded the development of the Harrier II Plus, which combined all the developments of the Marine Corps night-attack aircraft and added the APG-65 radar.

Most viewers focus on the Harrier II in its military role, but readers should also remember the major accomplishments of this substantial multinational aviation development program. The governments and aviation industries of the United States, the United Kingdom, and later Spain and Italy worked together on a major collaborative development and production program that has fielded more than three hundred AV-8B Harrier II V/STOL tactical aircraft of five different variants. The development and production of the Harrier II continued from the first design concepts in the early 1970s and the first flight of the YAV-8B in 1978 until the final production delivery of the Harrier II Plus to Spain in late 2003.

The USMC has long been a proponent of V/STOL for CAS and strike operations. Throughout the life of the first- and second-generation Harrier, the USMC maintained this V/STOL tactical aircraft force through ongoing improvements in systems, equipment, and training. During the past three decades the USMC Harrier II has successfully demonstrated the utility of V/STOL capability in operations supporting U.S. objectives from peacekeeping and humanitarian efforts to several major conflicts.

The second-generation Harrier II has played a major role in two wars (the Gulf wars) and many lesser-known contingency operations. Harrier IIs played a major role in Operation Enduring Freedom in Afghanistan and Operation Iraqi Freedom in support of allied ground assaults. In the late 1980s the AV-8B program office embarked on ways to upgrade USMC and allied Harrier IIs to improve their capabilities. First it was night-attack capabilities, and later the addition of the APG-65 radar, to improve CAS performance. USMC Harrier IIs have been equipped with the ARC-210 UHF radio, a GPS receiver, and the ATHS. Perhaps the most significant recent upgrade was the integration of the LITENING II targeting pod, which finally gave Harrier II pilots the ability to detect and designate point targets at night and in poor weather and to employ laser-guided munitions.

In 2000 a contract for the first of several Open System Core Avionics Requirement (OSCAR) upgrades was awarded. This effort expanded the Harrier II's computer and systems performance to allow for the addition of new weapons including the AIM-120 AMRAAM (advanced medium-range air-to-air missile) and JDAM bombs.[2]

At the end of 2006, about seventy Harrier IIs remained in service with the UK Joint Force Harrier. This included four operational squadrons (Nos. 1, 800, 801, IV) and No. 20, the OTU/reserve squadron. RAF/RN Harrier IIs have gone through many upgrades to maintain their utility for land and ship operations. GR Mk. 7 aircraft have been refitted to carry the TIALD pods and joint reconnaissance pods. New armaments include Paveway II/III laser-guided bombs, the AGM-65G Maverick air-to-surface missile, as well as conventional general-purpose and cluster bombs.

Thirty of the aircraft are currently being retrofitted to the GR Mk. 7A standard with the Rolls-Royce Pegasus Mk. 107 engine, which provides an additional 1,500 to 3,000 pounds of thrust. All RAF/RN Harrier IIs are being upgraded to the GR Mk. 9/9A standard, which adds a new computer, stores management system, GPS/INS to allow for the carriage of Brimstone air-to-surface missiles, and other new systems. Harrier IIs assigned to Joint Force Harrier will be deployed to support UK military assignments including flying from HMS *Ark Royal* and HMS *Illustrious*.

The U.S. Marine Corps, Royal Air Force, Spanish navy, and Italian navy have already demonstrated the combat utility of their Harrier II V/STOL forces and the benefits of the tactical and logistical benefits of interoperability. The long-term plan is to maintain and expand USMC capability with the introduction of an all-V/STOL JSF tactical aircraft force. However, until the V/STOL F-35B JSF is successfully developed and fielded (current plans call for Harrier IIs to remain in service beyond 2015 and beyond), the Harrier II will serve on the leading edge of the USMC tactical aircraft and remain the sole strike fighter capable of deploying on the dozen LHA/LHD amphibious assault ships of the U.S. Navy. The United Kingdom, Italy, and Spain have similar plans to maintain their naval carrier aviation forces well into the twenty-first century, relying on the Harrier II and transitioning to the JSF.

The initial P1127 was criticized as being unable to carry a handkerchief across the airfield. An awesome flexibility-based weapons systems has evolved from the P1127 Harrier II Plus. This capability is a tribute to a team like no other—the international collaboration among military, government, and industry and its single-minded drive to achieve the V/STOL vision.

Appendix A: Timeline

AV-8B Harrier II Key Dates

1957   **August:** Using company funds, engineers at Hawker Siddeley in England begin design of the P.1127, a small jet fighter capable of vertical takeoff and landing (VTOL) capabilities.

1959   **March:** Hawker begins construction, again at its own expense, of two P.1127 prototype aircraft.

1959   **September:** Bristol Engines begins bench testing of the BE.53 Pegasus 1 engine.

1960   **June:** The British government issues contracts to cover the two Hawker P.1127 prototypes and provides additional funding for four more development aircraft.

1960   **October:** First vertical takeoff of the first P.1127 at Dunsford, England, with pilot Bill Bedford at the controls. The plane is designated XP831 as an experimental aircraft powered by a Pegasus 2 vectored-thrust turbofan.

1961   **March:** Conventional takeoff of the first prototype at Royal Aircraft Establishment, Bedford.

1961   **September:** First full transitions from vertical to horizontal flight (accelerating and decelerating) take place.

1962   **April:** Maiden flight of the first of four development aircraft on the additional power of a Pegasus 3 engine.

1963   **February:** Nine militarized P.1127s are ordered for operational evaluation as the Hawker F(GA).Mk 1 Kestrel.

1964   **March:** The first Kestrel is delivered to RAF West Raynham.

1964   **October:** The Kestrel Evaluation Squadron is formed with pilots from the United Kingdom's Royal Air Force, Germany's Luftwaffe, and the U.S. Air Force, Navy, and Army. The unit receives its first aircraft in December and operates until the end of November 1965. The squadron accumulates a total of 938 missions and some 600 hours of flying.

1965   **February:** Development of the Hawker P.1154 supersonic VTOL combat aircraft is canceled. However, Parliament affirms the need for a fully militarized vertical and short takeoff and landing (V/STOL) version of the Kestrel for the RAF's ground attack squadrons. A contract for six development aircraft is issued. The aircraft is designated the GR.Mk 1 Harrier and is to be powered by the Pegasus 6 engine.

1965   **December:** Six Kestrels are shipped to the United States, where they are given the designation XV-6A. They are evaluated by pilots from the Air Force at Edwards AFB; by the Navy, including carrier trails aboard USS *Independence* (CV 62); and by NASA.

1966   Rolls-Royce acquires Bristol's engine division.

1966   **August:** Maiden flight of the first of six preproduction Harriers.

1967   **December:** Maiden flight of the first of 60 production GR.Mk1 Harriers.

1968   **September:** The U.S. Marine Corps sends two pilots to the Farnborough Air Show to conduct a preliminary evaluation of the GR.Mk 1 Harrier.

1969   **April 1:** The first GR. Mk 1 Harrier squadron enters service with the Royal Air Force's Harrier Operational Conversion Unit.

1969   **April:** The first two-seat trainer version of the Harrier, T.Mk 2, makes its maiden flight.

1969   **September 30:** The U.S. House of Representatives authorizes procurement of the Harrier for the Marine Corps as a close air support aircraft.

1969   **December:** McDonnell Douglas and Hawker Siddeley agree to cooperate in the development of advanced versions of the Harrier, with the intention that future aircraft will be built in St. Louis.

1969   **December 23:** The U.S. government signs a contract with Hawker Siddeley for an initial 12 Harriers, designated AV-8A.

1970   **January:** The world's first V/STOL combat squadron, the RAF's No. 1 Squadron based at Wittering, becomes operational.

1970   **January:** McDonnell Douglas enters into licensing agreement with Hawker Siddeley to support the 110 AV-8A Harriers that the British company will deliver to the U.S. Marine Corps.

1970   **November 20:** First USMC AV-8A makes its first flight.

1971   **January:** Deliveries of British-built AV-8A Harriers begin to the U.S. Marine Corps.

1971   **April:** USMC's first AV-8A Harrier squadron, VMA-531, is established at Beaufort, SC.

1971   **June:** First flight of the GR.Mk 1A Harrier with the Pegasus 10 power plant (F402-RR-400).

1975   **May:** McDonnell Douglas proposes a new version of the Harrier, AV-8B, to meet Marine Corps requirements for an advanced vectored thrust V/STOL light attack aircraft.

The objective is to approximately double the payload and range of the original AV-8A Harrier.

1976   **January:** First flight of the GR.Mk 3 Harrier with nose-mounted laser rangefinder and target-seeker, and tail mounted radar-warning receiver.

1976   **July 27:** The Defense Department approves the development of the AV-8B Harrier II.

1977   **April:** Hawker Siddeley becomes part of British Aerospace (BAe).

1978   **November 9:** The first St. Louis–built Harrier, a conversion prototype YAV-8B, makes its maiden flight with McDonnell test pilot Charlie Plummer at the controls. It hovers 130 feet above the pavement at Lambert International Airport in St. Louis, Mo., in the successful seven-minute inaugural flight.

1979   **May:** The two YAV-8B Harrier II prototypes complete their scheduled flight test program at Patuxent River, MD.

1979   **October:** The first YAV-8B prototype engages in hovering trials at sea.

1981   **August:** A Memorandum of Understanding between MDC and BAe is signed covering the production of Harrier IIs as Harrier GR. Mk 5s for the RAF.

1981   **November 5:** First of four full-scale development AV-8B Harrier IIs makes its first flight, with test pilot Charlie Plummer at the controls.

1983   **April:** With McDonnell Aircraft Company experimental pilot Bill Lowe keeping his hands off the control stick, an FSD AV-8B Harrier II makes the first vertical autopilot controlled automatic landing at Patuxent River, MD.

1983   **August 29:** First production version of AV-8B Harrier II makes its maiden flight.

1984   **January 12:** The first of 12 pilot production AV-8B Harrier IIs is delivered to the U.S. Marine Corps.

1984   **November:** McDonnell Douglas announces plans for a night attack version of AV-8B.

1985   **January 12:** The AV-8B is introduced at a rollout ceremony

1985   **January 30:** Marine Attack Squadron VMA-331, the "Bumblebees," is commissioned as the first operational AV-8B squadron.

1985   **March:** The AV-8B completes its Operational Evaluation (OPEVAL).

1985   **August:** The AV-8B achieves Initial Operational Capability (IOC).

1985   **September:** The Department of Defense approves full-rate production for the AV-8B.

1985   **November:** The first production AV-8B is delivered to the U.S. Marine Corps.

1986   **March:** The first nonstop transatlantic flight by the AV-8B Harrier II. Marine Attack Squadron VMA 331 makes the 3,500-mile flight from Marine Corps Air Station Cherry Point, NC, to Naval Air Station Rota, Spain.

1986   **October 23:** Six AV-8B Harrier IIs from VMA-331 successfully complete night carrier landing exercises aboard the amphibious assault ship USS *Belleau Wood* (LHA 3).

1986   **November 21:** The TAV-8B, two-seat trainer version of the Harrier II, makes its maiden flight with McDonnell test pilot Bill Lowe at the controls.

1987   **June 26:** First AV-8B Harrier II equipped for night attack missions makes maiden flight.

1987   **July 24:** The first TAV-8B Harrier II is delivered to Marine Corps Air Station Cherry Point, NC.

1987   **September 16:** Rollout of the first EAV-8B for the Spanish navy. In Spain, the planes receive the designation VA.2 Matador II.

1987   **October 6:** The first three EAV-8Bs touch down at Naval Air Station Rota, Spain.

1988   **January:** The 100th AV-8B Harrier II is delivered. Marine Corps squadron VMA-542, based at Cherry Point, NC, accepts the aircraft.

1989   **June 10:** Marine Attack Squadron VMA-331 becomes first AV-8B squadron to deploy to Japan.

1989   **September 11:** A Harrier II shatters four time-to-climb records for V/STOL aircraft, including one that had been standing for 18 years. BAe and Rolls-Royce test pilots break the records in a Harrier GR Mk.5 during flights at Filton, England.

1989   **September 29:** Fourteen Harrier IIs from Marine Corps Air Station Cherry Point, NC, park on the McDonnell Douglas flight ramp during a visit to St. Louis. It is the largest number of AV-8Bs to gather at the site of their origin.

1990   **September 28:** A memorandum signed by the United States, Spain, and Italy formalizes a plan to jointly develop the radar-equipped AV-8B Harrier II Plus aircraft.

1991   **January 17:** With the opening air campaign of Operation Desert Storm, Marine Corps squadron VMA-311 becomes the first U.S. unit to fly the AV-8B Harrier II in combat. Two more Harrier II squadrons plus an additional six-plane detachment later joined the squadron. A fourth AV-8B squadron operates in the Persian Gulf from an amphibious assault ship.

1991   **August 23:** The Italian navy receives its first TAV-8B.

1992   **June 3:** The U.S. Navy authorizes production of the AV-8B Harrier II Plus.

1992   **September 22:** AV-8B Harrier II Plus makes first flight one month ahead of schedule.

1992   **November 17:** Italy signs a contract for the production of 16 Harrier II Plus aircraft. Final assembly of 13 of these aircraft will be in Italy.

1993   **March:** Spanish government authorizes purchase of eight Harrier II Plus aircraft.

1993   **August 5:** The first three operational AV-8B Harrier II Plus aircraft are delivered to VMA-542 at Marine Corps Air Station Cherry Point, NC.

1993   **December 21:** Marine Squadron VMA-223 picks up its first Harrier II Plus aircraft from McDonnell Douglas facilities in St. Louis.

1994   **April 20:** The Italian navy takes delivery of its first AV-8B Harrier II Plus. Formal delivery of the first three Harrier II Plus aircraft takes place on June 10 at Marine Corps Air Station Cherry Point, NC.

1994   **May:** The Navy signs a contract with McDonnell Douglas to begin remanufacture of 74 existing AV-8B aircraft into the Harrier II Plus configuration.

1996   **January:** The Harrier II Plus is introduced to the Spanish navy.

1997   **July:** The Spanish navy takes delivery of its eighth and last Harrier II Plus assembled at Construcciones Aeronauticas, S.A. (CASA) in Seville. The Spanish navy flies 10 AV-8B Harrier II day-attack aircraft and is considering remanufacturing them to the II Plus configuration.

1997   **November 25:** In a ceremony attended by the chief of staff of the navy, Italy accepts the 13th and final AV-8B Harrier II Plus assembled at Alenia's Aeronautics Division in Turin. This brings to 16 the total number of Harrier II Plus aircraft and two TAV-8B two-seat trainers flown by the Italian navy.

2000   **May 11:** The Boeing Company and the U.S. Naval Air Systems Command sign a contract that begins the remanufacturing program for Spain's EAV-8B day-attack Harriers. The contract calls for the remanufacture of two Harriers with an option for an additional seven currently in the Spanish navy's fleet. This effort will standardize the fleet to a common Harrier II Plus configuration.

2001   **June 1:** USMC first tests AMRAAM on an AV-8B Harrier II Plus aircraft.

2001   **July:** The Harrier TAV-8B Upgrade program completes its first aircraft.

2001   **July 26:** Spain announces plans for an Advanced Acquisition Contract to purchase an additional three remanufactured AV-8B Harrier II Plus aircraft.

2001   **November 3:** AV-8B Harrier IIs begin conducting combat missions in support of the war on terrorism in Afghanistan, Operation Enduring Freedom, operating from USS *Peleliu* (LHA-5) and *Bataan* (LHD-5).

2001   **December:** The U.S. Marine Corps accepts delivery of the first Litening II pods for AV-8B Harrier II aircraft.

2002   **May:** During a test at the Naval Warfare Center at China Lake, CA, an AV-8B successfully releases a 1,000-lb. JDAM.

2002   **October:** Harrier IIs from VMA-513 and supporting units are deployed from MCAS Yuma to Bagram air base, Afghanistan, in support of the war on terrorism.

2003   **March 17:** The U.S. Navy releases photos of AV-8B Harrier aircraft operating on amphibious assault ship decks in support of Operation Iraqi Freedom. USMC Harrier IIs operating from the amphibious assault ships USS Bataan (LHD 5), *Bonhomme Richard* (LHD 6), *Tarawa* (LHA-1), and *Nassau* (LHA 4) plus aircraft from the Marine Corps and RAF fly from land bases in Kuwait in support of operations in Iraq.

2003   **April:** The final AV-8B Harrier II Plus aircraft begins its move down the line in the final assembly area of Building 2 in St. Louis.

2003   **September 22:** The last remanufactured AV-8B Harrier II Plus moves from final assembly to ramp operations in Building 42 in St. Louis.

2003   **October 30:** The last remanufactured AV-8B Harrier II Plus makes its maiden flight from St. Louis Lambert International Airport.

2003   **December 5:** In a ceremony at Boeing facilities in St. Louis, MO, the final remanufactured AV-8B II Plus is delivered to the Spanish navy. Vice Admiral Enrique Valdes, assistant chief of staff, resources and logistics, Spanish navy, accepts the aircraft.

2004   **May:** Harrier IIs and personnel from USMC units VMA-214 and VMA-542 deploy to Iraq and provide support for continuing coalition operations.

2004   **September:** RAF GR. Mk. 7 Harrier IIs and support personnel from No. 3 Squadron and support personnel from various units deploy to Kandahar air base, Afghanistan, for ongoing peacekeeping operations.

Harrier II Squadrons

U.S. Marine Corps

MCAS Cherry Point, North Carolina

VMAT-203

Known as the Hawks, this Marine Corps Air Station Cherry Point, North Carolina–based unit has served as the Harrier training squadron for the U.S. Marine Corps, Spain and Italy, since 1976. The squadron received its first Harrier II in 1984. All Harrier II pilots rotate through this squadron for training in simulators, two-seat TAV-8Bs, and Harrier IIs before assignment to operational squadrons.

VMA-223

The Bulldogs squadron converted from the A-4M Skyhawk to the Harrier II in 1987. Located at MCAS Cherry Point, the unit has made numerous deployments on amphibious assault ships. In 1991 a detachment of Bulldogs provided cover for Operation Sharp Edge in Liberia. In 1994 the squadron received the radar-equipped Harrier II Plus aircraft. This squadron also was the first Marine Harrier II squadron to fly fifty thousand mishap-free flight hours. The Bulldogs flew in support of Operation Iraqi Freedom in 2003 from the USS *Bataan*.

VMA-231

The Aces flew the AV-8A Harrier starting in 1973 at MCAS Cherry Point, and transitioned to the AV-8B Harrier II in 1985. The squadron deployed to Kuwait for Operation Desert Shield, and its pilots flew 987 combat sorties in Operation Desert Storm. An AV-8B detachment on board amphibious ships supported the rescue of Capt. Scott O'Grady, an F-16 pilot shot down over Bosnia, and participated in Operation Deny Flight to support NATO operations in that region. The squadron received its first Harrier II Plus aircraft in 1995. A detachment from the Aces flew in support of Operation Iraqi Freedom from the USS *Nassau* in 2003.

VMA-331

Named the Bumblebees, VMA-331 converted from the A-4M Skyhawk to the AV-8B, at MCAS Cherry Point and stood up on January 30, 1983, as the first operational Harrier II squadron. The squadron deployed aboard the USS *Belleau Wood* in 1987; moved to Iwakuni, Japan, in 1989; and contributed 975 combat sorties in Operation Desert Storm in 1990. In 1992 the squadron was decommissioned.

VMA-542

In 1972 this unit converted to the AV-8A Harrier from the F-4 Phantom II at MCAS Beaufort, South Carolina. Known as the Tigers, the squadron moved to MCAS Cherry Point in 1974 and flew the Harrier until 1987, when the unit converted to the AV-8B. The Tigers flew more than one thousand combat sorties in support of Operations Desert Shield and Desert Storm. The squadron received the Harrier II Plus in 1995. In 2003 the Tigers flew in support of Operation Iraqi Freedom from the USS *Bataan*. In 2004 and 2005 the squadron deployed to Iraq and provided air support for ongoing Marine Corps peacekeeping operations.

MCAS Yuma, Arizona

VMA-211

The Wake Island Avengers, located at MCAS Yuma, Arizona, transitioned from the A-4M Skyhawk to the Night Attack model of the Harrier II in 1990. In 1992 a detachment from VMA-211 embarked on the first AV-8B Night Attack deployment overseas, aboard the USS *Tarawa*. The Wake Island Avengers flew from the USS *Bonhomme Richard* during Operation Iraqi Freedom. Today the unit flies a mix of Night Attack and radar-equipped Harrier II Plus aircraft.

VMA-214

Known as the Black Sheep squadron from its days flying Corsairs in World War II, VMA-214 is located at MCAS Yuma. The squadron transitioned from the A-4M Skyhawk to the Harrier II in 1989, becoming the first operational Night Attack squadron. In 1994, the squadron deployed in support of Operation Southern Watch in Southwest Asia and Operation United Shield off the coast of Somalia. In 1998 and 1999 the Black Sheep participated in Operation Desert Fox in the North Arabian Sea, and in 2003 flew in support of Operation Iraqi Freedom. The Black Sheep deployed to Iraq again in 2004 and 2005 and currently support Marine Corps operations in Operation Iraqi Freedom II.

VMA-311

Named the Tomcats, this squadron, based in Yuma, transitioned from the A-4M Skyhawk to the AV-8B in 1989. A year later the unit was deployed to Operation Desert Shield and became the first Harrier II squadron to see combat in Desert Storm, where its pilots flew one thousand combat sorties. In 1992 the Tomcats received Night Attack Harrier IIs. The squadron flew in support of Operation Iraqi Freedom from the USS *Bonhomme Richard* and the USS *Tarawa*. Today the squadron flies a mix of Night Attack and Harrier II Plus aircraft.

VMA-513

The Nightmares were the first Marine Corps squadron to fly the AV-8A, operating from MCAS Beaufort in 1971. In 1976 the unit moved to MCAS Cherry Point, and in 1984 it moved to MCAS Yuma, flying the upgraded AV-8C. In 1987 this unit became the first West Coast squadron to receive the Harrier II. Pilots from a detachment of VMA-513 aircraft aboard the USS *Tarawa* flew 130 combat missions during Operation Desert Storm. The unit also saw extensive service operating from amphibious assault ships in Operation Enduring Freedom and a 2002–03 deployment on the ground in Afghanistan.

Royal Air Force/Royal Navy Joint Harrier II Force Squadrons

No. 1

The squadron's motto, "First in all things," is appropriate, as this unit became the first to put the Harrier into service in 1969. This squadron flew the GR Mk. 1 and later the GR Mk. 3. Its pilots provided air support for UK ground forces in the 1982 Falkland Islands operation. In 1988 the unit converted to the GR Mk. 5 Harrier II, which has since been upgraded to the Mk. 7/9 Night Attack version. The squadron moved to RAF Cottesmore, UK, in 2000, participated in Operation Telec in Iraq in 2003, and supported ongoing operations at Kandahar, Afghanistan, from 2004 to 2006.

No. 3

In 1972 this squadron received its first GR Mk. 1 and GR Mk. 3 Harriers, and served as a front-line unit in Germany. No. 3 squadron converted to the Harrier II in 1989. The squadron moved to RAF Cottesmore in April 1999. Harrier II aircraft from this unit supported NATO air cover operations over Iraq and participated in Operation Iraqi Freedom and the 2004–5 assignment to Afghanistan. In early 2006 No. 3 squadron ended more than thirty years of Harrier operations when it moved to RAF Coningsby and became the first operational Eurofighter Typhoon squadron.

No. IV

In 1970 this unit moved to Germany, operating GR Mk. 1 and later GR Mk. 3 Harriers. No. IV squadron received the GR Mk. 7 Night Attack Harrier II aircraft in 1990. Pilots from this unit supported NATO efforts over Yugoslavia in Operations Deliberate Force and Allied Force. The squadron moved to RAF Cottesmore in April 1999, and participated in Operation Iraqi Freedom in 2003 and ongoing operations in Kandahar, Afghanistan, from 2004 to 2006.

No. 20

This squadron was assigned GR Mk.1 and later GR Mk. 3 Harriers and operated in support of RAF Germany. Between 1977 and early 1992 the squadron operated first the Jaguar and then Tornado aircraft. In late 1992 this unit took over Harrier II training from No. 233 Operational Conversion Unit, and today the unit operates a mix of GR Mk. 7 and T Mk. 10 Harrier IIs from RAF Wittering, UK.

800 Naval Air Squadron

After the retirement of the F/A2 Sea Harrier and departure from Yeovil in early 2006, 800 Squadron was reactivated at RAF Wittering and became part of Joint Force Harrier as a part of No. 1 Group, RAF Strike Command, flying the GR Mk. 7 Harrier II.

801 Naval Air Squadron

Following the retirement of the F/A2 Sea Harrier, 801 Squadron was reactivated in 2006 at RAF Wittering as a part of the Joint Force Harrier flying GR Mk. 9 Harrier IIs.

Spanish Navy, Arma Aerea de la Armada Española

9 Squadron

This squadron was established in 1987 and received the first of twelve EAV-8B Harrier IIs. In 1990, Spain signed a memorandum of understanding with the United States and Italy for the development of the Harrier II Plus. Spain ordered eight Harrier II Plus aircraft, and the first of these was delivered from the CASA Seville plant in 1996. Five older AV-8B aircraft have been upgraded to the Harrier II Plus configuration. Harriers and Harrier IIs operated from the Rota Naval Base in Spain and the carrier *Príncipe de Asturias*.

8 Squadron

This pioneering tactical unit flew the thirteen AV-8S and TAV-8S Matador Harrier aircraft operated by the naval air arm from 1976 to 1996 from its base at Rota, and from the carrier *Dedalo*. In 1998, the Spanish navy sold nine AV-8S and two TAV-8S aircraft to the Royal Thai Navy.

Italian Navy, Gruppo Aerei Imbarcati

In 1989 the Italian parliament approved procure-ment by the Italian navy of fixed-wing aircraft for operations from their ski jump–equipped aircraft carrier, Giuseppe Garibaldi. In 1991 two Italian navy TAV-8Bs landed on Giuseppe Garibaldi, and the air arm was in the aviation business. Sixteen Harrier II Plus aircraft were delivered beginning in 1995. In 1995 a detachment of Italian Harrier IIs assisted the evacuation of the UN peace-keeping force from Somalia. An Italian task force led by Giuseppe Garibaldi deployed with eight Harrier II Plus aircraft and three escorts in support of Operation Enduring Freedom in Afghanistan in 2002.

The first Hawker P1127 prototype demonstrating its hover capability. This series of aircraft demonstrated the V/STOL and growth capability of the Harrier design. *Photo: BAeS*

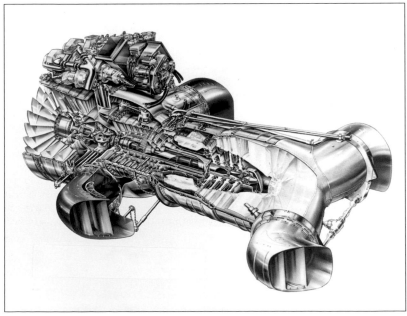

The cutaway view of the Rolls-Royce Pegasus engine. The compact engine with four rotating nozzles made possible the Harrier's V/STOL capability. *Photo: Rolls-Royce*

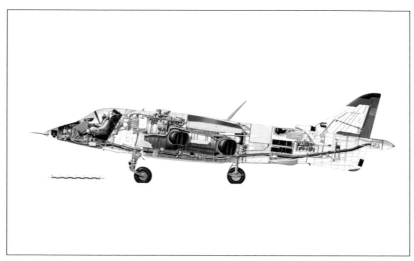

This side view of the Hawker Siddeley Marrier Mk. 50 demonstrates the central engine placement and compact configuration of the aircraft. *Photo: BAeS*

An RAF GR Mk. 3 Harrier located in Germany showing its unique hover capability. Several RAF Harrier squadrons were forward based in Germany in support of NATO for the latter part of the Cold War. *Photo: BAeS*

Royal Navy Sea Harrier refueling on an *Invincible*-class aircraft carrier. The Sea Harrier demonstrated its air combat performance by downing twenty Argentine aircraft for zero losses during the 1982 Falkland Islands conflict. *Photo: BAeS*

This photograph taken in December 1987 shows one of the two YAV-8B prototypes in flight with a U.S. Marine Corps AV-8A Harrier. The YAV-8B demonstrated the improved performance of the larger composite supercritical wing. *Photo: McDonnell Douglas*

One of the YAV-8B prototypes during a 1982 weapons test flight dropping twenty-four Mk.82, 500-pound bombs. *Photo: McDonnell Douglas*

AV-8Bs on the assembly line at the McDonnell Aircraft Company plant in St. Louis, Mo., 1982. More than 300 AV-8B aircraft were built on this production line from 1980 to 2003. *Photo: McDonnell Douglas*

The first flight of the AV-8B with test pilot Charlie Plummer at the controls in St. Louis, Mo., November 5, 1981. *Photo: McDonnell Douglas*

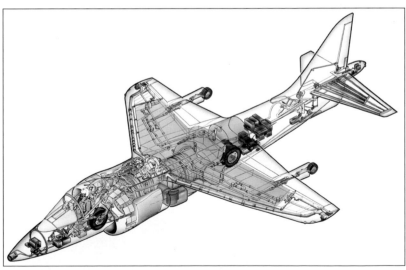

A cutaway drawing showing the configuration of the AV-8B day-attack aircraft. This shows the location of the major systems–including the engine, fuel, avionics, and reactions control systems–and pilot. *Photo: McDonnell Douglas*

Image of a Spanish navy AV-8B Matador climbing. The Spanish navy bought a dozen AV-8Bs, which were delivered in 1987–88. *Photo: McDonnell Douglas*

A two-seat TAV-8B trainer in hover assigned to VMAT-203 at MCAS Cherry Point, N.C. All USMC and many international Harrier II pilots have been trained by this training squadron. *Photo: USMC*

An AV-8B hovering near the U.S. Capitol Building during a U.S. Marine Corps aviation demonstration following the Gulf War in May 1991. *Photo: McDonnell Douglas*

U.S. Marine Corps AV-8B Harrier IIs deployed at a remote site. One of the major advantages of the Harrier and Harrier II was its capability to operate from short strips located near the battle zone. Marine Corps squadrons held regular exercises to practice this capability. *Photo: McDonnell Douglas*

An AV-8B from VMA-311, the Tomcats, flying over burning oil wells in Kuwait at the end of the 1991 Gulf War. *Photo: USMC*

An RAF GR Mk. 7 Harrier II in flight over the English countryside while on a pre-delivery test flight. The RAF bought ninety-six Harrier II aircraft. *Photo: BAeS*

Three of the thirteen T. Mk. 10 two-seat Harrier II aircraft delivered to the RAF. These aircraft are equipped with the full mission suite to allow them to perform both training and operational missions. *Photo: BAeS*

On August 23, 1991, two TAV-8B Harrier II aircraft landed on the Italian navy aircraft carrier *Giuseppe Garibaldi*, docked at Norfolk, Va. The delivery of these aircraft equipped the Italian navy with a modern fighter aircraft. Italy became the fourth customer for the Harrier II. *Photo: McDonnell Douglas*

The first AV-8B Night Attack aircraft on a test flight in May 1987. The Night Attack aircraft was the first major update for the Harrier II. Eventually all RAF aircraft and sixty-six USMC aircraft incorporated night-attack systems.
Photo: McDonnell Douglas

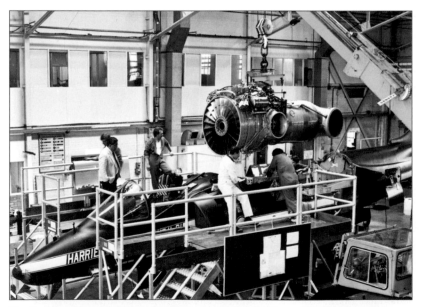

The first Pegasus -408 improved engine being installed in an RAF GR Mk. 5 test aircraft ZD402 in April 1989. This aircraft and engine went on to achieve four time-to-climb records. *Photo: Rolls-Royce*

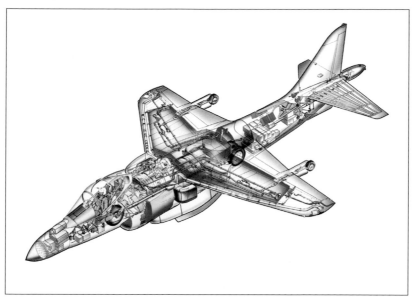

Cutaway view of the AV-8B Harrier II Plus aircraft which included the night-attack sensors and systems plus the APG-65 radar. The USMC, Spanish navy, and Italian navy fly the Harrier II Plus. *Photo: McDonnell Douglas*

British Aerospace, McDonnell Douglas, and Rolls-Royce personnel in front of the 96th single-seat Harrier II for the RAF. This photo taken on December 17, 1987, highlights the transatlantic team involved with the development and production of the Harrier II. *Photo: BAeS*

Part of the Spanish production team responsible for the assembly of the Harrier II Plus aircraft at the CASA plant in Spain. *Photo: CASA*

A GR Mk. 7 of RAF No. 1 Squadron on the ground at Al Jabber Air Base Kuwait. RAF Harrier II pilots provided close air and strike support for coalition forces during Operation Iraqi Freedom, and a Harrier II detachment also operated in Afghanistan. *Photo: Wing Commander Suddards*

Appendix B: Production History, Part 1

Part 1: AV-8 Procurement

AV-8B HARRIER II

CALENDAR DELIVERIES	YR	80	81	82	83	84	85	86	87	88	89	90	91	92	93	94	95	96	97	98	99	00	01	02	03
USMC	YR			4	1	12	24	30	35	46	39	24	22	17	16	16									
	CUM			4	5	17	41	71	106	152	191	215	237	254	270	286									
USMC REMAN.	YR																	4	4	10	12	12	12	14	6
	CUM																	4	8	18	30	42	54	68	74
GR-Mk.5 ASSY	YR					3	2	5	22	20	23	20	1												
	CUM					3	5	10	32	52	75	95	96												
SPAIN	YR								6	6								5	3						5
	CUM								6	12								17	20						5
T-Mk.10	YR														6	6	1								
	CUM														6	12	13								
ITALY	YR																2	5	6						
	CUM																2	7	13						
TOTAL	YR			4	1	15	26	35	63	72	62	44	23	17	22	22	3	14	13	10	12	12	12	14	11
	CUM			4	5	20	46	81	144	216	278	322	345	362	384	406	409	423	436	446	458	470	482	496	507

Does not include 2 YAV-8B prototypes built in 1978 and 1979

Appendix B: Production History, Part 2

U.S. Marine Corps

(These tables are reproduced courtesy of the Royal Air Force Charitable Trust Enterprises.)

Serial	Variant	Build No	First Fit	Delivery	Operator, location or fate
Fiscal Year 1979					
161396	AV-8B-1	512001/1	05-Nov-81	22-Apr-82	Naval Test and Evaluation Museum, NAS Pensacola
161397	AV-8B-1	512002/2	07-Apr-82	23-Apr-82	MDA, St. Louis
161398	AV-8B-1	512003/3	10-Apr-82	16-Apr-82	Indian Head, preserved
161399	AV-8B-1	512004/4	04-Jun-83	08-Jun-82	Patuxent River, preserved
Fiscal Year 1982					
161573	AV-8B-2	512005/5	29-Aug-83	14 Nov-83	USMC, cr Kuwait, 23-Feb-91 (VMA-542) (Failed to recover from a high angle, night weapons delivery on a tank park near Ali Al Salem Airfield)
161574	AV-8B-2	512006/6	14-Nov-83	03-Feb-84	USMC VMAT-203, Cherry Point
161575	AV-8B-2	512007/7	17-Jan-84	23-Feb-84	USMC NADEP, Cherry Point
161576	AV-8B-2	512008/8	04-Jun-84	16-Jul-84	MDA, St. Louis
161577	AV-8B-2	512009/9	22-May-84	12-Jul-84	USMC MALS-14, Cherry Point
161578	AV-8B-2	512010/10	21-Jun-84	26-Jul-84	USMC, cr 31-Mar-85 (VMAT-203)
161579	AV-8B-3	512011/11	16-Jul-84	24-Aug-84	USMC NADEP, Cherry Point
161580	AV-8B-3	512012/12	20-Jul-84	14-Sep-84	USMC NADEP, Cherry Point
161581	AV-8B03	512013/13	02-Aug-84	07-Sep-84	USMC
165306	AV-8B+-23	264		May-96	MDA
161582	AV-8B-3	512014/14	24-Aug-84	28-Nov-84	USMC, cr Cherry Point, 13-Jul-88 (VMAT-203)
161583	AV-8B-3	512015/15	12-Sep-84	21-Dec-84	USMC
165307	AV-8B+-23	265		Aug-96	MDA
161584	AV-8B-3	512016/16	15-Oct-84	03-Jan-85	USMC, AMARC stored, Davis-Monthan AFB

Legend:

cr: crash

R: remanufacture

SR: Spanish remanufacture

*VMA-231 deployed to Yuma, a/c delivered to them in Yuma

** SR-1-2 ferry to Spain 08-Aug-03

***SR-3-5 ferry to Spain 14-Dec-03

Serial	Variant	Build No	First Fit	Delivery	Operator, location or fate
Fiscal Year 1983					
162068	AV-8B-4	512017/17	03-Nov-84	19-Jan-85	USMC
165310	AV-8B+-24	268		May-97	USMC NADEP, Cherry Point
162069	AV-8B-4	512018/18	18-Dec-84	01-Mar-85	USMC VMAT-203, Cherry Point
162070	AV-8B-4	512019/19	30-Nov-84	27-Dec-84	USMC NADEP, Cherry Point
162071	AV-8B-4	512020/20	11-Dec-84	28-Dec-84	USMC, cr Nellis AFB, 11-Feb-88 (VMA-331) (Engine flamed-out)
162072	AV-8B-4	512021/21	17-Jan-85	18-Mar-85	USMC, AMARC stored, Davis-Monthan AFB
162073	AV-8B-4	512022/22	26-Feb-85	01-May-85	USMC, cr Barnegat Bay, NJ, 05-Jun-87 (VMA-331) (Engine flamed-out)
162074	AV-8B-4	512023/23	02-Mar-85	27-Mar-85	USMC
165311	AV-8B+-24	269		Jul-97	USMC NADEP, Cherry Point
162075	AV-8B-4	512024/24	11-Apr-85	06-May-85	USMC VMAT-203, Cherry Point
162076	AV-8B-4	512025/25	11-Apr-85	30-May-85	MDA, St. Louis
162077	AV-8B-5	512026/26	23-Apr-85	14-Jun-85	USMC NADEP, Cherry Point
162078	AV-8B-5	512027/27	15-May-85	26-Jul-85	USMC, cr 04-May-90 (VMAT-203)
162079	AV-8B-5	512028/28	18-May-85	26-Jun-85	USMC, cr Cherry Point, 27-Feb-86 (VMA-331) (Control lost)
162080	AV-8B-5	512029/29	08-Jun-85	30-Jun-85	USMC NADEP, Cherry Point
162081	AV-8B-5	512030/30	08-Jun-85	02-Jul-85	USMC, cr Central Kuwait, 09-Feb-91 (VMA-231) (Shot down by shoulder-launched SAM)
162082	AV-8B-5	512031/31	19-Jun-85	22-Jul-85	USMC
165308	AV-8B+-23	266	Nov-96		USMC
162083	AV-8B-5	512032/32	26-June-85	24-Jul-85	USMC
165309	AV-8B+-24	267		Feb-97	USMC NADEP, Cherry Point
162084	AV-8B-5	512033/33	16-Jul-85	15-Aug-85	USMC, AMARC stored, Davis-Monthan AFB
162085	AV-8B-5	512034/34	26-Jul-85	28-Aug-85	USMC NADEP, Cherry Point
162086	AV-8B-5	512035/35	5-Aug-85	16-Sep-85	USMC VMA-223, Cherry Point
162087	AV-8B-5	512036/36	17-Aug-85	09-Oct-85	USMC
165312	AV-8B+-24	270		Sep-97	USMC NADEP, Cherry Point
162088	AV-8B-5	512037/37	29-Aug-85	15-Oct-85	USMC VMA-231, Cherry Point
Fiscal Year 1984					
162721	AV-8B-6	512038/38	06-Sep-85	18-Oct-85	USN VX-9, China Lake
162722	AV-8B-6	512039/39	27-Sep-85	12-Nov-85	USMC, AMARC stored, Davis-Monthan AFB
162723	AV-8B-6	512040/40	17-Oct-85	07-Nov-85	USMC VMAT-203, Cherry Point

Serial	Variant	Build No	First Fit	Delivery	Operator, location or fate
162724	AV-8B-6	512044/41	24-Oct-85	04-Dec-85	USMC, cr Yuma Range, 17-Jan-86 (VMA-231) (Bird strike)
162725	AV-8B-6	512045/42	25-Oct-85	09-Jan-86	USMC VMAT-203, Cherry Point
162726	AV-8B-6	512046/43	16-Nov-85	14-Jan-86	USMC NADEP, Cherry Point
162727	AV-8B-6	512047/44	21-Nov-85	14-Jan-86	USMC, cr Villagarcia de la Torre, Spain, 11-Nov-91 (VMA-223)
162728	AV-8B-6	512048/45	07-Dec-85	20-Jan-86	USMC
165305	AV-8B+-23	263	29-Nov-95	Feb-96	USN VX-9, China Lake
162729	AV-8B-6	512049/46	07-Jan-86	20-Feb-86	USMC VMA-231, Cherry Point
162730	AV-8B-6	512050/47	10-Jan-86	27-Jan-86	USMC VMA-231, Cherry Point
162731	AV-8B-6	512051/48	18-Feb-86	08-Apr-86	USMC VMAT-203, Cherry Point
162732	AV-8B-6	512052/49	10-Feb-86	14-Apr-86	USMC, AMARC stored, Davis-Monthan AFB
162733	AV-8B-6	512053/50	26-Feb-86	08-Apr-86	USMC VMA-231, Cherry Point
162734	AV-8B-6	512054/51	26-Feb-86	27-Mar-86	USMC, cr 10-Feb-90 (VMAT-203)
162735	AV-8B-7	512055/52	13-Mar-86	21-Apr-86	USMC, cr Cherry Point, 19-Jun-90 (VMA-331) (Aborted take-off)
162736	AV-8B-7	512056/53	02-Apr-86	09-May-86	USMC, cr off South Carolina coast, 18-Sep-95 (VMAT-203) (Collided with TAV-8B 164138)
162737	AV-8B-7	512057/54	22-Apr-86	13-Jun-86	USMC VMAT-203, Cherry Point
162738	AV-8B-7	512058/55	07-May-86	17-Jun-86	USMC VMAT-203, Cherry Point
162739	AV-8B-7	512059/56	27-May-86	14-Jul-86	USMC VMA-231, Cherry Point
162740	AV-8B-7	512060/57	10-Jun-86	25-Jul-86	USMC, cr NW Kuwait, 27-Feb-91 (VMA-331) (Shot down by SA-7 surface-to-air-missile)
162741	AV-8B-7	512061/58	10-Jun-86	25-Jul-86	USMC VMA-231, Cherry Point
162742	AV-8B-7	512062/59	20-Jun-86	28-Aug-86	USMC VMAT-203, Cherry Point
162743	AV-8B-7	512063/60	27-Jun-86	08-Aug-86	USMC, cr in Red Sea, 20-Mar-91 (VMA-331)
162744	AV-8B-7	512064/61	01-Aug-86	02-Oct-86	USMC VMA-231, Cherry Point
162745	AV-8B-7	512065/62	07-Aug-86	29-Aug-86	USMC, cr 04-Nov-86 (VMA-542) (Collided with F/A-18A 161981)
162746	AV-8B-7	512066/63	27-Aug-86	17-Oct-86	USMC, cr Cherry Point, 12-Jan-87 (VMAT-203)
162747	AV-8B-7	212201/T1	21-Oct-86	09-Dec-86	MDA, St. Louis
Fiscal Year 1985					
162942	AV-8B-8	512067/64	20-Sep-86	27-Oct-86	USMC, cr 23 miles NE of Ie Shima Island, Pacific Ocean, 26-Jan-90 (VMA-542)
162943	AV-8B-8	512068/65	22-Sep-86	24-Oct-86	USMC VMAT-203, Cherry Point
162944	AV-8B-8	512069/66	06-Oct-86	07-Nov-86	USMC VMAT-203, Cherry Point
162945	AV-8B-8	512070/67	13-Nov-86	11-Dec-86	USMC, cr in Atlantic, 150 km off NC coast, 10-Oct-95 (VMAT-203)
162946	AV-8B-8	512074/68	08-Nov-86	30-Nov-86	USMC VMAT-203, Cherry Point
162947	AV-8B-8	512075/69	21-Nov-86	22-Dec-86	USN NAWS, China Lake

Serial	Variant	Build No	First Fit	Delivery	Operator, location or fate
162948	AV-8B-8	512076/70	21-Nov-86	13-Dec-86	USMC, AMARC stored, Davis-Monthan AFB
162949	AV-8B-8	512077/71	05-Dec-86	15-Jan-87	USMC VMAT-203, Cherry Point
162950	AV-8B-8	512078/72	13-Dec-86	16-Jan-87	USMC NADEP, Cherry Point
162951	AV-8B-8	512079/73	31-Dec-86	24-Feb-87	USMC NADEP, Cherry Point
162952	AV-8B-8	512080/74	22-Jan-87	20-Feb-87	USMC, cr in Mediterranean off Turkey, 08-Oct-88 (VMA-331)
162953	AV-8B-8	512081/75	26-Jan-87	23-Feb-87	USMC VMAT-203, Cherry Point
162954	AV-8B-8	512082/76	03-Feb-87	20-Mar-87	USMC, cr during Desert Storm, 22-Jan-97 (VMA-331) (Flew into sea on night approach to USS Nassau)
162955	AV-8B-8	512083/77	21-Feb-87	25-Mar-87	USMC, cr Cherry Point, 10-Aug-93 (VMA-231)
162956	AV-8B-8	512084/78	14-Feb-87	12-Mar-87	USMC VMA-211, Yuma
162957	AV-8B-8	512085/79	04-Mar-87	10-Apr-87	USMC VMA-214, Yuma
162958	AV-8B-8	512086/80	12-Mar-87	23-Apr-87	USMC VMA-214, Yuma
162959	AV-8B-8	512087/81	03-Apr-87	30-Apr-87	USMC VMA-211, Yuma
162960	AV-8B-8	512088/82	08-Apr-87	11-May-87	USMC VMA-211, Yuma
162961	AV-8B-8	512089/83	08-Apr-87	07-May-87	USMC, cr Twenty-Nine Palms range, CA, 09-Oct-87 (VMA-542)
162962	AV-8B-8	512090/84	24-Apr-87	29-May-87	USMC VMAT-203, Cherry Point
162963	TAV-8B-9	212202/T2	12-Jun-87	23-Jul-87	USMC, Cherry Point
162964	AV-8B-8	512091/85	14-May-87	08-Jun-87	USMC VMA-542-Cherry Point
162965	AV-8B-9	512092/86	15-May-87	08-Jun-87	USMC VMA-513, Iwakuni
162966	AV-8B-9	512093/87	26-Jun-87	26-Jun-87	USN, cr near China Lake, 27-Sep-94 (NAWS)
162967	AV-8B-9	512094/88	04-Jun-87	30-Jul-87	USMC VMAT-203, Cherry Point
162968	AV-8B-9	512095/89	09-Jun-87	01-Jul-87	USMC VMA-214, Yuma
162969	AV-8B-9	512096/90	26-Jun-87	18-Jul-87	USMC VMA-513, Iwakuni
162970	AV-8B-9	512097/91	17-Jul-87	18-Aug-87	USMC, cr 08-Aug-90 (VMA-513)
162971	TAV-8B-9	212203/T3	18-Sep-87	03-Oct-87	USMC NADEP, Cherry Point
162972	AV-8B-9	512098/92	23-Jul-87	13-Aug-87	USMC VMA-223, Cherry Point
162973	AV-8B-9	512099/93	28-Aug-87	25-Sep-87	USMC VMA-223, Cherry Point

Fiscal Year 1986

Serial	Variant	Build No	First Fit	Delivery	Operator, location or fate
163176	AV-8B-10	512100/94	06-Oct-87	29-Oct-87	USMC VMA-513, Iwakuni
163177	AV-8B-10	512101/95	11-Oct-87	31-Oct-87	USMC, cr Cherry Point, 21-Jun-94 (VMA-223) (Engine failure)
163178	AV-8B-10	512102/96	21-Oct-87	06-Nov-87	USMC VMA-214, Yuma
163179	AV-8B-10	512103/97	09-Nov-87	30-Nov-87	USMC VMA-223- Cherry Point
163180	TAV-8B-10	212204/T4	28-Oct-87	30-Nov-87	USMC NADEP, Cherry Point
163181	AV-8B-10	512104/98	14-Nov-87	19-Dec-87	USMC, cr 09-Dec-92 on a flight from Yuma (VMA-214)
163182	AV-8B-10	512105/99	15-Nov-87	12-Dec-87	USMC, cr Piney Island range, 01-Mar-88 (VMA-542)
163183	AV-8B-10	512106/100	03-Dec-87	22-Dec-87	USMC VMA-223-Cherry Point

Serial	Variant	Build No	First Fit	Delivery	Operator, location or fate
163184	AV-8B-10	512107/101	02-Dec-87	17-Dec-87	USMC, cr Maxwell AFB, AL, 05-Nov-88 (VMA-542)
163185	AV-8B-10	512108/102	09-Dec-87	29-Dec-87	USMC, cr Parris Island, SC, 03-May-89 (VMA-542)
163186	TAV-8B-10	212205/T5	28-Jan-88	23-Mar-88	USMC VMAT-203, Cherry Point
163187	AV-8B-10	512109/103	16-Dec-87	17-Jan-88	USMC, cr Twenty-Nine Palms ranges, CA, 12-Feb-90 (VMA-223)
163188	AV-8B-10	512110/104	20-Dec-87	15-Jan-88	USMC VMA-223, Cherry Point
163189	AV-8B-10	512111/105	22-Jan-88	01-Mar-88	USMC VMA-231, Cherry Point
163190	AV-8B-10	106	22-Jan-88	07-Mar-88	USMC, cr Al Jaber airfield, Kuwait, 25-Feb-91 (VMA-542) (Shot down by shoulder-launched SAM)
163191	TAV-8B-10	T6	30-Mar-88	28-Apr-88	USN NAWS, China Lake
163192	AV-8B-10	107	09-Feb-88	07-Mar-88	USMC VMA-214, Yuma
163193	AV-8B-10	108	25-Feb-88	28-Mar-88	USMC VMA-214, Yuma
163194	AV-8B-10	109	23-Feb-88	16-Mar-88	USMC VMA-214, Yuma
163195	AV-8B-10	110	10-Mar-88	31-Mar-88	USMC, cr Cherry Point, 16-Feb-96 (VMA-231)
163196	TAV-8B-11	T7	20-June-88	15-Jul-88	USMC VMAT-203, Cherry Point
163197	AV-8B-11	111	16-Mar-88	04-May-88	USMC VMA-542, Cherry Point
163198	AV-8B-11	112	30-Mar-88	02-May-88	USMC VMA-231, Cherry Point
163199	AV-8B-11	113	12-Apr-88	08-Jun-88	USMC VMA-542, Cherry Point
163200	AV-8B-11	114	21-Apr-88	22-May-88	USMC VMA-223, Cherry Point
163201	AV-8B-11	115	21-Apr-88	26-May-88	USMC VMA-231, Cherry Point, cr 16-Jul-03
163202	TAV-8B11	T8	30-Aug-88	20-Sep-88	USMC, cr Cherry Point, 28-Aug-89 (VMAT-203)
163203	AV-8B-11	116	13-May-88	04-Jun-88	USMC VMA-211, Yuma
163204	AV-8B-11	117	12-May-88	16-Jun-88	USMC VMA-211, Yuma
163205	AV-8B-11	118	18-May-88	15-Jul-88	USMC VMA-223, Cherry Point
163206	AV-8B-11	119	26-May-88	07-Jul-88	USMC VMA-223, Cherry Point, cr 07-Oct-96, AZ
163207	TAV-8B-11	T9	22-Oct-88	14-Dec-88	USMC NADEP, Cherry Point

Fiscal Year 1987

Serial	Variant	Build No	First Fit	Delivery	Operator, location or fate
163419	AV-8B-11	120	25-May-88	22-Jun-88	USMC NADEP, Cherry Point, cr 03-Feb-01 (VMAT-203)
163420	AV-8B-11	121	10-Jun-88	01-Jul-88	USMC, cr off Cox's Bazaar, Bangladesh, 15-May-91 (VMA-513)
163421	AV-8B-11	122	20-Jun-88	14-Jul-88	USMC, cr Raleigh, NC, 15-Oct-93 (VMA-231) (Bird strike)
163422	AV-8B-11	123	23-Jun-88	30-Jul-88	USMC, cr 18-Feb-95 (VMA-542)
163423	AV-8B-11	124	12-Jul-88	29-Sep-88	USMC VMA-211, Yuma
163424	AV-8B-11	125	14-Jul-88	04-Aug-88	USMC VMA-223, Cherry Point
163425	AV-8B-11	126	27-Jul-88	23-Aug-88	USMC, cr Camp Lejeune, NC, 22-Sep-93 (VMA-231)
163426	AV-8B-11	127	01-Aug-88	26-Aug-88	USMC VMA-542, Cherry Point

Serial	Variant	Build No	First Fit	Delivery	Operator, location or fate
163514	AV-8B-11	128	23-Jul-88	10-Aug-88	USMC, cr 19-Aug-92 (VMA-231)
163515	AV-8B-11	129	08-Aug-88	16-Sep-88	USMC VMA-542, Cherry Point
163516	AV-8B-11	130	22-Aug-88	16-Sep-88	USMC, cr East China Sea, 01-Sep-95 (VMA-542)
163517	AV-8B-11	131	31-Aug-88	29-Sep-88	USMC VMA-513, Iwakuni
163518	AV-8B-11	132	10-Sep-88	30-Sep-88	USMC, cr Southern Kuwait, 24-Jan-91 (VMA-311) (Shot down by shoulder-launched SAM)
163519	AV-8B-11	133	16-Sep-88	05-Oct-88	USMC VMA-311, Yuma

Fiscal Year 1988

Serial	Variant	Build No	First Fit	Delivery	Operator, location or fate
163659	AV-8B-12	134	04-Oct-88	02-Nov-88	USMC VMA-542, Cherry Point
163660	AV-8B-12	135	02-Oct-88	02-Nov-88	USMC VMA-214, Yuma
163661	AV-8B-12	136	15-Oct-88	11-Nov-88	USMC VMA-311, Yuma
163662	AV-8B-12	137	18-Oct-88	17-Nov-88	USMC VMA-542, Cherry Point
163663	AV-8B-12	138	26-Oct-88	21-Nov-88	USMC VMA-542, Cherry Point
163664	AV-8B-12	139	07-Nov-88	21-Nov-88	USMC VMA-311, Yuma
163665	AV-8B-12	140	01-Nov-88	29-Nov-88	USMC VMA-231, Cherry Point
163666	AV-8B-12	141	07-Nov-88	29-Nov-88	USMC, cr Twenty-Nine Palms ranges, CA, 31-Oct-89 (VMA-311) (Engine fire)
163667	AV-8B-12	142	17-Nov-88	06-Dec-88	USMC, cr 16-Dec-89
163668	AV-8B-12	143	04-Jan-89	23-Mar-89	USMC VMA-513, Iwakuni
163669	AV-8B-12	144	21-Nov-88	13-Dec-88	USMC NADEP, Cherry Point
163670	AV-8B-12	145	15-Dec-88	01-May-89	USMC VMA-223, Cherry Point
163671	AV-8B-12	146	14-Dec-88	18-Apr-89	USMC, cr Chocolate Mountains range, AZ, 02-Feb-90 (VMA-311)
163672	AV-8B-12	147	17-Jan-89	24-Apr-89	USMC VMA-311, Yuma
163673	AV-8B-12	148	20-Jan-89	25-May-89	USMC VMA-542, Cherry Point
163674	AV-8B-13	149	30-Jan-89	23-May-89	USMC VMA-311, Yuma
163675	AV-8B-13	150	16-Feb-89	26-Apr-89	USMC VMA-311, Yuma
163676	AV-8B-13	151	22-Feb-89	20-May-89	USMC VMA-542, Cherry Point
163677	AV-8B-13	152	15-Mar-89	04-May-89	USMC VMA-513, Iwakuni
163678	AV-8B-13	153	17-Mar-89	28-Apr-89	USMC VMA-311, Yuma
163679	AV-8B-13	154	23-Mar-89	28-Apr-89	USMC, cr Pimlico Sound, NC, 25-Feb-94 (VMA-542)
163680	AV-8B-13	155	31-Mar-89	22-May-89	USMC NADEP, Cherry Point
163681	AV-8B-13	156	21-Apr-89	06-Jun-89	USMC, cr 17-Aug-94 (VMA-311)
163682	AV-8B-13	157	16-May-89	15-Jun-89	USMC VMA-231, Cherry Point
163683	AV-8B-13	158	09-Jun-89	06-Jul-89	USMC VMA-211, Yuma
163684	AV-8B-13	159	09-Jun-89	13-Jul-89	USMC, cr Yuma, 13-Jul-92 (VMA-311) (Left the runway)
163685	AV-8B-13	160	28-Jun-89	31-Jul-89	USMC, cr off San Diego, CA, 21-Feb-90 (VMA-311)
163686	AV-8B-13	161	17-Jul-89	16-Aug-89	USMC VMA-231, Cherry Point
163687	AV-8B-13	162	12-Jul-89	14-Aug-89	USMC VMA-231, Cherry Point
163688	AV-8B-13	163	29-Jul-89	21-Aug-89	USMC VMA-311, Yuma
163689	AV-8B-13	164	18-Aug-89	31-Aug-89	USMC VMA-223, Cherry Point

Serial	Variant	Build No	First Fit	Delivery	Operator, location or fate
163690	AV-8B-13	165	31-Aug-89	20-Sep-89	USMC VMA-513, Iwakuni
Fiscal Year 1989					
163852	AV-8B-13	166	16-Sep-89	30-Sep-89	USMC VMA-231, Cherry Point, cr 16-Sep-96, NC
163853	AV-8B-13	167	08-Jul-89	15-Sep-89	USMC NADEP, Cherry Point
163854	AV-8B-13	168	20-Sep-89	10-Oct-89	USN NAWS, China Lake
163855	AV-8B-13	169	04-Oct-89	02-Nov-89	USMC VMA-311, Yuma, cr 07-Mar-02, CA
163856	TAV-8B-12	T10	22-Nov-88	22-Mar-89	USMC, cr South Carolina, 21-Apr-90 (VMAT-203) (Bird strike)
163857	TAV-8B-12	T11	23-May-89	22-Jun-89	USMC VMAT-203, Cherry Point
163858	TAV-8B-12	T12	25-Jul-89	31-Aug-89	USMC VMAT-203, Cherry Point
163859	TAV-8B-13	T13	20-Oct-89	22-Nov-89	USMC VMAT-203, Cherry Point
163860	TAV-8B-13	T14	20-Oct-89	22-Nov-89	USMC VMAT-203, Cherry Point
163861	TAV-8B-13	T15	17-Nov-89	20-Dec-89	USMC VMAT-203, Cherry Point
163862	AV-8B-14	170	27-Oct-89	20-Nov-89	USMC VMA-311, Yuma, cr 31-Dec-98
163863	AV-8B-14	171	25-Oct-89	14-Nov-89	USMC VMA-513, Iwakuni, cr 03-Oct-98, Pacific
163864	AV-8B-14	172	01-Nov-89	29-Nov-89	USMC VMA-311, Yuma
163865	AV-8B-14	173	09-Nov-89	18-Dec-89	USMC VMA-513, Iwakuni
163866	AV-8B-14	174	17-Nov-89	18-Dec-89	USMC VMA-214, Yuma, cr 14-Jun-99
163867	AV-8B-14	175	07-Nov-89	18-Dec-89	USMC VMA-513, Iwakuni
163868	AV-8B-14	176	30-Nov-89	19-Dec-89	USMC, cr Chocolate Mountains range, AZ, 29-Feb-96 (VMA-214)
163869	AV-8B-14	177	13-Jan-90	14-Feb-90	USMC VMA-214, Yuma
163870	AV-8B-14	178	10-Jan-90	31-Jan-90	USMC VMA-214, Yuma
163871	AV-8B-14	179	23-Mar-90	23-Mar-90	USN NAWS, China Lake
163872	AV-8B-14	180	23-Jan-90	01-Mar-90	USMC VMA-311, Yuma
163873	AV-8B-15	181	07-Feb-90	06-Mar-90	USMC, cr Twenty-Nine Palms range, CA, 04-Feb-91 (VMA-214)
163874	AV-8B-15	182	16-Feb-90	20-Mar-90	USMC VMA-311, Yuma
163875	AV-8B-15	183	13-Mar-90	05-Apr-90	USMC, cr Davenport, IO, 29-Jun-92 (VMA-214)
163876	AV-8B-15	184	26-Mar-90	01-May-90	USMC VMA-311, Yuma
163877	AV-8B-15	185	03-Apr-90	01-May-90	USMC VMA-513, Iwakuni
163878	AV-8B-15	186	18-Apr-90	31-May-90	USMC, cr 06-Nov-90 (VMA-211)
163879	AV-8B-15	187	23-May-90	12-Jun-90	USMC VMA-214, Yuma
163880	AV-8B-15	188	05-Jun-90	27-Jun-90	USMC VMA-214, Yuma
163881	AV-8B-15	189	05-Jun-90	29-Jun-90	USMC VMA-311, Yuma
163882	AV-8B-15	190	22-Jun-90	16-Jul-90	USMC, cr Pasir Gudang, Johore, Malaysia, 06-Mar-92 (VMA-214)
163883	AV-8B-15	191	07-Aug-90	30-Aug-90	USMC VMA-311, Yuma
Fiscal Year 1990					
164113	TAV-8B-16	T16	11-Apr-90	23-May-90	USMC VMAT-203, Cherry Point

Serial	Variant	Build No	First Fit	Delivery	Operator, location or fate
164114	TAV-8B-16	T17	13-Oct-90	07-Nov-90	USMC VMAT-203, Cherry Point
164115	AV-8B-15	192	10-Sep-90	26-Sep-90	USMC VMA-311, Yuma, cr 04-Jun-99, Kadina, Okinawa
164116	AV-8B-15	193	11-Oct-90	29-Oct-90	USMC VMA-311, Yuma, cr 24-Oct-97, Japan
164117	AV-8B-16	194	17-Oct-90	09-Nov-90	USMC VMA-311, Yuma
164118	AV-8B-16	195	30-Oct-90	10-Dec-90	USMC, cr near Cherry Point, 19-Aug-92 (VMA-211) (Flew into sea)
164119	AV-8B-16	196	17-Nov-90	10-Dec-90	USMC VMA-311, Yuma
164120	AV-8B-16	197	28-Nov-90	17-Dec-90	USMC, cr Barry Goldwater range, AZ, 13-Apr-92 (VMA-211) (Collided with AV-8B 164133)
164121	AV-8B-16	198	14-Jan-91	02-Feb-91	USMC VMA-311, Yuma
164122	TAV-8B-16	T18	10-Nov-90	20-Dec-90	USMC VMAT-203, Cherry Point
164123	AV-8B-17	199	01-Feb-91	13-Jun-91	USMC VMA 513, Iwakuni, cr 07-Dec-05, FL
164124	AV-8B-17	200	14-Jun-91	05-Jul-91	USMC VMA-214, Yuma, cr 22-Jul-02, NC
164125	AV-8B-17	201	25-Jun-91	26-Jul-91	USMC, cr Yuma, 12-May-93 (VMA-211) (Engine failure)
164126	AV-8B-17	202	17-Jul-91	07-Aug-91	USMC VMA-211, Yuma
164127	AV-8B-17	203	22-Jul-91	02-Aug-91	USMC VMA-214, Yuma, cr 15-Jun-05
164128	AV-8B-17	204	12-Aug-91	29-Aug-91	USMC VMA-211, Yuma
164129	AV-8B+-17	205	22-Sep-92	25-Sep-92	USN NAWS, China Lake (Radar integration aircraft)
164130	AV-8B-17	206	15-Aug-91	04-Sep-91	USMC VMA-211, Yuma
164131	AV-8B-17	207	03-Feb-92	27-Mar-92	USMC VMA-513, Iwakuni
164132	AV-8B-17	208	26-Mar-92	27-Apr-92	USMC VMA-513, Iwakuni, cr 08-Oct-96, (Engine failure)
164133	AV-8B-17	209	10-Feb-92	18-Mar-92	USMC, cr Barry Goldwater range, AZ, 13-Apr-92 (VMA-211) (Collided with AV-8B 164120)
164134	AV-8B-17	210	23-Mar-92	09-Apr-92	USMC VMA-513, Iwakuni, cr 29-Jun-99
164135	AV-8B-17	211	31-Mar-92	27-Apr-92	USMC VMA-211, Yuma
164138	TAV-8B-17	T21	16-Feb-92	02-Apr-92	USMC VMAT-203, Cherry Point
164139	AV-8B-18	212	28-Apr-92	21-May-92	USMC VMA-513, Iwakuni
164140	AV-8B-18	213	30-Apr-92	21-May-92	USMC VMA-211, Yuma
164141	AV-8B-18	214	05-May-92	11-Jun-92	USMC VMA-513, Iwakuni
164142	AV-8B-18	215	05-Jun-92	28-Jul-92	USMC VMA-513, Iwakuni
164143	AV-8B-18	216	01-Oct-92	14-Oct-92	USMC VMA-214, Yuma
164144	AV-8B-18	217	11-Aug-92	16-Sep-92	USMC VMA-211, Yuma, cr 15-Apr-00
164145	AV-8B-18	218	20-Aug-92	15-Sep-92	USMC VMA-211, Yuma
164146	AV-8B-18	219	16-Sep-92	01-Oct-92	USMC VMA-211, Yuma
164147	AV-8B-18	220	12-Oct-92	08-Dec-92	USMC VMA-211, Yuma
164148	AV-8B-18	221	08-Nov-92	09-Feb-93	USMC VMA-211, Yuma

Serial	Variant	Build No	First Fit	Delivery	Operator, location or fate
164149	AV-8B-18	222	29-Nov-92	29-Jan-93	USMC VMA-513, Iwakuni, cr 11-Feb-98, Yuma
164150	AV-8B-18	223	28-Nov-92	21-Dec-92	USMC VMA-211, Yuma, cr 14-Jul-05, NC
164151	AV-8B-18	224	27-Mar-93	30-Apr-93	USMC VMA-513, Iwakuni
164152	AV-8B-18	225	15-May-93	22-Jun-93	USMC VMA-211, Yuma
164153	AV-8B-18	226	26-Jun-93	10-Aug-93	USMC VMA-214, Yuma
164154	AV-8B-18	227	28-Oct-93	03-Dec-93	USMC VMA-214, Yuma
Fiscal Year 1991					
164540	TAV-8B-18	T22	17-Jun-92	25-Aug-92	USMC VMAT-203, Cherry Point, cr 02-Mar-03
164541	TAV-8B-18	T23	25-Jun-92	25-Aug-92	USMC, cr Rocky Mount, NC, 14-Jan-95 (VMAT-203)
164542	TAV-8B-18	T24	08-Nov-92	20-Jan-93	USMC VMAT-203, Cherry Point
164543	AV-8B-18	228	02-Dec-92	02-Feb-93	USMC VMA-211, Yuma
164544	AV-8B-18	229	05-Mar-93	07-Apr-93	USMC VMA-214, Yuma
164545	AV-8B-18	230	22-Apr-93	13-May-93	USMC VMA-214, Yuma
164546	AV-8B-18	231	05-Jun-93	15-Jul-93	USMC VMA-211, Yuma
164547	AV-8B-18	232	09-Nov-93	29-Jan-93	USMC, cr Red Sea, 30-Jan-95 off USS Essex (VMA-214)
164548	AV-8B+-19	233	17-Mar-93	16-Apr-93	USN NAWS, China Lake, cr 17-Jun-97
164549	AV-8B+-19	234	27-Mar-93	07-May-93	USN VX-9, China Lake
164550	AV-8B+-19	235	13-May-93	10-Jun-93	USMC VMA-542, Cherry Point, cr 16-Oct-97, OH
164551	AV-8B+-19	236	05-Jun-93	30-Jun-93	USMC VMA-223, Cherry Point
164552	AV-8B+-19	237	09-Jul-93	28-Jul-93	USMC VMA-542, Cherry Point
164553	AV-8B+-19	238	09-Jul-93	29-Jul-93	USMC VMA-542, Cherry Point
164554	AV-8B+-19	239	06-Aug-93	31-Aug-93	USMC VMA-542, Cherry Point
164555	AV-8B+-19	240	25-Aug-93	01-Oct-93	USMC VMA-542, Cherry Point, cr 11-Aug-97, Yuma
164556	AV-8B+-19	241	17-Sep-93	06-Oct-93	USMC VMA-542, Cherry Point
164557	AV-8B+-19	242	08-Nov-93	21-Dec-93	USMC VMA-223, Cherry Point
164558	AV-8B+-19	243	15-Jan-94	24-Feb-94	USMC VMA-223, Cherry Point
164559	AV-8B+-19	244	01-Feb-94	08-Apr-94	USMC VMA-541, Cherry Point
164560	AV-8B+-19	245	25-Mar-94	23-May-94	USMC VMA-231, Cherry Point
164561	AV-8B+-19	246	18-May-94	23-Jun-94	USMC VMA-231, Cherry Point, cr 22-Jun-02, NC
164562	AV-8B+-19	247	15-Jan-94	31-Jan-94	USMC VMA-223, Cherry Point
164566	AV-8B+-19	251	16-Apr-94	29-Jul-94	USMC VMA-223, Cherry Point
164567	AV-8B+-19	252	14-Jun-94	16-Aug-94	USMC VMA-223, Cherry Point
164568	AV-8B+-19	253	01-Jul-94	06-Oct-94	USMC VMA-231, Cherry Point, cr 01-May-99, Adriatic Sea
164569	AV-8B+-19	254	22-Jul-94	21-Sep-94	USMC VMA-223, Cherry Point
164570	AV-8B+-19	255	13-Sep-94	19-Oct-94	USMC VMA-231, Cherry Point
164571	AV-8B+-19	256	04-Oct-94	10-Nov-94	USMC VMA-231, Cherry Point
Fiscal Year 1994					
165001	AV-8B+-21	257	02-Dec-94	23-Feb-95	USMC VMA-231, Cherry Point
165002	AV-8B+-21	258	08-Feb-95	30-Mar-95	USMC VMA-231, Cherry Point

Serial	Variant	Build No	First Fit	Delivery	Operator, location or fate
165003	AV-8B+-21	259	31-Mar-95	19-Apr-95	USMC VMA-223, Cherry Point
165004	AV-8B+-21	260	14-Apr-95	26-May-95	USMC VMA-231, Cherry Point
165005	AV-8B+-21	261	07-Jul-95	14-Aug-95	USMC VMA-231, Cherry Point
165006	AV-8B+-21	262	07-Sep-95	04-Oct-95	USMC VMA-231, Cherry Point
165305-R1	B-263	284	29-Nov-95	22-Jan-96	VX-9, China Lake
165306-R2	B-264	285	18-Mar-96	23-Apr-96	VMA-231, Cherry Point
165307-R3	B-265	286	08-Aug-96	24-Sep-96	VMA-231, Cherry Point
165308-R4	B-266	287	11-Nov-96	04-Dec-96	VMA-231, Cherry Point
165309-R5	B-267	288	20-May-97	08-Jul-97	VMA-542, Cherry Point
165310-R6	B-268	289	21-Aug-97	11-Sep-97	VMA-231, Cherry Point
165311-R7	B-269	290	06-Oct-97	04-Nov-97	VMA-542, Cherry Point
165312-R8	B-270	291	11-Nov-97	18-Dec-97	VMA-231, Cherry Point
165354-R9	B-271	292	20-Jan-98	13-Feb-98	VMA-542, Cherry Point
165355-R10	B-272	293	09-Feb-98	12-Jun-98	VMA-223, Cherry Point
165356-R11	B-273	294	27-Mar-98	18-Jun-98	VMA-223, Cherry Point
165357-R12	B-274	295	05-May-98	12-Jun-98	VMA-223, Cherry Point
165380-R13	B-275	296	17-Jun-98	08-Jul-98	VMA-223, Cherry Point
165381-R14	B-276	297	21-Jul-98	05-Aug-98	VMA-223, Cherry Point
165382-R15	B-277	298	16-Aug-98	31-Aug-98	VMA-223, Cherry Point
165383-R16	B-278	299	04-Sep-98	29-Sep-98	VMA-223, Cherry Point
165384-R17	B-279	300	20-Oct-98	23-Nov-98	VMA-223, Cherry Point
165385-R18	B-280	301	18-Nov-98	15-Dec-98	VMA-223, Cherry Point
165386-R19	B-281	302	12-Jan-99	16-Feb-99	VMA-223, Cherry Point
165387-R20	B-282	303	08-Feb-99	26-Feb-99	VMA-223, Cherry Point
165388-R21	B-283	304	10-Mar-99	30-Jun-99	VMA-231, Cherry Point
165389-R22	B-284	305	22-Mar-99	07-Apr-99	VMA-542, Cherry Point
165390-R23	B-285	306	05-May-99	18-May-99	VMA-231, Cherry Point
165391-R24	B-286	307	26-May-99	11-Jun-99	VMA-542, Cherry Point
165397-R25	B-287	308	10-Jun-99	30-Jun-99	VMA-214, Yuma
165398-R26	B-288	309	11-Oct-99	25-Oct-99	VMA-214, Yuma
165417-R27	B-289	310	10-Jan-00	21-Jan-00	VMA-214, Yuma
165418-R28	B-290	311	01-Dec-99	13-Dec-99	VMA-214, Yuma, cr 01-Jan-05, Indian Ocean
165419-R29	B-291	312	11-Dec-99	16-Dec-99	VMA-214, Yuma
165420-R30	B-292	313	17-Mar-00	15-May-00	VMA-311, Yuma
165421-R31	B-293	314	27-Jan-00	10-Feb-00	VMA-214, Yuma
165422-R32	B-294	315	02-Jun-00	27-Jun-00	VMA-211, Yuma
165423-R33	B-295	316	21-Jun-00	26-Jun-00	VMA-311, Yuma
165424-R34	B-296	317	27-Sep-00	17-Oct-00	VMA-311/VMA-211, cr 08-Dec-03, Chocolate Mountains, CA
165425-R35	B-297	318	21-Apr-00	10-May-00	VMA-311, Yuma
165426-R36	B-298	319	07-Jun-00	15-Jun-00	VMA-311/VMA-214, cr 01-Dec-04, Yuma, AZ
165427-R37	B-299	320	17-Aug-00	29-Aug-00	VMA-211, Yuma
165428-R38	B-300	321	25-Aug-00	31-Aug-00	VMA-211, Yuma
165429-R39	B-301	322	27-Sep-00	02-Sept-00	VMA-311, Yuma
165430-R40	B-302	323	23-Mar-01	06-Apr-01	VMA-211, Yuma
165566-R41	B-303	324	02-Mar-01	16-Mar-01	VMA-513, Yuma
165567-R42	B-304	325	04-May-01	08-Jun-01	VMA-211, Yuma
165568-R43	B-305	326	06-Aug-01	06-Sep-01	VMA-513, Yuma

Serial	Variant	Build No	First Fit	Delivery	Operator, location or fate
165569-R44	B-306	327	15-Oct-01	25-Oct-01	VMA-214, Yuma
165570-R45	B-307	328	03-Dec-01	30-Apr-02	VMA-214, Yuma
165571-R46	B-308	329	12-Apr-01	26-Apr-01	VMA-311, Yuma, cr 03-Dec-03, Yuma
165572-R47	B-309	330	07-Jun-01	27-Jun-01	VMA-211, Yuma
165573-R48	B-310	331	16-May-01	30-May-01	VMA-311, Yuma
165574-R49	B-311	332	02-Jul-01	31-Jul-01	VMA-513, Yuma
165575-R50	B-312	333	02-Aug-01	15-Aug-01	VMA-513, Yuma
165576-R51	B-313	334	28-Aug-01	28-Sep-01	VMA-513, Yuma
165577-R52	B-314	335	21-Sep-01	28-Sep-01	VMA-513, Yuma
165578-R53	B-315	336	09-Nov-01	21-Nov-01	VMA-214, Yuma
165579-R54	B-316	337	27-Oct-01	31-Oct-01	VMA-214, Yuma
165580-R55	B-317	338	10-Jan-02	18-Jan-02	VMA-214, Yuma
165581-R56	B-318	339	22-Feb-02	05-Mar-02	VMA-214, Yuma
165582-R57	B-319	340	13-Mar-02	20-Mar-02	VMA-311, Yuma
165583-R58	B-320	341	21-Mar-02	28-Mar-02	VMA-311, Yuma
165584-R59	B-321	342	11-Jun-02	01-Jul-02	VMA-513, Yuma
165585-R60	B-322	343	15-May-02	22-May-02	VMA-513, via PAX and China Lake, Yuma
165586-R61	B-323	344	04-Jun-02	25-Jun-02	VMA-311, Yuma
165587-R62	B-324	345	28-Jun-02	18-Jul-02	VMA-211, Yuma
165588-R63	B-325	346	02-Aug-02	15-Aug-02	VMA-211, Yuma
165589-R64	B-326	347	06-Sep-02	30-Sept-02	VMA-214, Yuma
165590-R65	B-327	348	11-Sep-02	20-Sep-02	VMA-211, Yuma
165591-R66	B-328	349	15-Oct-02	31-Oct-02	VMA-311, Yuma
165592-R67	B-329	350	14-Nov-02	26-Nov-02	VMA-214, Yuma
165593-R68	B-330	351	15-Dec-02	19-Dec-02	VMA-542, CHPT, NC
165594-R69	B-331	352	26-Jan-03	31-Jan-03	VMA-231, CHPT, NC
165595-R70	B-332	353	08-Feb-03	20-Feb-03	VMA-231, CHPT, NC
165596-R71	B-333	354	09-Apr-03	16-May-03	VMA-231, CHPT, NC
165597-R72	B-334	355	09-May-03	31-May-03	VMA-231, CHPT, NC
166287-R73	B-335	356	29-Jul-03	20-Aug-03	*VMA-231, CHPT, NC
166288-R74	B-336	357	05-Sep-03	27-Sep-03	VMA-231, CHPT, NC

Italy

164563	AV-8B+-19	248	10-Feb-94		McDonnell Douglas
MM7199	AV-8B+-19			20-Apr-94	McDonnell Douglas/Italian Navy, Cherry Point
	AV-8B+-19			17-Jun-95	Italian Navy 1° Gruppo Aerie Imbarcati, Grottaglie
164564	AV-8B+-19	249	25-Mar-94		McDonnell Douglas
MM7200	AV-8B+-19			17-May-94	McDonnell Douglas/Italian Navy, Cherry Point
	AV-8B+-19			16-Jan-95	Italian Navy 1° Gruppo Aerie Imbarcati, Grottaglie
164565	AV-8B+-19	250	30-Mar-94		McDonnell Douglas
MM7201	AV-8B+-19			12-May-94	McDonnell Douglas/Italian Navy, Cherry Point
	AV-8B+-19			16-Jan-95	Italian Navy 1° Gruppo Aerie Imbarcati, Grottaglie
165007	AV-8B-+-22	IT001	27-Jul-95	11-Oct-95	McDonnell Douglas

Serial	Variant	Build No	First Fit	Delivery	Operator, location or fate
MM7212	AV-8B+-22			Nov-95	Italian Navy 1° Gruppo Aerie Imbarcati, Grottaglie
165008	AV-8B+-22	IT002	13-Dec-05	18-Dec-95	McDonnell Douglas
MM7213	AV-8B+-22			18-Dec-95	Italian Navy 1° Gruppo Aerie Imbarcati, Grottaglie
165009	AV-8B+-22	IT003	08-Feb-96	07-Mar-96	McDonnell Douglas
MM7214	AV-8B+-22			07-Mar-96	Italian Navy
165010	AV-8B+-22	IT004			McDonnell Douglas
MM7215	AV-8B+-22			May-96	Italian Navy
165011	AV-8B+-22	IT005			McDonnell Douglas
MM7216	AV-8B+-22			Jul-96	Italian Navy
165012	AV-8B+-22	IT006			McDonnell Douglas
MM7217	AV-8B+-22			Sep-96	Italian Navy
165013	AV-8B+-22	IT007			McDonnell Douglas
MM7218	AV-8B+-22			Nov-96	Italian Navy
165014	AV-8B+-22	IT008			McDonnell Douglas
MM7219	AV-8B+-22			Jan-97	Italian Navy
165015	AV-8B+-22	IT009			McDonnell Douglas
MM7220	AV-8B+-22			Mar-97	Italian Navy
165016	AV-8B+-22	IT010			McDonnell Douglas
MM7221	AV-8B+-22			May-97	Italian Navy
165017	AV-8B+-22	IT011			McDonnell Douglas
MM7222	AV-8B+-22			Jul-97	Italian Navy
165018	AV-8B+-22	IT012			McDonnell Douglas
MM7223	AV-8B+-22			Sep-97	Italian Navy
165019	AV-8B+-22	IT013			McDonnell Douglas
MM7224	AV-8B+-22			Nov-97	Italian Navy
164136	TAV-8B+-17	T19	07-May-91	25-Mar-91	McDonnell Douglas
MM55032	TAV-8B+-17				McDonnell Douglas/Italian Navy, Cherry Point
	TAV-8B+-17			16-Jan-95	Italian Navy 1° Gruppo Aerie Imbarcati, Grottaglie
164137	TAV-8B+-17	T20	01-May-91	30-May-91	McDonnell Douglas
MM55033	TAV-8B+-17				McDonnell Douglas/Italian Navy, Cherry Point
	TAV-8B+-17			16-Jan-95	Italian Navy 1° Gruppo Aerie Imbarcati, Grottaglie
Spain					
163010	EAV-8B-9	E1	21-Jul-87		McDonnell Douglas
VA.2-1	EAV-8B-9			28-Aug-87	Spanish Navy, cr 18-Dec-89 (Esc 009)
163011	EAV-8B-9	E2	18-Aug-87		McDonnell Douglas
VA.2-2	EAV-8B-9			21-Sep-87	Spanish Navy Esc 009, Rota
163012	EAV-8B-9	E3	02-Sep-87		McDonnell Douglas
VA.2-3	EAV-8B-9			01-Oct-87	Spanish Navy Esc 009, Rota
163013	EAV-8B-9	E4	01-Sep-87		McDonnell Douglas
VA.2-4	EAV-8B-9			09-Oct-87	Spanish Navy Esc 009, Rota
163014	EAV-8B-9	E5	18-Sep-87		McDonnell Douglas
VA.2-5	EAV-8B-9			31-Oct-87	Spanish Navy Esc 009, Rota
163015	EAV-8B-9	E6	01-Oct-87		McDonnell Douglas

Serial	Variant	Build No	First Fit	Delivery	Operator, location or fate
VA.2-6	EAV-8B-9			01-Dec-87	Spanish Navy Esc 009, Rota
163016	EAV-8B-9	E7	22-Dec-87		McDonnell Douglas
VA.2-7	EAV-8B-9			27-Feb-88	Spanish Navy ESC 009, Rota
163017	EAV-8B-9	E8	04-Feb-88		McDonnell Douglas
VA.2-8	EAV-8B-9			02-Mar-88	Spanish Navy, cr 26-Nov-93 (Esc 009)
163018	EAV-8B-9	E9	16-Mar-88		McDonnell Douglas
VA.2-9	EAV-8B-9			25-Apr-88	Spanish Navy Esc 009, Rota
163019	EAV-8B-9	E10	19-Apr-88		McDonnell Douglas
VA.2-10	EAV-8B-9			31-May-88	Spanish Navy Esc 009, Rota
163020	EAV-8B-9	E11	14-Jul-88		McDonnell Douglas
VA.2-11	EAV-8B-9			31-Aug-88	Spanish Navy Esc 009, Rota
163021	EAV-8B-9	E12	04-Aug-88		McDonnell Douglas
VA.2-12	EAV-8B-9			31-Aug-88	Spanish Navy Esc 009, Rota
165028	EAV-8B+-22	E13	11-Dec-95	29-Jan-96	McDonnell Douglas
VA.2-14	EAV-8B+-22			15-Jan-96	Spanish Navy Esc 009, Rota
165029	EAV-8B+-22	E14	15-Mar-96		McDonnell Douglas
VA.2-15	EAV-8B+-22			29-Mar-96	Spanish Navy
165030	EAV-8B+-22	E15			McDonnell Douglas
VA.2-16	EAV-8B+-22			May-96	Spanish Navy
165031	EAV-8B+-22	E16			McDonnell Douglas
VA.2-17	EAV-8B+-22			Jul-96	Spanish Navy
165032	EAV-8B+-22	E17			McDonnell Douglas
VA.2-18	EAV-8B+-22			31-Oct-96	Spanish Navy
165033	EAV-8B+-22	E18			McDonnell Douglas
VA.2-19	EAV-8B+-22			Jan-97	Spanish Navy
165034	EAV-8B+-22	E19			McDonnell Douglas
VA.2-20	EAV-8B+-22			Apr-97	Spanish Navy
165035	EAV-8B+-22	E20			McDonnell Douglas
VA.2-21	EAV-8B+-22			Jul-97	Spanish Navy
165652-SR1	SR-1		09-Jun-03	24-Jun-03 to cpnc	**Spain via cpnc
165653-SR2	SR-2		08-Jul-03	22-Jul-03 to cpnc	**Spain via cpnc
166411-SR3	SR-3		23-Sep-03	09-Oct-03 to cpnc	***Spain via cpnc
166412-SR4	SR-4		22-Oct-03	13-Jan-04 to cpnc	
166413-SR5	SR-5		30-Oct-03	20-Nov-03 to cpnc	***Spain via cpnc

Appendix B: Production History, Part 3

UK, BAe Systems

Serial	Variant	Build No	First Fit	Delivery	Operator, location or fate
ZD318	GR5	512041/DB1			
			30-Apr-85		MoD(PE)
	GR7		29-Nov-89		MoD(PE)/BAe Dunsfold
ZD319	GR5/GR5A	512042/DB2			
			31-Jul-85		MoD(PE)/BAe
ZD320	GR5/GR5A	512043/P1	14-Mar-86	23-Sep-86	MoD(PE)/BAe
ZD321	GR5/GR5A	512071/P2	12-Apr-88	20-Jun-88	MoD(PE)/BAe Dunsfold
ZD322	GR5	512072/P3	11-Mar-87	04-Oct-88	RAF
	GR7			15-Dec-95	RAF No 1 Sqn, Wittering
ZD323	GR5	512073/P4	27-Apr-87	29-May-87	RAF
	GR7				RAF HOCU/No 20(R) Sqn, Wittering
ZD324	GR5	512112/P5	25-May-87	01-Jul-87	RAF
	GR7			Apr-94	RAF HOCU/No 20(R) Sqn, Wittering
ZD325	GR5	512113/P6			RAF, cr Atlantic Ocean, 22-Oct-87 (Involuntary ejection)
ZD326	GR5	512114/P7	08-Apr-88	06-May-88	RAF
	GR7		17-Feb-94	20-Apr-94	RAF No 3 Sqn/No 4 Sqn, Laarbruch
ZD327	GR5	512115/P8	25-Apr-88	02-Jun-88	RAF
	GR7		08-Jul-93	01-Feb-94	RAF No 3 Sqn, Laarbruch
ZD328	GR5	512116/P9	17-May-88	26-Jul-88	RAF
	GR7		22-Sep-93	01-Oct-93	RAF No 1 Sqn, Wittering
ZD329	GR5	P10	06-Jul-88	22-Aug-88	RAF
	GR7		01-Dec-94	22-Jul-95	RAF HOCU/No 20(R) Sqn, Wittering
ZD330	GR5	P11	16-Jun-88	02-Aug-88	RAF
	GR7		03-Dec-93	13-Feb-94	RAF No 3 Sqn, Laarbruch
ZD345	GR5	P12	10-Aug-88	01-Sep-88	RAF
	GR7		21-Dec-94	05-Feb-95	RAF HOCU/No 20(R) Sqn, Wittering
ZD346	GR5	P13	23-May-88	18-Jul-88	RAF
	GR7		08-Dec-94	28-Jan-95	MoD(PE)/BAe Dunsfold
ZD347	GR5	P14	18-Aug-88	03-Mar-89	RAF
	GR7		07-Dec-94	14-Sep-95	MoD(PE)/BAe Dunsfold
ZD348	GR5	P15	09-Aug-88	02-Sep-88	RAF
	GR7		27-Jul-94	17-Sep-94	RAF HOCU/No 20(R) Sqn, Wittering
ZD349	GR5	P16	19-Sep-88	30-Sep-88	RAF, cr near Evesham 14-Jan-94 (20(R) Sqn) (Bird strike)
ZD350	GR5	P17	24-Aug-88	10-Nov-88	RAF, cr 07-Aug-92
9189M	GR5				RAF St. Athan, BDRT
ZD351	GR5	P18	06-Oct-88	31-Oct-88	RAF
	GR7				MoD(PE)/BAe Dunsfold

Serial	Variant	Build No	First Fit	Delivery	Operator, location or fate
ZD352	GR5	P19	22-Sep-88	07-Oct-88	RAF
	GR7		10-Dec-93	03-Feb-94	MoD(PE)/BAe Dunsfold
ZD353	GR5	P20	21-Oct-88	11-Nov-88	RAF, damaged by fire, 29-Jul-91
ZD354	GR5	P21	04-Nov-88	05-Dec-88	RAF
	GR7		18-Oct-94	18-Dec-94	RAF No 1 Sqn, Wittering
ZD355	GR5	P22	25-Oct-88	04-Nov-88	RAF, cr on take-off Aalborg, Denmark, 17-Oct-90
ZD375	GR5	P23	10-Oct-88	27-Oct-88	RAF
	GR7		22-Jan-95	08-Feb-95	RAF No 3 Sqn/No 4 Sqn, Laarbruch
ZD376	GR5	P24	26-Oct-88	21-Nov-88	RAF
	GR7		15-Dec-94	10-Feb-95	MoD(PE)/BAe Dunsfold
ZD377	GR5	P25	03-Nov-88	02-Dec-88	RAF
	GR7		31-Jan-94	07-Feb-95	RAF St Athan
ZD378	GR5	P26	16-Nov-88	13-Dec-88	RAF
	GR7		26-Jan-94	23-May-94	RAF HOCU/No 20(R) Sqn, Wittering
ZD379	GR5	P27	22-Nov-88	12-Dec-88	RAF
	GR7		24-Feb-94	02-May-94	MoD(PE)BAe Dunsfold
ZD380	GR5	P28	16-Nov-88	06-Dec-88	RAF
	GR7		10-Dec-90	09-Oct-91	MoD(PE)/BAe Dunsfold
ZD400	GR5	P29	24-Nov-88	12-Dec-88	RAF
	GR7				MoD(PE)/BAe Dunsfold
ZD401	GR5	P30	12-Dec-88	20-Dec-88	RAF
	GR7			10-May-94	RAF No 1 Sqn, Wittering
ZD402	GR5	P31	05-Dec-88		Rolls-Royce, Filton (Pegasus 11-61 test-bed)
	GR7			17-Aug-93	RAF HOCU/No 20(R) Sqn, Wittering
ZD403	GR5	P32	17-Dec-88	22-Dec-88	RAF
	GR7			Jun-93	RAF St Athan
ZD404	GR5	P33	17-Dec-88	22-Dec-88	RAF
	GR7			Apr-93	RAF HOCU/No 20(R) Sqn, Wittering
ZD405	GR5	P34	12-Dec-88	23-Dec-88	RAF
	GR7				RAF No 1 Sqn, Wittering
ZD406	GR5	P35	07-Feb-89	27-Jun-89	RAF
	GR7		08-Apr-93	Jul-93	RAF St Athan
ZD407	GR5	P36	14-Feb-89	27-Jun-89	RAF
	GR7		19-Dec-92	Jan-93	RAF St Athan
ZD408	GR5	P37	27-Feb-89	13-Jul-89	RAF
	GR7		11-Feb-93	Mar-93	RAF No 4 Sqn, Laarbruch
ZD409	GR5	P38	13-Mar-89	04-Jul-89	RAF
	GR7		12-Jan-93	Mar-93	RAF St Athan
ZD410	GR5	P39	10-Apr-89	27-Jul-89	RAF
	GR7		14-Jan-93		RAF No 4 Sqn, Laarbruch
ZD411	GR5	P40	18-Apr-89	19-Jul-89	RAF
	GR7		07-May-93	Jun-93	MoD(PE)/BAe Dunsfold
ZD412	GR5	P41	31-Aug-89	05-Oct-89	RAF, cr Gütersloh, 30-Sep-91 (3 Sqn) (Landing accident)
ZD430	GR5A	P42	04-Sep-89	20-Sep-89	RAF
	GR7		26-Mar-91	09-Apr-91	RAF, cr Heckington, Lincs, 13-Jun-93

Serial	Variant	Build No	First Fit	Delivery	Operator, location or fate
ZD431	GR5A	P43	01-Aug-89	24-Oct-89	RAF
	GR7		05-Dec-91	13-Dec-91	RAF No 1 Sqn, Wittering
ZD432	GR5A	P44	30-Jun-89	10-Jul-89	RAF
	GR7		06-Jul-90	21-Aug-90	RAF, cr Dahuk, Northern Iraq, 23-Nov-93 (Mechanical failure)
ZD433	GR5A	P45	08-Aug-89	05-Sep-89	RAF
	GR7		20-Nov-91	26-Nov-91	MoD(PE)/BAe Dunsfold
ZD434	GR5A	P46	17-Oct-89	02-Nov-89	RAF
	GR7		05-Dec-91	13-Dec-91	RAF No 4 Sqn, Laarbruch
ZD435	GR5A	P47	03-Oct-89	24-Oct-89	RAF
	GR7		27-Dec-91	06-Jan-92	RAF No 4 Sqn, Laarbruch
ZD436	GR5A	P48	29-Sep-89	20-Nov-89	RAF
	GR7				MoD(PE)/BAe Dunsfold
ZD437	GR5A	P49	03-Nov-89	29-Nov-89	RAF
	GR7		06-Dec-91	06-Jan-92	RAF HOCU/No 20(R) Sqn, Wittering
ZD438	GR5A	P50	12-Dec-89	17-Jan-90	RAF
	GR7		18-Dec-91	06-Jan-92	RAF No 1 Sqn, Wittering
ZD461	GR5A	P51	10-Oct-89	16-Nov-89	RAF
	GR7		21-Feb-92	13-Mar-92	RAF HOCU/No 20(R) Sqn, Wittering
ZD462	GR5A	P52	03-Nov-89	22-Nov-89	RAF
	GR7		10-Jun-92	04-Aug-92	RAF No 1 Sqn, Wittering
ZD463	GR5A	P53	08-Nov-89	07-Dec-89	RAF
	GR7		31-Jul-92	19-Aug-92	RAF HOCU/No 20(R) Sqn, Wittering
ZD464	GR5A	P54	22-Nov-89	21-Dec-89	RAF
	GR7		11-Sep-92	03-Nov-92	RAF HOCU/No 20(R) Sqn, Wittering
ZD465	GR5A	P55	15-Feb-90	18-Apr-90	RAF
	GR7		07-Aug-92	17-Aug-92	RAF No 1 Sqn, Wittering
ZD466	GR5A	P56	24-Nov-89	24-Jan-90	RAF
	GR7		16-Dec-92	05-Feb-93	RAF No3 Sqn/No 4 Sqn, Laarbruch
ZD467	GR5A	P57	08-Jan-90	09-Feb-90	RAF
	GR7		02-May-91	04-Jun-91	RAF AWC/SAOEU, DTEO Boscombe Down
ZD468	GR5A	P58	12-Feb-90	30-Mar-90	RAF
	GR7		06-Oct-92	10-Nov-92	RAF No 1 Sqn, Wittering
ZD469	GR5A	P59	05-May-90	19-Mar-90	RAF
	GR7		26-Oct-92		RAF HMF, Laarbruch
ZD470	GR5A	P60	21-Mar-90	19-Jun-90	RAF
	GR7		28-Jun-91	07-Nov-91	RAF No 1 Sqn, Wittering
ZG471	GR7	P61	23-Jul-90	14-Aug-90	RAF No 1 Sqn, Wittering
ZG472	GR7	P62	15-Jul-90	17-Aug-90	RAF AWC/SAOEU, DTEO Boscombe Down
ZG473	GR7	P63	27-Jul-90	12-Sep-90	RAF, cr 6 miles S of Gütersloh, 29-May-91 (4 Sqn)
ZG474	GR7	P64	28-Jul-90	24-Sep-80	RAF No 1 Sqn, Wittering
ZG475	GR7	P65	02-Aug-90	29-Aug-90	RAF, cr Solway Firth, 01-Jun-95 (SAOEU)

Serial	Variant	Build No	First Fit	Delivery	Operator, location or fate
ZG476	GR7	P66	15-Sep-90	28-Nov-90	RAF, cr nr Wittering, 19-Feb-96 (20(R) Sqn)
ZG477	GR7	P67	03-Sep-90	05-Nov-90	RAF No 3 Sqn, Laarbruch
ZG478	GR7	P68	17-Sep-90	05-Nov-90	RAF St. Athan
ZG479	GR7	P69	01-Oct-90	30-Nov-90	RAF No 4 Sqn, Laarbruch
ZG480	GR7	P70	05-Oct-90	05-Dec-90	RAF No 3 Sqn, Laarbruch
ZG500	GR7	P71	19-Nov-90	13-Dec-90	RAF No 4 Sqn, Laarbruch
ZG501	GR7	P72	13-Dec-90	20-Dec-90	RAF AWC/SAOEU, DTEO Boscombe Down
ZG502	GR7	P73	17-Dec-90	21-Dec-90	RAF No 4 Sqn, Laarbruch
ZG503	GR7	P74	18-Dec-90	21-Dec-90	MoD(PE)/BAe Dunsfold
ZG504	GR7	P75	15-Jan-91	26-Feb-91	RAF St Athan
ZG505	GR7	P76	21-Jan-91	12-Mar-91	RAF No 1 Sqn, Wittering
ZG506	GR7	P77	16-Apr-91	19-Jun-91	RAF No 3 Sqn, Laarbruch
ZG507	GR7	P78	26-Jun-91	04-Nov-91	RAF No 3 Sqn/No 4 Sqn, Laarbruch
ZG508	GR7	P79	29-Jul-91	04-Nov-91	RAF No 3 Sqn, Laarbruch
ZG509	GR7	P80	05-Jul-91	25-Jul-91	RAF No 3 Sqn, Laarbruch
ZG510	GR7	P81	17-Aug-91	07-Nov-91	RAF No 3 Sqn, Laarbruch
ZG511	GR7	P82	05-Oct-91	04-Nov-91	MoD(PE)/BAe Dunsfold
ZG512	GR7	P83	21-Oct-91	08-Jan-92	RAF No 4 Sqn, Laarbruch
ZG530	GR7	P84	30-Oct-91	10-Dec-91	RAF No 3 Sqn, Laarbruch
ZG531	GR7	P85	10-Nov-91	28-Nov-91	RAF St Athan
ZG532	GR7	P86	12-Oct-91	12-Feb-92	RAF St Athan
ZG533	GR7	P87	10-Oct-91	10-Dec-91	RAF No 3 Sqn, Laarbruch
ZG856	GR7	P88	09-Oct-91	22-Nov-91	RAF No 4 Sqn, Laarbruch
ZG857	GR7	P89	22-Nov-91	20-Jan-92	RAF No 3 Sqn, Laarbruch
ZG858	GR7	P90	01-Dec-91	24-Dec-91	RAF No 3 Sqn, Laarbruch
ZG859	GR7	P91	13-Dec-91	18-Jan-92	MoD(PE)/BAe, Dunsfold
ZG860	GR7	P92	21-Dec-91	14-Jan-92	RAF St Athan
ZG861	GR7	P93	16-Feb-92	11-May-92	RAF St Athan
ZG862	GR7	P94	22-Apr-92	02-Jun-92	RAF No 3 Sqn, Laarbruch
ZH653	T10	TX001	07-Apr-94		MoD(PE)/FJTS, DTEO Boscombe Down
ZH654	T10	TX002			MoD(PE)/BAe, Dunsfold
ZH655	T10	TX003	19-Aug-94	27-Mar-95	RAF, stored Wittering (damaged)
ZH656	T10	TX004	19-Oct-94	30-Oct-95	RAF No 3 Sqn, Laarbruch
ZH657	T10	TX005	05-Dec-94	30-Jan-95	RAF HOCU/No 20(R) Sqn, Wittering
ZH658	T10	TX006	29-Nov-94	06-Feb-95	RAF HOCU/No 20(R) Sqn, Wittering
ZH659	T10	TX007	14-Dec-94	17-Feb-95	RAF HOCU/No 20(R) Sqn, Wittering
ZH660	T10	TX008	23-Feb-95	06-Mar-95	RAF HOCU/No 20(R) Sqn, Wittering
ZH661	T10	TX009	31-Mar-95	12-Apr-95	RAF No 1 Sqn, Wittering
ZH662	T10	TX010	12 May-95	25-May-95	RAF HOCU/No 20(R) Sqn, Wittering
ZH663	T10	TX011	07-Jul-95	24-Aug-95	RAF HOCU/No 20(R) Sqn, Wittering
ZH664	T10	TX012	21-Sep-95	28-Sep-95	RAF No 4 Sqn, Laarbruch
ZH665	T10	TX013	01-Oct-95	26-Oct-95	RAF HOCU/No 20(R) Sqn, Wittering

Appendix C: Technical Data on Harrier Versions

AV-8A/C (GR Mk. 1/3) Harrier

The Royal Air Force purchased more than 140 first-generation Harriers, and the aircraft served with four squadrons and several detachments. The U.S. Marine Corps bought 110 similar AV-8A Harriers, which equipped four squadrons. Forty-seven AV-8As were upgraded to the AV-8C configuration, which added ECM systems, improved communications and support features. The Spanish navy bought two TAV-8S and ten AV-8S aircraft through the U.S. Marine Corps and five more directly from BAe. The Spanish navy flew these aircraft until they were sold to the Royal Thai Navy in 1998.

Specification: Hawker Siddeley AV-8A Harrier (aircraft delivered: RAF, 1966–87; USMC, 1971–76)

Powerplant: one Rolls-Royce Pegasus 11 Mk 103, F402-RR-402 rated at 21,800 lb. thrust, 96.9 kN

Dimensions: wingspan 25 ft. 3 in., 7.6 m; length 47 ft. 2 in., 14.3 m; height 11 ft. 3 in., 3.4 m; wing area 201.1 sq. ft., 18.61 sq. m

Weights: operating empty, 12,200 lb., 5,533 kg; maximum takeoff, 26,000 lb., 11,790 kg for 1,330 ft., 405 m STO or 17,950 lb., 8,000 kg for VTO

Performance: maximum level speed, 635 knots, Mach .972, 1,186 km/h; combat radius, 200 nm, 320 km

Armament: two 30 mm Aden cannon with 130 rounds per gun; maximum ordnance 8,000 lb., 3,630 kg, including bombs, cluster bombs, and AIM-9Ls for self-defense

AV-8B Harrier II

The U.S. Marine Corps bought 166 AV-8B Day Attack aircraft between 1983 and 1993; these aircraft served with seven operational squadrons and the training squadron. The Royal Air Force ordered sixty-two similar GR Mk. 5/5A Harrier II aircraft fitted with a different ECM suite, communications systems, and Martin Baker ejection seat, and enhanced bird strike capability. The Spanish navy ordered twelve AV-8B Harrier II aircraft, which were delivered in 1987 and 1988.

Specification: Boeing AV-8B Harrier II (BAe was the prime contractor for RAF aircraft)

Powerplant: one Rolls-Royce Pegasus F402-RR-406/406A (USMC); Pegasus 105 (RAF) turbofan rated at 21,800 lb. thrust, 96.9 kN

Dimensions: wing span 30 ft. 4 in., 25 m; length 46 ft. 4 in., 14.12 m; height 11 ft. 8 in., 3.55 m; wing area 343.40 sq. ft., 22.61 sq. m.

Weights: operating empty, 13,175 lb., 5,967 kg; normal takeoff, 22,950 lb., 10,410 kg; maximum takeoff, 31,000 lb., 14,061 kg for 1,330 ft., 405 m STO or 18,021 lb., 8,174 kg for VTO

Performance: maximum level speed, 561 knots, 650 mph, 1,065 km/h; maximum rate of climb, 14,715 ft., 4,485 m per minute; combat radius, 300 nm, 480 km

Armament: one GAU-12A 25mm cannon with three hundred rounds; maximum ordnance 13,235 lb., 6,003 kg, including AGM-65s, cluster bombs, and AIM-9Ls for self defense

TAV-8B Harrier II

The U.S. Marine Corps procured twenty-two two-seat TAV-8B aircraft between 1986 and 1992 to support conversion training. Most of these aircraft are located at VMAT-203, with one aircraft assigned to a test unit. Spain and Italy also fly the TAV-8B for training. The Marine Corps TAV-8B fleet is being upgraded to incorporate the higher-thrust Pegasus -408 plus life extension, support, and avionics enhancements.

Specification: Boeing TAV-8B Harrier II

Powerplant: one Rolls-Royce F402-RR-406 turbofan rated at 21,800 lb. thrust, 96.9 kN; upgraded; one Rolls-Royce F402-RR-408 turbofan rated at 23,800 lb. thrust, 104 kN

Dimensions: wing span, 30 ft. 4 in., 9.25 m; length 50 ft. 6 in., 15.4 m; height 13 ft. 1 in., 3.8 m; wing area 343.4 sq. ft., 22.61 sq. m

Weights: operating empty, 14,500 lb., 6,577 kg; normal takeoff, 22,950 lb., 10,410 kg; maximum takeoff, 29,750 lb., 13,494 kg for 1,330 ft., 405 m STO or 14,500 lb., 6,577 kg for VTO

Performance: maximum level speed, 575 knots, 662 mph, 1,065 km/h; maximum rate of climb, 14,715 ft., 4,485 m per minute; combat radius 300 nm, 486 km

Armament: Practice bombs, 2 pylons

AV-8B Night Attack

The U.S. Marine Corps purchased sixty-six AV-8B Night Attack aircraft; these first entered service with VMA-214 and VMA-211. The Marine Corps Night Attack Harrier II included an integrated FLIR system, improved HUD, and provision for night-vision goggles, plus self-defense and support enhancements. The Royal Air Force Harrier II fleet is equipped with GR Mk. 7 aircraft with Night Attack systems.

Specification: Boeing AV-8B Harrier II (Night Attack aircraft delivered between 1986 and 1993)

Powerplant: one Rolls-Royce Pegasus F402-RR-408 turbofan rated at 23,500 lb. thrust, 104 kN

Dimensions: wing span, 30 ft. 4 in., 9.25 m; length 46 ft. 4 in., 14.12 m; height 11 ft. 8 in., 3.55 m; wing area 343.40 sq. ft., 22.61 sq. m
Weights: operating empty, 13,968 lb., 6,336 kg; normal takeoff, 22,950 lb., 10,410 kg; maximum takeoff, 31,000 lb., 14,061 kg for 1,330 ft., 405 m STO or 18,950 lb., 8,596 kg for VTO

Performance: maximum level speed, 575 knots, 662 mph, 1,065 km/h; maximum rate of climb, 14,715 ft., 4,485 m per minute; combat radius, 300 nm, 480 km

Armament: one GAU-12A 25mm cannon with three hundred rounds; maximum ordnance 13,235 lb., 6,003 kg, including AGM-65s, cluster bombs, and AIM-9L/Ms for self-defense

Harrier II Plus

The U.S. Marine Corps, Italy, and Spain cooperatively funded the development and testing of an improved version of the Harrier II equipped with the APG-65 radar, night-attack systems, an improved Pegasus -408 engine, and other systems enhancements. The Marine Corps bought forty-two of these aircraft and remanufactured seventy-four AV-8B Day Attack aircraft to the Plus configuration. The Spanish navy bought eight Harrier II Plus aircraft and remanufactured five AV-8Bs. The Italian navy purchased sixteen Harrier II Plus aircraft.

Specification: Boeing AV-8B Harrier II Plus

Powerplant: one Rolls-Royce F402-RR-408 turbofan rated at 23,500 lb. thrust, 104 kN

Dimensions: wing span 30 ft. 4 in., 9.25 m; length 47 ft. 8 in., 14.40 m; height 11 ft. 8 in., 3.55 m; wing area 343.4 sq. ft., 22.61 sq. m

Weights: operating empty, 14,912 lb., 6,764 kg; normal takeoff, 22,950 lb., 10,410 kg; maximum takeoff, 31,000 lb., 14,061 kg for 1,330 ft., 405 m STO or 19,999 lb., 9,071 kg

for VTO

Performance: maximum level speed, 575 knots, 662 mph, 1,065 km/h; maximum rate of climb, 14,715 ft., 1,065 km/h per minute; combat radius, 300 nm, 480 km

Armament: one GAU-12A 25mm cannon with three hundred rounds; maximum ordnance 13,235 lb., 6,003 kg, including AGM-65s, cluster bombs, AIM-120 AMRAAM, and AIM-9L/Ms for self-defense

Harrier II Remanufacture Program

In an effort to provide fleet Marine squadrons with the most capable Harrier II available, the U.S. Marine Corps launched the Harrier II Plus Remanufacture Program in 1994. Seventy-four AV-8B Harrier IIs were converted into the more capable Harrier II Plus aircraft, with a renewed service life. In addition, the Spanish navy joined the program to remanufacture five of its AV-8B Harrier II aircraft. Combined with the Harriers already in service, this fleet will serve the U.S. Marine Corps, the Spanish navy, and the Italian navy well into the twenty-first century.

GR Mk. 5/7/9 Harrier II

The RAF ordered ninety-six GR Mk. 5/5A Harrier IIs, fitted with an RAF-specific internal ECM suite, communications systems, additional underwing pylons for Sidewinder missiles, and a Martin Baker ejection seat. Thirty-four GR Mk. 7 aircraft were delivered with the Night Attack system, and the operational GR Mk. 5s were converted to the GR Mk. 7 configuration. Thirty GR Mk. 7s are being configured to accept the higher-thrust Pegasus Mk. 107 engine, becoming GR Mk. 7As. RAF Harrier IIs will be upgraded to the GR Mk. 9 configuration with system and software changes that allow use of "smart" weapons, and improved navigation and communications systems, in addition to the higher-thrust engines.

Airframe: BAe Systems GR Mk. 5/7/9 Harrier II

Powerplant: one rolls-Royce Pegasus Mk. 105, 21,750 lb. thrust, 96.7 kN; retrofit GR Mk. 7/ GR Mk. 9; Rolls-Royce Pegasus Mk. 107; 24,750 lb. thrust, 104 kN, GR Mk. 7A/GR Mk. 9A

Dimensions: wing span 30 ft., 4 in., 9.25 m; length 46 ft. 4 in., 14.12 m; height 11 ft. 8 in., 3.55 m; wing area 343.4 sq. ft., 22.61 sq. m

Weights: operating empty, 15,409 lb., 6,990 kg; normal takeoff, 22,950 lb., 10,410 kg; maximum takeoff 31,000 lb., 14,061 kg for 1,330 ft., 405 m STO or 18,950 lb., 8,595 kg for VTO

Performance: maximum level speed, 575 knots, 662 mph, 1,065 km/h; maximum rate of climb 14,715 ft., 4,485 m per minute; combat radius, 300 nm, 480 km

Armament: maximum ordnance 13,235 lb., 6,003 kg, including AGM-65s, bombs, and AIM-9Ls for self-defense

T Mk. 10

The RAF bought thirteen T Mk. 10s two-seat aircraft, equipped with the full GR Mk. 7 avionics suite, in 1994 and 1995 for training and operational support. The T Mk. 10 is undergoing an avionics and systems upgrade, bringing them to the T Mk. 12 configuration.

Airframe: BAe Systems T Mk. 10

Powerplant: one Rolls-Royce Pegasus 105, 21,800 lb. thrust, 96.9 kN

Dimensions: wing span 30 ft. 4 in., 9.25 m; length 50 ft. 3 in., 15.3 m; height 11 ft. 8 in., 3.55 m; wing area, 343.4 sq. ft., 22.61 sq. m

Weights: operating empty, 17,020 lb., 7,720 kg; maximum takeoff, 30,000 lb., 13,607 kg for 1,330 ft., 405 m STO or 14,500 lb., 6,577 kg for VTO

Performance: maximum level speed, 575 knots, 662 mph, 1,065 km/h; maximum rate of climb 14,715 ft., 4,485 m per minute; combat radius, 300 nm, 480 km

Armament: maximum ordnance 10,000 lb., 4,535 kg, including bombs and AIM-9Ls for self-defense

USMC Program Managers

Col. Edwin Harper, USMC (Ret.)
Col. William Traynor, USMC (Ret.)
Col. Richard Marsh, USMC (Ret.)
Col. John Braddon, USMC (Ret.)
Col. Stanley Lewis, USMC (Ret.)
Col. James Orr, USMC (Ret.)
Col. Harry Blot, USMC (Ret.)
Col. Lewis Watt, USMC (Ret.)
Col. James Hart, USMC (Ret.)
Col. Richard Priest, USMC (Ret.)
Col. Judson Mason, USMC (Ret.)
Col. Thomas White III, USMC (Ret.)
Col. David R. Heinz, USMC

Industry Team Program Managers

The Boeing Company

Ed Harper	Darryl Davis
Roger Mathews	Robert Krieger
Patrick Finneran	David Bowman
Charles Allen	Robert Feldmann

BAe Systems

Ray Searle	Mike Sharland
Maurice Carlile	Martin Rushton
Dick Wise	Tom Mather
Dave Nelson	Nigel Davey

Rolls-Royce Pegasus Project Directors

John Schroeder	Chris Fairhead
Tom Hartmann	Brian Evans
Phil Wilkins	Brian Miller
Chris Pratt	Peter Calder

Notes

CHAPTER 1

1. Peter Mersky, *U.S. Marine Corps Aviation:* 1912–Present (Baltimore, Md.: Nautical and Aviation Publishing, 1997), 13–106.
2. Ibid.
3. Ray Bonds, ed., *U.S. War Machine: An Encyclopedia of American Military Equipment and Strategy* (London: Salamander Books, 1985), 206–19.
4. Richard P. Hallion, *The Naval Air War in Korea* (Baltimore, Md.: Nautical and Aviation Publishing, 1986), 72–92.
5. R. A. Gustafson, "The Marine Corps View," *Armed Forces Journal* (April 1981): 58.
6. Mersky, *U.S. Marine Corps Aviation:* 1912–Present, 217–27.
7. Hearings Before the Special Subcommittee on Close Air Support of the Preparedness Investigating Subcommittee of the Committee on Armed Services, United States Senate, Ninety-Second Congress, First Session, Hearings, 22 October 1971, 252–72.
8. U.S. Department of Defense, "Joint Tactics, Techniques, and Procedures for Close Air Support," Joint Publication 3-09.3, 1 December 1995.

CHAPTER 2

1. Bruce Myles, *Jump Jet: The Revolutionary Harrier* (San Rafael, Calif.: Presidio Press, 1978), 5–19.
2. Author's interview with Ian Milne, London, 17 Sept. 2003.
3. Paul Jackson, "Harrier," *World Airpower Journal*, no. 6 (summer 1991): 48–51.
4. Roy Braybrook, *Harrier: Vertical Reality* (Fairford, UK: Royal Air Force Benevolent Fund, 1996), 5–25.
5. Sg. Ldr. G. R. Pitchfork, "Harrier in Support of the Close-in Battle," technical paper, 11th Aerospace Symposium, Maxwell Air Force Base, Ala., 9–10 March 1987.
6. Peter E. Davies and Anthony M. Thornborough, *Harrier Story* (Naval Institute Press, 1996), 68–115, 160–78.
7. "Falklands Campaign: The Lessons," UK government document presented to Parliament by the Secretary for Defence, December 1982, Her Majesty's Stationery Office, ISBN 0101875800, 19.
8. Ibid.
9. *V/STOL in the Roaring Forties,* British Aerospace Publication (UK: Polygraphic Ltd., 1982).
10. Rolando Alano, "St. Barbara: What a Debut," *Aeroespacio Revista Nacional Aeronautica y Espacial* (1986), 44–55.
11. V/STOL in the Roaring Forties, 33.
12. Paul Jackson, "Strike Force South," *Australian Aviation* (December 1982), 60.
13. Salvador Mafe Huertas, "Spanish Harriers," *Air Forces Monthly* (September 1999), 21–23.
14. Jackson, "Harrier," 72–74.
15. Pushpindar S. Chopra, "India and the MiG-21," *Air Enthusiast* (July 1973), 7.

16. Christopher M. Centner, "Ignorance Is Risk: The Big Lesson from Desert Storm Air Base Attacks," *Airpower Journal* (winter 1992): 12–18.
17. John Stillion and David Orletsky, *Airbase Vulnerability to Conventional Cruise Missile and Ballistic Attacks* (Santa Monica, Calif.: RAND study prepared for the U.S. Air Force, 1999).

CHAPTER 3

1. Author's interview with Lt. Gen. Thomas Miller, USMC (Ret.), Arlington, Va., 14 January 2004. All of the following information and quotes from Lieutenant General Miller are from this interview.
2. Author's interview with Col. Edwin Harper, USMC (Ret.), St. Louis, Mo., 20 August 2003. All of the following information and quotes from Colonel Harper are from this interview.
3. Harper interview.
4. Miller interview.
5. Bert H. Cooper, "V/STOL Developments: Background and Status of Navy/Marine Corps Vertical and Short Take-off and Landing Aircraft Programs," U.S. Congressional Research Service Study 78-51F, 1 March 1978, 32–35.
6. Harper interview.
7. Ibid.
8. "Close Air Support: Cheyenne vs. Harrier vs. A-X?" *Armed Forces Journal* (October 1970): 19–20.
9. "Close Air Support for the U.S. Armed Forces," *International Defense Review* 4 (October 1971): 433.
10. Hearings before the Special Subcommittee on Close Air Support of the Preparedness Investigating Subcommittee of the Committee on Armed Services, U.S. Senate, Ninety Second Congress, 1 November 1971, 252–72.
11. Ibid.
12. Bert H. Cooper, "The British Harrier V/STOL Aircraft: Analysis of Operational Experience and Relevance to U.S. Tactical Aviation," U.S. Congressional Research Service Study 81–180, 15 August 1981 (hereafter Cooper, CRS study 1981), 78–80.
13. John W. Fozard, "The Origin of a U.S. Species: Entry of the AV-8A Harrier into the Marine Corps," *Marine Corps Gazette* (May 1992), 77–85.
14. Author's interview with Bob Nidiffer, Rolls-Royce, Yuma, Ariz., 1 October 2003.
15. Author's interview with Capt. Bud Orr, USN (Ret.), Washington, D.C., 13 August 2003.
16. Ibid.
17. Davies and Thornborough, *Harrier Story*, 65.
18. Author's interview with Maj. Gen. Harry Blot, USMC (Ret.), Washington, D.C., 20 October 2003; Harry W. Blot, "A New Dimension in Air Combat," *Rolls-Royce Magazine* 6 (1980), 3–7.
19. Ibid.
20. Author's interview with Col. Greg Kuzniewski, USMC (Ret.), Washington, D.C., 13 August 2003.
21. Orr interview.
22. "The Marines' Bad Luck Plane: Why the Harrier Keeps Crashing," *Time* magazine, 15 August 1977, 16.
23. Author's interview with Lt. Col. W. R. Spicer, USMC (Ret.), 28 December 2005 (electronic).
24. Author's interview with Maj. Gen. Joe Anderson, USMC (Ret.), Washington, D.C., 13 August 2003.

CHAPTER 4

1. Cooper, CRS study 1981, 81–84.
2. Harper interview.
3. Interview with Ray Searle, London, 27 September 2003.
4. Braybrook, *Harrier: Vertical Reality*, 67–73.

5. Cooper, CRS study 1981, 82.
6. Harper interview.
7. Jackson, "Harrier," 72–78.
8. Searle interview.
9. Roy Braybrook, "AV-8B Harrier II: Stepping-Stone to an Anglo-American Supersonic V/STOL Aircraft?" *Air International* (February 1982), 64–69.
10. Russell Murray, "The AV-8B Controversy: Rising Vertically Through the List of Priorities Invulnerable to Systems Analysts," *Armed Forces Journal International* (April 1981): 50–61.
11. Ibid.
12. Cooper, CRS study 1981, 82–83.
13. Miller interview.
14. Joel L. Goza, "The AV-8B Decision," master's thesis, June 1982, U.S. Naval Postgraduate School, Monterey, Calif., 44.
15. "Marines to Purchase F/A-18s After Losing Bid for AV-8Bs," *Aviation Week and Space Technology* (5 February 1979),18.
16. Goza thesis, 60.

CHAPTER 5

1. Braybrook, *Harrier: Vertical Reality*, 101–4.
2. Interview with Jack Jackson, St. Louis, Mo., 20 May 2003.
3. Bert H. Cooper, "V/STOL Aviation in the U.S. Navy," *Navy International* (September 1984), 12–16.
4. Author's interview with Col. Richard H. Priest (Ret.), 23 May 2005 (electronic).
5. Braybrook, *Harrier: Vertical Reality*, 91–95.
6. Davies and Thornborough, *Harrier Story*, 118.
7. Ibid.
8. Author's interview with Jerry Kauffman, 20 May 2005 (electronic). BAe Systems Technical Paper, Harrier II Wing Delamination Programme, 2005.
9. Harper interview.
10. Cooper, "V/STOL Aviation."
11. Author's interview with Fred Chana, St. Louis, Mo., 14 May 2004.
12. Russ Stromberg, "The AV-8B OPEVAL: Mission Complete, the Best Ever," *Wings of Gold* (summer 1985), 36–42; author's interview with Lt. Col. Russ Stromberg (Ret.), 11 October 2004 (electronic).
13. Jackson interview.
14. Searle interview.
15. H. Wall, "AV-8B: An International Success Story," AIAA paper, 1989.
16. Author's interview with Darryl Carpenter, St. Louis, Mo., 23 June 2004.

CHAPTER 6

1. Stromberg, "The AV-8B OPEVAL: Mission Complete."
2. Jackson interview.
3. Davies and Thornborough, *Harrier Story*, 128–30.
4. Author's interview with Maj. Gen. Michael Ryan, USMC (Ret.), Washington, D.C., 13 August 2003.
5. Richard Butcher, "Training Pilots to Think AV-8B," *Rolls-Royce Magazine* 25 (June 1985), 2–7; Brendan Greeley, "Improved VTOL Performance of TAV-8B Adds Realism to Attack Force Training," *Aviation Week and Space Technology* (3 August 1987), 68–72.
6. Author's interview with Lt. Col. John Capito, USMC (Ret.), 15 May 2004 (electronic).
7. Richard Butcher, "First Operational AV-8B Squadron," *Rolls-Royce Magazine* 30 (September 1986), 15–19.
8. Ibid.

9. VMA-231 history, online source: www.2maw.usmc.mil, official website for the 2nd Marine Aircraft Wing.

10. VMA-542 history, online source: www.2maw.usmc.mil.

11. Author's interview with Col. Richard H. Priest, 23 May 2005 (electronic); VMA-223 history, online source: www.2maw.usmc.mil.

12. VMA-513 history, online source: www.3maw.usmc.mil, official website for the 3rd Marine Aircraft Wing.

13. VMA-311 history, online source: www.3maw.usmc.mil.

14. VMA-214 history, online source: www.3maw.usmc.mil.

15. VMA-211 history, online source: www.3maw.usmc.mil.

16. "Matador: Spearhead of Spanish Naval Strike Power," *Rolls-Royce Magazine* 7 (1980).

17. Alan Laws, "Harrier: European Operators," *Combat Aircraft* (January 1999), 58–63.

18. David A. Brown, "Britain Weighs U.S. AV-8B Buy," *Aviation Week and Space Technology* (2 February 1981), 14.

19. Author's interview with John Parker, Washington, D.C., 31 October 2003.

20. Paul Jackson, "Twice Three Makes Five," *Air International* (August 1989), 59–67.

21. Ibid.

22. Ibid.

23. No. 1 Squadron history, online source: www.raf.mod.uk/squadrons/, Royal Air Force: squadron page.

24. No. 3 Squadron history, online source: www.raf.mod.uk/squadrons/.

25. No. IV Squadron history, online source: www.raf.mod.uk/squadrons/.

26. No. 20 Squadron history, online source: www.raf.mod.uk/rafwittering/sqn20.

CHAPTER 7

1. Committee on Armed Services, United States Senate, 100th Congress, DOD Authorization for Appropriations for Fiscal Year 1989 Hearings, 21 March 1988, 48–54.

2. Lon Nordeen, "The Marines AV-8B Gulf Deployment," *Air Forces Monthly* (February 1992), 42.

3. Ibid.

4. Norman Friedman, *Desert Victory: The War For Kuwait* (Annapolis, Md.: Naval Institute Press, 1991), 75–146.

5. Ibid.

6. Nordeen, "Marines AV-8B," 43.

7. Ibid.

8. Tom Clancy and Chuck Horner, *Every Man a Tiger: The Gulf War Air Campaign* (New York: Berkley Books, 1999), 234–80.

9. Nordeen, "Marines AV-8B," 44.

10. Ibid.

11. Ibid.

12. Ibid.

13. Nordeen, "Marines AV-8B," 45.

14. Ibid.

15. Jeffrey Janowiec, "The Gulf War: A Marine POW," *Marine Corps Aviation Association Journal* (September 2002): 85–87.

16. Nordeen, "Marines AV-8B," 45.

17. GAO/NSIAD-93-15, Washington, D.C., December 1992. "Operation Desert Storm," GAO Report 1992, 94.

18. Thomas Cohen, "Statistics from the Storm," *Air Force Magazine* (April 1998), 184–85.

19. Davies and Thornborough, *Harrier Story*, 133–48.

CHAPTER 8

1. Friedman, *Desert Victory,* 343–46.
2. Author's interview with Lt. Col. Terry Mattke, USMC (Ret.), Washington, D.C., 20 August 2004.
3. Ibid.
4. Ibid.
5. Interview with Clint Moore, St. Louis, Mo., 23 June 2005.
6. Interview with Ben Park, 22 June 2005 (electronic).
7. Interview with Col. Lewis C. Watt (Ret.), 25 May 2005 (electronic).
8. Braybrook, *Harrier: Vertical Reality,* 110–11.
9. David J. Martin, "Progress in Certifying F402-RR-408: The Improved Pegasus Engine for the AV-8B and the Harrier II Plus," Rolls-Royce technical paper, London, 1990.
10. Watt interview.
11. Interview with Michael Gladwin (Rolls-Royce Pegasus program manager), Washington, D.C., 22 July 2003.
12. A. Street, "V/STOL Engine Design Evolution: Growth of the Pegasus Engine for the Harrier," Rolls-Royce technical paper delivered at the International Powered Lift Conference, Royal Aeronautical Society, London, 29–31 August 1990.
13. Davies and Thornborough, *Harrier Story,* 153–55.
14. Ibid.
15. Interview with Mike Gladwin.
16. Richard Burgess, "Precise and Lethal: The AV-8B in the USMC," *Air Forces Monthly* (July 2004), 66–72; Boeing Historical Office, St. Louis, Mo.
17. Interview with Lt. Col. Russ Stromberg (Ret.), 11 October 2004 (electronic).
18. Paul Jackson, "Twice Five Makes Seven," *Air International* (May 1994), 272–79.
19. Henri-Pierre Grolleau, "Vertical Masters," *Combat Aircraft* (May 2002), 524–35.
20. Alan Dawes, "Sea Harrier Axed," *Air Forces Monthly* (March 2002); Nick Weighman, "Joint Force Harrier toward Joint Strike Fighter," UK Ministry of Defense briefing, London, June 2004.

CHAPTER 9

1. Author's interview with Roger Mathews, 22 June 2005 (electronic); R. Speth, "Harrier II Plus, a Product of Multinational Cooperation: Managing the Change," AIAA technical paper 93-4837, 1–3 December 1993.
2. Author's interview with Dick Wise, St. Louis, Mo., 12 July 2005.
3. Mathews interview.
4. John Hutchinson, "Italian Navy Regains Its Wings with the Harrier II Plus," *Rolls-Royce Magazine* 54 (September 1992), 8–12.
5. Author's interview with Pat Finneran, St. Louis, Mo., 19 April 2005.
6. Author's interview with Bob White, Raytheon, Amberly, Australia, 25 March 2003.
7. Riccardo Niccoli, "Italian Navy Regains Its Wings," *Air International* (June 1996).
8. Author's interview with Col. Richard H. Priest, 15 May 2005 (electronic).
9. Author's interview with Jackie Jackson, St. Louis, Mo., 16 October 2004.
10. Speth, "Harrier II Plus."
11. Henri-Pierre Grolleau, "Vertical Masters," *Combat Aircraft* (May 2002), 524–35.
12. J. Maxwell and D. Arbuthnot, "AV-8B Harrier II Plus: Program Success," AIAA Paper 94-2109, 20 June 1994.
13. Salvador Mafe Huertas, "Spanish Harriers," *Air Forces Monthly* (September 1999), 21–23.
14. Finneran interview.
15. Director, Operational Test and Evaluation FY 1997 Annual Report, "AV-8B Remanufacture."
16. "AV-8B Remanufacture Effort Cuts Accident Rate, Marines Say," *Aerospace Daily* (17 April 1996), 100–101.
17. Finneran interview.

CHAPTER 10

1. Davies and Thornborough, *Harrier Story*, 203–4.
2. John Tirpak, "Deliberate Force," *Air Force Magazine* (October 1997), 23–27.
3. Michael K. Hile, "Evolution of the Harrier II," *Air International* (January 2004), 16–20.
4. RAF Campaign Histories: Operation Allied Force 1999, online source: www.raf.mod.uk/history.
5. Kosovo: Operation Allied Force, UK House of Commons Research Paper 99/48, 29 April 1999.
6. RAF Campaign Histories: Operation Allied Force 1999, online source: www.raf.mod.uk/history.
7. Ruggero Stanglini and Marco Amatimaggio, "Harrier Italia," *Rolls-Royce Magazine* 10 (June 2004), 2–7.
8. Kosovo: Lessons Learned from the Crisis, Chapter 7, "Air Operations," online source: www.kosovo.mod.uk/lessons. UK Ministry of Defense report, 1999.
9. Ibid.
10. David Hunter, "Mavericks on RAF Harriers," *Air Forces Monthly* (May 2001), 6–8.
11. Steve Bowman, "Bosnia: U.S. Military Operations," Congressional Research Service Paper B93056, Washington, D.C., 2001.
12. Tom Clancy, *Marine: A Guided Tour of a Marine Expeditionary Unit* (New York: Berkley Books, 1996), 149–230.
13. Bowman, "Bosnia: U.S. Military Operations."
14. Vice Adm. Daniel J. Murphy, Jr., USN, presentation to the Seapower Subcommittee, U.S. Senate Armed Services Committee, Washington, D.C., 13 October 1999.
15. Maj. Gen. Robert M. Flanagan, USMC, statement to the Senate Armed Services Committee, 26 October 1999.
16. Ibid.
17. Ibid.

CHAPTER 11

1. Clancy, *Marine*.
2. Lt. Col. Lee Schram, "AV-8B Harrier," APW-22, HQMC briefing, 2003. Author's email communication with Colonel Schram, 10 August 2003.
3. Author's interview with Lt. Col. Bob Claypool, Yuma, Ariz., 1 October 2003.
4. Michael Hughes, "Further Enhancements for LITENING Targeting Pod Developed," *International Defense Review* (December 2002): 62.
5. Author's interview with Jerry Dolvin, St. Louis, Mo., 15 June 2005.
6. Author's interview with James Mason, St. Louis, Mo., 24 June 2005.
7. Author's interview with Col. Lee Buland, 10 June 2006 (electronic).
8. Ibid.
9. Ibid.
10. Finneran interview.
11. Author's interview with Col. Chuck Allen (Ret.), 20 June 2005 (electronic).
12. Ibid.
13. Buland interview.
14. Rick Burgess, "Precise and Lethal: Harrier II Development and Service with the U.S. Marine Corps," *Air Forces Monthly* (July 2004), 67–72.
15. Alan C. Miller and Kevin Sack, "Far from the Battlefield, Marines Lose One-Third of Harrier Fleet, *Los Angeles Times* (15 December 2002).
16. Harrier II Review Panel, first annual report (location: USMC HQ, September 1998), http://www.usmc.mil/harp.
17. Claypool interview.
18. Author's interview with Maj. James Coppersmith, 22 June 2006 (electronic).

CHAPTER 12

1. Paul White, "Crisis after the Storm," Washington Institute for Near East Policy, research paper no. 2, 2 November 1999.
2. "A Second Storm," *Air Forces Monthly* (March 2003), 20–24.
3. Davies and Thornborough, *Harrier Story*, 196–200.
4. Ibid.
5. Lt. Col. Lee Schram, USMC, "AV-8B Harrier," APW-22, HQMC briefing, 2003.
6. John Rahe, "Flying Nightmares Go Around the Clock: VMA-513 Night Attack Deploy with NVGs," *World Airpower Journal* 37 (1999): 31–33.
7. Ellen Knickmeyer, "Ships Become Harrier Platforms," AP story accessed 12 March 2003, online source: www.militarycity.com.
8. Claypool interview.
9. Lt. Col. Michael K. Hile, "Tomcats Operation Iraqi Freedom," VMA-311, squadron briefing, 1 October 2003.
10. Jamie Hunter and Tony Holmes, *Gulf War II: Operation Iraqi Freedom, the Air War* (Surrey, UK: Tomcat Publishing, 2004), 94–99.
11. Sq. Cdr. Andy McKeon, Joint Force Harrier, UK Ministry of Defense briefing, London, 2005.
12. Anthony Cordesman, "The Instant Lessons of the Iraq War," Center for Strategic and International Studies Report, 14 April 2003.
13. Steve Bowman, "Iraq: U.S. Military Operations," Congressional Research Service Paper RL31701, 2 October 2003.
14. Robert Wall, "Lessons Emerge: Interdiction-Heavy Marine Air Operations Clear Opposition for Ground Force," *Aviation Week and Space Technology* (14 April 2003).
15. Author's interview with Lt. Col. Michael K. Hile (Ret.), Yuma, Ariz., 1 October 2003.
16. Cordesman, "The Instant Lessons of the Iraqi War."
17. Claypool interview.
18. Hile interview.
19. Claypool interview.
20. Ibid.
21. Hunter and Holmes, *Gulf War II*, 70–71.
22. David A. Bryant, "Harriers Win the Day for Marine Corps Aviation During Iraqi Freedom," USMC press release, 17 July 2003.
23. Claypool interview.
24. Hile, VMA-311 briefing.
25. Ibid.
26. Mark Elfers, "Support the Harrier Transformation," U.S. Naval Institute *Proceedings* (October 2003), 48–51.
27. Tim Ripley, "Iraq War by the Numbers," *Air Forces Monthly* (August 2003), 26–29.
28. Hunter and Holmes, *Gulf War II*, 94.
29. Bryant, "Harriers Win the Day."
30. Nathan LaForte, "VMA-542, VMA-214 Bring Marine Attack Jets to Iraq," USMC press release, 3rd Marine Aircraft Wing, 22 May 2004.
31. Jonathan Keiler, "Who Won the Battle of Fallujah?" U.S. Naval Institute *Proceedings* (January 2005), 57–61.
32. Cpl. Paul Leidec, "Marine Harrier Pilots Fly into History over Iraq," Marine Corps press release, 3rd Marine Aircraft Wing, 12 November 2004.

CHAPTER 13

1. "Operation Enduring Freedom Gets Underway," *Air International* (November 2001), 258–67.
2. Richard Burgess, "Navy and Marine Corps Units Continue Hunt for Terrorists," Navy League report, *Seapower* magazine (February 2002).
3. Sgt. Joseph R. Chenelly, "Harrier Jets Conduct Air Strikes in Afghanistan," USMC press release, 15th MEU, 4 November 2001.

4. 26th MEU Unit History, online: www.global.security.org.military/agency/usmc/26thmeu.
5. Thomas M. Corcoran, "Harrier Fighters Make First Combat Footprint for the 26th MEU (SOC) in Afghanistan," USMC press release, 14 December 2001.
6. Marco Amatimaggio and Ruggero Stanglini, "Harrier Italian," *Rolls-Royce Magazine* 101 (June 2004), 2–7.
7. Arthur Brill, "Afghan Diary: Marine Corps Considerations, Lessons Learned in Phase One," *Seapower* magazine (April 2002).
8. Sgt. Keith A. Milks, "22nd MEU (SOC) Harriers Fly Combat Missions over Afghanistan," Marine Corps press release, 12 July 2002.
9. Michael V. Franzak, "Nightmares in Afghanistan," *Naval Aviation News* (May–June 2003), 18–23.
10. Interview with Col. James Dixon, MCAS Yuma, Ariz., 1 October 2004.
11. Capt. Eric Dent, "22nd MEU Harriers Mark 1,000 Combat Flight Hours," USMC press release, 30 June 2004.
12. Sgt. Keith Milks, "FACs Bring Fire from Above to Support 22nd MEU Infantry," USMC press release, 22 June 2004.
13. Ibid.
14. Ibid.
15. "Deployment of UK RAF Harrier GR Mk. 7 Aircraft to Afghanistan," UK Ministry of Defense release, 25 August 2004; Royal Air Force News, Events and Current Operations, online source: www.raf.mod.uk/news, accessed August 2004.
16. Graham Bond, "A Short Flight in the Hind Kush: Harriers Provide Close Air Support in the Hunt for al Qaeda and Taliban," *Focus Newspaper* (12 November 2004), 12.
17. "Embarked Harriers Support Operation Herrick," Royal Air Force news release, 3 March 2005.
18. Alan Warnes, "RAF Harriers in Afghanistan: Operation Herrick," *Air Forces Monthly* (November 2005), 30–32.

CHAPTER 14

1. Stromberg, *The Marine Corps AV-8 Program*, 12–14.
2. Charlotte Adams, "AV-8B Open Systems Pioneer," *Avionics Magazine* (July 2002), 21–27.

Bibliography

Books

Bonds, Ray, ed. *U.S. War Machine: An Encyclopedia of American Military Equipment and Strategy*. London: Salamander Books, 1985.

Braybrook, Roy. *Harrier: Vertical Reality*. Fairford, UK: Royal Air Force Benevolent Fund, 1996.

Campbell, Douglas N. *The Warthog and the Close Air Support Debate*. Annapolis, Md.: Naval Institute Press, 2003.

Clancy, Tom. *Marine: A Guided Tour of a Marine Expeditionary Unit*. New York: Berkley Books, 1996.

Clancy, Tom, and Chuck Horner. *Every Man a Tiger:* The Gulf War Air Campaign. New York: Berkley Books, 1999.

Friedman, Norman. *Desert Victory: The War For Kuwait*. Annapolis, Md.: Naval Institute Press, 1991.

Hallion, Richard P. *The Naval Air War in Korea*. Baltimore, Md.: Nautical and Aviation Publishing, 1986.

————. *Strike from the Sky: History of Battlefield Air Attack, 1911–1945*. Washington, D.C.: Smithsonian Institution Press, 1989.

Hunter, Jamie, and Tony Holmes. *Gulf War II: Operation Iraqi Freedom, the Air War*. Surrey, UK: Tomcat Publishing, 2004.

Myles, Bruce. *Jump Jet: The Revolutionary Harrier*. San Rafael, Calif.: Presidio Press, 1978.

Thornborough, Anthony M., and Peter E. Davies. *Harrier Story*. Annapolis, Md.: Naval Institute Press, 1996.

Periodicals

"A Second Storm," *Air Forces Monthly*, March 2003, 20–24.

Adams, Charlotte. "AV-8B Open Systems Pioneer," *Avionics Magazine*, July 2002, 21–27.

Alano, Rolondo. "St. Barbara: What a Debut," *Aeroespacio Revista Nacional Aeronautica Espacial*, 1986, 44–55.

"AV-8B Remanufacture Effort Cuts Accident Rate, Marines Say," *Aerospace Daily*, 17 April 1996, 100–101.

Blot, Harry, W. "A New Dimension in Air Combat," *Rolls-Royce Magazine* 6, 1980, 3–7.

Bond, Graham. "A Short Flight in the Hind Kush: Harriers Provide Close Air Support in the Hunt for al Qaeda and Taliban," *Focus* newspaper, 12 November 2004, 12.

Braybrook, Roy. "AV-8B Harrier II: Stepping-Stone to an Anglo-American Supersonic V/STOL Aircraft?" *Air International*, February 1982, 64–69.

Brill, Arthur. "Afghan Diary: Marine Corps Considerations, Lessons Learned in Phase One," *Seapower* magazine, April 2002.

Brown, David. "Britain Weighs U.S. AV-8B Buy," *Aviation Week and Space Technology*, 2 February 1981, 14.

Burgess, Richard. "Navy and Marine Corps Continue Hunt for Terrorists," Navy League report, *Seapower* magazine, February 2002.

———. "Precise and Lethal: Harrier II Development and Service with the U.S. Marine Corps," Air *Forces Monthly*, July 2004, 67–72.

Butcher, Richard. "Training Pilots to Think AV-8B," *Rolls-Royce Magazine* 25, June 1985, 2–7.

———."First Operational AV-8B Squadron," *Rolls-Royce Magazine* 30, September 1986, 15–19.

Centner, Christopher M. "Ignorance Is Risk: The Big Lesson from Desert Storm Air Base Attacks," *Airpower Journal*, winter 1992, 12–18.

Chopra, Pushpindar. "India and the MiG-21," *Air Enthusiast*, July 1973, 7–11.

"Close Air Support: Cheyenne vs. Harrier vs. A-X?" *Armed Forces Journal* 19, October 1970, 19–20.

"Close Air Support for the U.S. Armed Forces," *International Defense Review* 4, October 1971, 433.

Cohen, Thomas. "Statistics from the Storm," *Air Force Magazine*, April 1998, 184–85.

Cooper, Bert, H. "V/STOL Aviation in the U.S. Navy," *Navy International*, September 1984, 12–16.

Dawes, Alan. "Sea Harrier Axed," *Air Forces Monthly*, March 2002, 7–12.
Elfers, Mark. "Support the Harrier Transformation," U.S. Naval Institute *Proceedings*, October 2003, 48–51.

Fozard, John. "The Origin of a U.S. Species: Entry of the AV-8A Harrier into the U.S. Marine Corps," *Marine Corps Gazette*, May 1992, 77–85.

Franzak, Michael V. "Nightmares in Afghanistan," *Naval Aviation News*, May–June 2003, 18–23.

Greeley, Brendan. "Improved VTOL Performance of TAV-8B Adds Realism to Attack Force Training," *Aviation Week and Space Technology*, 3 August 1987, 68–72.

Grolleau, Henri-Pierre. "Vertical Masters," *Combat Aircraft*, May 2002, 524–35.

Gustafson, R. A. "The Marine Corps View," *Armed Forces Journal*, April 1981, 58.

Hile, Michael K. "Evolution of the Harrier II," *Air International*, January 2004, 16–20.

Huertas, Salvador Mafe. "Spanish Harriers," *Air Forces Monthly*, September 1999, 21–23.

Hughes, David. "Further Enhancements for the LITENING Targeting Pod Developed," *International Defense Review*, December 2002, 62.

Hutchinson, John. "Italian Navy Regains Its Wings with the Harrier II Plus," *Rolls-Royce Magazine* 54, September 1992, 8–12.

Hunter, David. "Mavericks on the RAF Harriers," *Air Forces Monthly*, May 2001, 6–8.

Jackson, Paul. "Strike Force South, *Australian Aviation*, December 1982, 60.

———. 'Twice Three Makes Five," *Air International*, August 1989, 59–67.

———. "Harrier," *World Airpower Journal* 6, 1991, 48–64.

———. "Twice Five Makes Seven," *Air International*, May 1994, 272–79.

Janowiec, Sgt. Jeffrey. "The Gulf War: A Marine POW," *Marine Corps Aviation Association Journal*, September 2002, 85–87.

Keiler, Jonathan. "Who Won the Battle of Fallujiah?" Naval Institute *Proceedings*, January 2005, 57–61.

Knickmeyer, Ellen. "Ships Become Harrier Platforms," AP story accessed 12 March 2003, online source: www.militarycity.com.

Laws, Alan. "Harrier: European Operations," *Combat Aircraft*, January 1999, 58–63.

"Marines Bad Luck Airplane: Why the Harrier Keeps On Crashing," *Time* magazine, 15 August 1977, 16.

"Marines to Purchase F/A-18s after Losing Bid for the AV-8Bs," *Aviation Week and Space Technology*, 5 February 1979, 18.

"Matador: Spearhead of Spanish Naval Strike Power," *Rolls-Royce Magazine* 7, 1980.

Miller, Alan C., and Kevin Sack. "Far from the Battlefield, Marines Lose One-Third of Harrier Fleet," *Los Angeles Times*, 15 December 2002.

Miller, Thomas H. "Harrier: How and Why," *Foundation*, spring 1991, 20–25.

Murray, Russell. "The AV-8B Controversy: Rising Vertically Through the List of Priorities Invulnerable to Systems Analysis," *Armed Forces Journal International*, April 1981, 50–61.

Niccoli, Riccardo. "Italian Navy Regains Its Wings," *Air International*, June 1996, 24–29.

Nordeen, Lon. "The Marines' AV-8B Gulf Deployment," *Air Forces Monthly*, February 1992, 42.

"Operation Enduring Freedom Gets Underway," *Air International*, November 2001, 258–67.

Rahe, John. "Flying Nightmares Go Around the Clock: VMA-513 Night Attack Deploy with NVGs," *World Airpower Journal* 37, 1999, 31–33.

Ripley, Tim. "Iraq War by the Numbers," *Air Forces Monthly*, August 2003, 26–29.

Stanglini, Ruggero, and Marco Amatimaggio. "Harrier Italia," *Rolls-Royce Magazine* 10, June 2004, 2–7.

Stromberg, Russ. "The AV-8B OPEVAL: Mission Complete, the Best Ever," *Wings of Gold*, summer 1985, 36–42.

Tirpak, John. "Deliberate Force," *Air Force Magazine*, October 1997, 23–27.

Wall, Robert. "Lessons Emerge: Interdiction-Heavy Marine Air Operations Clear Opposition for Ground Forces," *Aviation Week and Space Technology*, 14 April 2003.

Warran, Alan. "RAF Harriers in Afghanistan: Operation Herrule," *Air Force Monthly*, November 2005, 30–32.

Government Hearings, Special Reports, Releases, and Technical Papers

Bowman, Steve. "Bosnia: U.S. Military Operations," Congressional Research Service report B93056, 2001.

———. "Iraq: U.S. Military Operations," Congressional Research Service report RL31701, October 2, 2003.

Committee on Armed Services, United States Senate, One Hundredth Congress, DOD Authorization for Appropriations for Fiscal Year 1989, Hearings, 21 March 1988, 48–54.

Cooper, Bert. "The British Harrier V/STOL Aircraft: Analysis of Operational Experience and Relevance to U.S. Tactical Aviation," Congressional Research Service Report, 15 August 1981, no. 81–180 F.

Cordesman, Anthony. "Lessons of the Iraqi War," Center for Strategic and International Studies, Washington, DC, 2003.

Director, Operational Test and Evaluation FY 1997 Annual Report, "AV-8B Remanufacture." Systems Description and Contribution to Joint Vision 2010.

"Falklands Campaign: The Lessons," UK government document presented to Parliament by the Secretary for Defence, December 1982, Her Majesty's Stationery Office, ISBN 0101875800, 19.

Flanagan, Maj. Gen. Robert M., USMC. Statement to the U.S. Senate Armed Services Committee, 26 October 1999.

Gibson, Maj. Mark J. "USMC Close Air Support Must Be Complementary, Not Competitive," master's thesis, U.S. Marine Corps Command and Staff College, 1995.

Goza, Maj. Joel L. "The AV-8B Decision," master's thesis, U.S. Naval Postgraduate School, Monterey, Calif., June 1982.

Hagee, Gen. Michael M, USMC. "Marine Corps Concepts and Programs: 2004," report.

Haley, Maj. S. D., USMC. "Close Air Support and the Marine Air/Ground Team," master's thesis, U.S. Marine Corps Command and Staff College, 2 April 1984.

Hearing before the Special Subcommittee on Close Air Support of the Preparedness Investigating Subcommittee of the Committee on Armed services, United States Senate, Ninety-Second Congress, First Session, Hearings, 22 October 1971, 252–72.

Hile, Lt. Col. Michael K., commanding officer VMA-311. "Tomcats in Operation Iraqi Freedom," squadron briefing, 1 October 2003.

Jones, Maj. W. M. "Marine Corps Close Air Support: What Aircraft Are Really Needed?" master's thesis, U.S. Marine Corps Command and Staff College, 1988.

Kosovo: Lessons Learned from the Crisis, Chapter 7, "Air Operations," online source: www.kosovo. mod.uk/lessons. UK Ministry of Defense report, 1999.

"Kosovo: Operation Allied Force," UK House of Commons Research Paper 99/48, 29 April 1999.

McKeon, Andy, Sq. Cdr. Joint Force Harrier, UK Ministry of Defense briefing, London, 2005.

Martin, David J. "Progress in Certifying F402–RR–408: The Improved Pegasus Engine for the AV-8B and the Harrier II Plus," Rolls-Royce technical paper, London, 1990.

Maxwell, J., and D. Arbuthnot. "AV-8B Harrier II Plus: Program Success," AIAA paper 94–2109, 20 June 1994.

Murphy, Adm. Daniel J., Jr. Presentation to the Seapower Subcommittee, U.S. Senate Armed Services Committee, Washington, D.C., 13 October 1999.

Operation Desert Storm, General Accounting Office Report, 1992.

Pitchfork, G. R., Sq. Cdr. "Harrier in Support of the Close-in Battle," technical paper, 11th Aerospace Symposium, Maxwell Air Force Base, Ala., 9–10 March 1987.

RAF Campaign History, Operation Allied Force, 1999. Online source: www.raf.mod.uk/history.
Schram, Lt. Col. Lee. "AV-8B Harrier II," HQ USMC briefing, 2003.

Speth, R. "Harrier II Plus, a Product of Multinational Cooperation: Managing the Change," AIAA technical paper 93–4837, 1 December 1993.

Stillion, John, and David Orletsjy. Airbase Vulnerability to Conventional Cruise Missiles and Ballistic Missiles. Santa Monica, Calif.: RAND study prepared for the U.S. Air Force, 1999.

Street, A. "V/STOL Engine Design Evolution: Growth of the Pegasus Engine for the Harrier," Rolls-Royce technical paper delivered at the International Powered Lift Conference, Royal Aeronautical Society, London, 29–31 August 1990.

U.S. Department of Defense Joint Tactics, Techniques and Procedures for Close Air Support, Joint Publications 3–09.3, 1 December 1995.

U.S. Marine Corps AV-8 V/STOL Program, 5th ed. Boeing Gold Book, April 2002.

V/STOL in the Roaring Forties, British Aerospace Publication, UK: Polygraphic Ltd., 1982.

Weighman, Nick. "Joint Force Harrier toward Joint Strike Fighter," UK Ministry of Defense briefing, London, June 2004.

White, Paul. "Crisis after the Storm," Washington Institute for Near East Policy, research paper no. 2, 2 November 1999.

Military Press Releases

Bryant, Sgt. David A. "Harriers Win the Day for Marine Corps Aviation During Iraqi Freedom," USMC press release, 17 July 2003.

Chenelly, Joseph R. "Harrier Jets Conduct Air Strikes in Afghanistan," USMC press release, 4 November 2001.

Corcoran, Sgt. Thomas M., USMC. "Harrier Fighters Make First Footprint for the 26th MEU (SOC) in Afghanistan," USMC press release, 14 December 2001.

Dent, Capt. Eric, USMC. "22nd MEU Harriers Mark 1,000 Combat Flight Hours," USMC press release, 30 June 2004.

"Deployment of UK RAF Harrier GR Mk. 7 to Afghanistan," UK Ministry of Defense, 25 August 2004.

"Harriers Support Operation Herrick," UK Ministry of Defense, 3 March 2005.

LaForte, Sgt. Nathan. "VMA-542, VMA214 Bring Marine Attack Jets to Iraq," USMC press release, 22 May 2004.

Milks, Sgt. Keith, USMC. "22nd MEU Harriers Fly Combat Missions over Afghanistan," USMC press release, 12 July 2002.

———. "FACs Bring Fire from Above to Support 22nd MEU Infantry," USMC press release, 22 June 2004.

Author Interviews

Anderson, Maj. Gen. Joseph (Ret.), Washington, D.C., 13 August 2004.
Blot, Maj. Gen. Harry (Ret.), Washington, D.C., 20 October 2003.
Buland, Col. David L., electronic, March–June 2005.
Capito, Lt. Col. John (Ret.), electronic, 12 May 2004.
Carpenter, Daryl, St. Louis, Mo., 23 June 2004.
Chara, Fred, St. Louis, Mo., 14 May 2004.
Claypool, Lt. Col. Bob, Yuma, Ariz., 1 October 2003.

Dixon, Lt. Col. James (Ret.), Yuma, Ariz., October 2003.

Dolvir, Jerry, St. Louis, Mo., 16 February 2005.

Finneran, Pat, St. Louis, Mo., 19 April 2005.

Gladwin, Michael, Washington, D.C., 22 July 2003.

Harper, Col. Edwin, St. Louis, Mo., 20 August 2003.

Herman, Lt. Col. Ted (Ret.), Cherry Point, N.C., November 1993.

Hile, Lt. Col. Michael K. (Ret.), Yuma, Ariz., October 2003, and subsequent.

Jackson, Jack, St. Louis, Mo., May 20, 2003, 15 June 2004.

Jones, Lt. Col. (Ret.), Cherry Point, N.C., November 1993.

Kauffman, Jerry, St. Louis, Mo., 18 June 2006.

Kuzniewski, Col. Greg (Ret.), Washington, D.C., 13 August 2004.

Mason, James, St. Louis, Mo., 14 June 2005.

Mathews, Roger, electronic, 22 June 2005.

Mattke, Lt. Col. Terry (Ret.), electronic, August/September 2004.

Miller, Lt. Gen. Thomas (Ret.), Arlington, Va., 14 January 2004.

Milne, Ian, London, UK, September–October 2003.

Moore, Clint, St. Louis, Mo., 23 June 2005.

Nidiffer, Robert, Yuma, Ariz., 1 October 2003.

Orr, Capt. Bud (Ret.), Washington, D.C., 13 August 2003.

Parker, John, Washington, DC, 31 October 2003.

Priest, Col. Richard H. (Ret.), electronic, May–June 2005.

Ryan, Maj. Gen. Michael (Ret.), Washington, D.C., 13 August 2003.

Saverese, Col. Mark (Ret.), electronic, February 2005.

Searle, Ray, London, September–October 2003.

Street, Martin, UK, 22 October 2003.

Stromberg, Lt. Col. Russ (Ret.), electronic, 11 October 2004; March–April 2005.

Watt, Col. Lewis C. (Ret.), electronic, May–June 2005.

White, Bob, Amberly, Australia (Raytheon), 25 March 2003.

White, Lt. Col. (Ret.), Cherry Point, N.C., November 1993.

Wise, Dick, St. Louis, Mo., 12 July 2005.

Index

About the Author

Lon O. Nordeen has been active in the aerospace industry for more than thirty years, initially on the staff of the American Institute of Aeronautics and Astronautics (AIAA) and later with McDonnell Douglas and Boeing. He is the author of *Air Warfare in the Missile Age* (Smithsonian Institution Press 1986; 2nd ed. 2002), *Fighters Over Israel: The Story of the Israeli Air Force from the War of Independence to the Bekaa Valley* (Crown 1990), *Phoenix over the Nile: A History of Egyptian Airpower, 1933-1994* (Smithsonian Institution Press 1996), and numerous articles and technical conference presentations.